MW01013548

MONTH-BY-MONTH GARDENING

# PENNSYLVANIA

First published in 2015 by Cool Springs Press, an imprint of Quarto Publishing Group USA Inc.,
400 First Avenue North, Suite 400, Minneapolis, MN USA 55401

© 2015 Quarto Publishing Group USA Inc.

Cool Springs Press titles are also available at discounts in bulk quantity for industrial or sales-promotional use.
For details write to Special Sales Manager at Quarto Publishing Group USA Inc., 400 First Avenue North, Suite 400,
Minneapolis, MN 55401 USA. To find out more about our books, visit us online at www.coolspringspress.com.

Library of Congress Cataloging-in-Publication Data

Ball, Liz, author.
  Pennsylvania month-by-month gardening : what to do each month to have a beautiful garden all year / Liz
Ball and George Weigel.
     pages cm
  ISBN 978-1-59186-630-5 (sc)
  1. Gardening--Pennsylvania. I. Weigel, George, author. II. Title. III. Title: Pennsylvania month-by-month
gardening.

  SB453.2.P4B37 2015
  635.09748--dc23

                                                                                    2014050258

ISBN: 978-1-59186-630-5

Acquisitions Editor: Billie Brownell
Art Director: Cindy Samargia Laun
Layout: Danielle Smith-Boldt
Front Cover Photo: George Weigel

Printed in China
10 9 8 7 6 5 4 3 2 1

MONTH-BY-MONTH GARDENING

# PENNSYLVANIA

### What to Do Each Month to Have
### a Beautiful Garden All Year

LIZ BALL & GEORGE WEIGEL

COOL
SPRINGS
PRESS
*Home and Garden Experts*™

# Dedication

Liz: To the Garden Writers Association and its member community of supportive, knowledgeable colleagues who have encouraged my writing over many years.

George: To Suze, my lifelong love, who is co-propagator of my other loves, daughter Erin and son Andy, who's grown the family landscape to include daughter-in-law Julie and a little sweet pea named Leona Pearl.

# Acknowledgments

Liz: My deepest gratitude to George for being willing to take on the task of reorganizing and updating my book *Month-by-Month Gardening in Pennsylvania*. His willingness to do this work has assured that gardeners and homeowners in our state will have access to the newest information in a way that I could never have achieved. A special thanks to Billie Brownell for her support and guidance over the years, and particularly, her encouragement of my collaboration with George on this project.

George: Thanks, first, to Liz for suggesting me as the torch-bearer for this second-generation collaboration of *Month-By-Month Gardening in Pennsylvania*. As a reader of the original, I thought it was such a useful tool—very specific and very timely for gardeners throughout Pennsylvania.

I'd also like to thank the production team at Cool Springs Press and especially editor Billie Brownell, who somehow manages to juggle multiple book projects at the same time and keep them all organized and flowing.

And third, thanks to the army of info-suppliers who contributed the many bits and pieces that make up this book—the assorted Master Gardeners, horticulturists, growers, garden-center folks, hort professors, public-garden staffers, Extension educators, home gardeners, and yes, even my own backyard bugs and voles, who assisted with the Problem-Solve section.

# Contents

# Introduction

*It doesn't help that few people have had any classes or other training in the fine art of yard care. Those without parents or grandparents to show them what to do are basically left to wing it. That wastes time, energy, and money in the effort to figure out how to get it right.*

"When do I do that?" That's the perplexing question asked by many a Pennsylvania yard-owner—right after figuring out what to plant where (the subject of the companion book to this title, Cool Springs' *Pennsylvania Getting Started Garden Guide*.)

Uncertainty over when to do what often leads to "horticultural paralysis." People fear they'll do the wrong thing at the wrong time and thereby kill off all landscape life. And so they do nothing.

Experienced gardeners know that's a recipe for jungledom. When a gardener turns his or her back for long, Mother Nature takes over.

Think of this book as a way to fast-forward through years of trial and error. Though it touches on the basics of how-to, it's primarily a *when-to* book. Use it as a detailed playbook or "honey-do" list to refer to throughout the year. Feel free to mark it up or whittle it down into your own specific gardening planner, based on your own observations and timing that experience teaches in each little corner of the Earth.

Such a gardening calendar is not groundbreaking (figuratively speaking). One of America's first best-selling gardening books was Bernard M'Mahon's 1806 *The American Gardener's Calendar*, a compendium of the most advanced horticultural knowledge of the day. M'Mahon emigrated from Ireland and founded a successful seed and nursery business in Philadelphia. He quickly realized the need for practical gardening advice based on the climate, weather, and soil conditions peculiar to the New World. For the subsequent fifty years and eleven editions, his book was the best gardening resource available. The idea of gardening and plant care laid out in a monthly calendar is as useful today as during M'Mahon's time.

## GARDENING BY CALENDAR

Caring for plants is not rocket science (although rockets might cross your mind when browsing deer get bad enough). Most gardening tasks are not difficult. The tricky part is the timing—knowing when to do them. The second trickiest is carving out time to get the jobs done.

Timing relates to an understanding of the way plants grow in your particular area and how factors such as weather, soil, light, moisture, and even insect/plant interactions affect that.

Learning these things would be easy if they stayed the same from year to year. None of them do, of course, which makes gardening fun and challenging to the avid gardener but maddening and "@%!*#!" to those who just want to get the work done and get back to golfing.

Gardening involves being willing to make time to do certain tasks when the time is right. That's a common trait of successful gardeners. Caring for plants is a team effort, and the other member of the team, the aforementioned Mother Nature, is extremely organized, often erratic, and always ready. So, Lesson No. 1 is to be flexible enough to adapt to Mother's whims.

Just as the optimal task dates can vary depending on what part of Pennsylvania is your home, so can these dates vary from season to season. A mild winter or an unusually early spring warm-up can advance care needs by two weeks or more. Similarly, a cold winter and slow start can push back jobs two weeks or more beyond the norm. Over time, gardeners learn to roll with the punches that inevitably come with each gardening year.

Lesson No. 2 is that no garden is ever really done. That's a blessing to the avid gardener who enjoys the process as much as the results, but a curse to the reluctant gardener who just wants to "git 'er done" once and for all.

## GARDENING IN PENNSYLVANIA

Pennsylvanians are fortunate garden-wise, although it may not always seem so during a stifling summer drought or a tree-cracking December ice storm. Situated between colder Northern states with their long, dark winters, and warmer Southern states with their brutal, humid summers, Pennsylvanians tread in the more moderate middle ground. Despite our own weather swings, an awesome number of plants grow well throughout Pennsylvania.

Add to that the legacy of rich soil from the protective eastern hardwood forest that carpeted the state for eons—plus the relatively generous rainfall throughout most years—and we end up with excellent gardening conditions.

As it stretches from the Delaware River to Lake Erie, Pennsylvania's varied topography influences the climate statewide. Climatic variation is most obvious and significant in winter. Generally, average temperatures cool moving from east to west. The dates of expected fall frost are earlier in much of the western part of the state, while dates for the last spring frost are later.

■ *A little snow won't hurt your tulips if the temperature doesn't go too low.*

Pennsylvania encompasses six U.S. Department of Agriculture cold-hardiness zones, ranging from average winter lows of -15 to -20 degrees Fahrenheit in the highest reaches of northern Pennsylvania (Zone 5a) to average winter lows of 5 to 10 degrees Fahrenheit in the southeast corner (Zone 7b). Most of the state falls in the moderate Zones 6a and 6b, meaning lows bottom out in the range of 0 to -10 degrees Fahrenheit.

The warmest area of Pennsylvania is in and around Philadelphia. There, proximity to the Delaware River and the city's heat-trapping concrete and asphalt creates a Zone 7b climate that's akin to northern Virginia. West and north toward the Allegheny Mountains, the increasing elevation promotes a Zone 6 climate, marked by slightly chillier mornings and evenings and earlier fall frosts. As the mountains yield to the Allegheny Plateau, a Zone 5 climate prevails with even earlier fall-frost dates that cut short the outdoor growing season. Knowing which zone you live in helps with timing your jobs as well as knowing which plants to select in the first place. Keep in mind that the USDA hardiness ratings used throughout the plant industry are *averages.* Many winters never hit zero, meaning it's possible to grow plants rated for warmer zones. But it's also possible for a rogue winter to go *below* the average, killing plants that normally survive.

## GROWING LOCAL

Regional climate is just one factor that influences gardening success. In many cases, it's not even the most important one. All gardening is local, *quite* local in fact. The conditions that prevail on your particular property at any given time are the ones that carry the most weight. Those include type of soil, amount of light, presence of wind, frequency of rainfall, how well that rain drains, and the incidence of deer or rabbit visits. Such factors not only vary from yard to yard but even in different parts of the same yard.

The better you're able to observe, recognize, and address these "microclimates," the better your plants will perform. Microclimates are small areas where conditions are modified by the presence of buildings, natural springs, walls, large trees, rows of shrubs, and more. Second-story balconies and roof-overhang environments, for example, are significantly different from open lawn areas and garden beds near pavement.

## PENNSYLVANIA'S CLIMATE

**Frost Dates**

**Zone 5** (i.e. Scranton)

Average first fall frost: Sept. 28

Average last spring frost: May 15

Latest fall frost: Oct. 14

Latest spring frost: May 31

**Zone 6** (i.e. Harrisburg)

Average first fall frost: Oct. 18

Average last spring frost: April 24

Latest fall frost: Nov. 4

Latest spring frost: May 11

**Zone 7** (i.e. Philadelphia)

Average first fall frost: Oct. 24

Average last spring frost: April 18

Latest fall frost: Nov. 12

Latest spring frost: April 26

**Average Frost-Free Growing Season**

**Zone 5:** 138 days

**Zone 6:** 179 days

**Zone 7:** 191 days

**Precipitation**

Average annual precipitation statewide is 41.45 inches.

To see your city's month-by-month average totals: http://www.usclimatedata.com/climate/pennsylvania/united-states/3208

Source: National Climatic Data Center

These special areas offer opportunities for fine-tuning plant choices so that an even wider palette of plants can be used. Get to know plant options by reading, asking experts, visiting gardens, joining plant societies, and mostly by experience and experimentation. Any successful gardener will tell you about the number of plants that were killed over the years while learning gardening intricacies.

Keep in mind that your plants are part of a unique ecosystem, which is a community of living things both animal and vegetative that interact in a mutual effort to survive and stay healthy. Whether you're installing a new landscape or maintaining or enhancing an existing one, consider this bigger picture when planning.

Plants that mesh with the ecosystem are generally more vigorous, healthy, and "happy" than those unaccustomed to coping with the challenges of an unfamiliar environment. Free of stresses such as drought, poor soil, root competition, or insufficient light, plants' natural defense systems work at peak performance. That makes them better able to fend off pest and disease problems.

■ *You can create your own microclimate by planting a row of arborvitae, which can block the wind.*

Savvy gardeners know that healthy plants largely take care of themselves, reducing watering demands and virtually eliminating the need to spray.

It's much easier in the long run to learn what each plant prefers and then deliver it, rather than guess and create unnecessary work for yourself. In other words, a proactive approach, working *with* plants, is far easier than a reactive one, working *against* pest, disease, and environmental assaults.

## KNOW THEIR NEEDS

The first step in plant care is to plan an appropriate place for each plant in its new environment. A good strategy is to emulate each plant's natural environment as closely as possible. Most flowering bulbs, for example, prefer sun and well-drained soil. Astilbe, sedge, and turtlehead, on the other hand, would rather be in damp shade.

You'll have much better success with less work by identifying your conditions and matching plants to them than by buying whatever catches your eye and then trying to modify your conditions to meet their needs.

To use that approach, sketch a map of your yard. Include existing plants. Then observe each area, and mark them off by differing conditions. This will help you determine what to plant where—or in the case of struggling or troubled plants, what to *move* where.

Pay attention to:

- **Light.** Where is it sunny and where is it shady? At what time of day is it sunny and for how long? Keep in mind that afternoon sun is more taxing (at least on shade-preferrers) than morning sun.

- **Moisture.** Are some areas damper than others? Grass that stays greener longer in hot, dry weather is a good clue. Where does water run in a rain? How long does it take to dry out afterward? Are overhangs or other structures blocking any areas of rain? Any swales or low-lying areas that collect rain? All of this will help you know where to place moisture-lovers vs. drought-tough species. If *everything* is dry, locate plants that need regular watering closest to a faucet.

- **Soil.** You may not have consistent soil quality or soil nutrition throughout the landscape. Do a soil test in different areas to get an up-front read on major plant nutrients as well as each area's acidity level (pH). Also do one or more do-it-yourself checks of your soil's quality and drainage ability. (See "Here's How to Check the Quality of Your Soil," below.)

- **Wind.** Succulents and other plants adapted to dry and windy climates do fine out in the open. Others need some wind protection, especially borderline-hardy broadleaf evergreens that can take a beating in windy spots during a cold winter. Sites along an

## HERE'S HOW
### TO CHECK THE QUALITY OF YOUR SOIL

1. **Drainage test.** Before planting, dig a hole as big as the rootball of the plant you plan to plant. Fill it with water and give it twenty-four hours to drain. Then fill it again, and watch to see how many inches it drains per hour.

   If it's not going down by at least 1 inch per hour, plan on some serious "uncompacting" by adding compost or similar organic matter or by building raised beds.

2. **Soil-texture test.** Dig a tablespoon of soil and add enough water that you can roll it into a ball. If you can't form a ball, the soil is sandy. Next, squeeze the ball between your thumb and index finger to make a ribbon. The longer the ribbon goes before cracking, the more clay you've got. Less than 2 inches is a good composition. More than 2 inches means the soil is clayish and would benefit from improvement with compost or similar organic matter.

3. **Jar test.** Dig 2 to 3 cups of soil from 6 to 8 inches deep in your planting bed. Let it dry on newspaper for twenty-four hours. Use a sieve or colander to sift rocks, roots, and other debris out of the soil. Crush lumps of soil to sift them through. Pour 2 cups of the sifted soil into a quart jar or clean mayonnaise jar and add 1 tablespoon of powdered detergent. Fill the jar with water, seal, and shake vigorously for three minutes. After one hour, the biggest sand particles will settle out into a bottom layer. After two hours, the slightly smaller silt particles will settle out into a second layer. After twenty-four hours, the smallest clay particles will settle out into a third layer. Measure the thickness of each layer and the total depth. To figure the percentage of each layer, divide that layer's thickness by the total depth. (Example: If all three layers total 3 inches and 2 inches of that is the clay layer, then about 66 percent of your soil is clay.) Ideally, all three layers will be about the same. When any of the three exceed 60 percent, that type is becoming undesirably dominant, and amending with organic matter is advised.

■ *Take a handful of soil and dampen it with water until it is moldable, almost like moist putty, then squeeze it into a ribbon. If a ribbon of greater than 2 inches forms before it breaks, you have very heavy and poorly drained soil. It will not be suitable for a garden without some major amendments.*

■ *A simple jar test will help you determine what kind of soil you have.*

east- or south-facing wall or nestled in a courtyard will protect plants from winter's frigid winds, which prevail from the north and northwest.

- **What's nearby?** Scope out the surrounding area and make note of features that will have an impact on your plants and their care. This includes proximity to hot spots such as driveways and asphalt roads; nearby trees whose roots are creeping (those can spread twice or more the canopy of a tree); utility boxes that might limit plant choices; trees such as walnut or butternut that inhibit the growth of many species, and especially the presence of deer, rabbits, groundhogs, voles, and other plant-raiding critters.

## MATCH PLANTS AND CONDITIONS

Once you know what you've got, do your homework to choose plants that are appropriate for each site. *Pennsylvania Getting Started Garden Guide* highlights nearly 200 of the best plants for Pennsylvania gardens, including the specific sites and conditions that each prefers.

Do not fall for a plant simply because it is trendy, on sale, or gorgeous! Maybe you'll get lucky and guess right. Or maybe you won't. Increase your success odds by replacing guessing with homework.

Aim to have lots of different kinds of plants— trees, shrubs, bulbs, perennials—and lots of varieties of each. The more diverse the plants on your property, the more hosts you'll have for the beneficial organisms and insects that protect plants from predators.

Start with plants rated for your USDA cold-hardiness zone. For borderline ones or species where you're knowingly pushing the envelope, plant them in your most protected microclimates. Or accept that these may die back to the ground or croak in some years.

Lean toward varieties that have been bred or selected for their bug- and disease-resistance. This alone can go a long way toward eliminating spraying.

Choose plants that solve landscape problems rather than create new ones. This includes planting border plants in far enough from the line that you're not invading your neighbors' space or having to constantly trim to prevent it.

It also includes planting plants that screen out unwanted views but that don't block views you want to keep (such as the sight line while backing your car out of the driveway).

And it *especially* means picking plants that match the size of the space you have so you don't end up spending more time with your pruners than your significant other. Most pruning work isn't done because the plant or the gardener delights in it; it's done to keep a too-big plant from overgrowing a too-small space.

## DON'T CALL ME DIRT

Odds are good that you flunked the soil test. Especially in housing developments built since the mid-1900s, few yards are blessed with decent soil. Even if your land started out without heavy clay or copious rock, topsoil is often scraped off during construction and piled up. Then when the house is built, several inches of soil from the pile are usually spread on top of the graded, compacted subsoil. This layering of limited topsoil is plant death waiting to happen. Adding more fertilizer won't solve it.

Good soil is a living, breathing organism that's far more than a medium that keeps plants from falling over. Think of it as a microscopic factory of life that supplies nutrients, moisture, oxygen, and energy that plants absolutely need to live and thrive.

Unless you've lucked out and moved into a place where gardeners lived before, you'll need to improve the underlying structure of the soil to add nutrients and air pockets that allow the roots to "breathe." The best way to do that is by working 2 to 3 inches of compost, mushroom soil, chopped leaves, rotted cow manure and/or similar organic matter into at least the top 10 or 12 inches of the existing soil. That works out to about 20 to 25 percent "good stuff" worked into your lousy existing stuff.

## HERE'S HOW

### TO DRAW YOUR OWN LANDSCAPE PLAN

1. Start with the big-picture game plan by mapping out your yard on a piece of paper. Include its main features, such as the house, driveway, walks, existing trees, and any outbuildings.

2. Think about the desired uses for each part of the yard and mark off space for each use. You may want a patio area off the back door or a swimming pool in the back yard, for example.

3. Take exact measurements of areas where you'd like to design landscaping, and transfer the measurements to graph paper. Look for graph paper sized at four, five, or eight boxes per inch, and use a scale in which one box equals 1 foot.

■ *Sketch the landscape features you're considering on a photocopy or tracing paper copy of your site map.*

4. Mark features that affect plant placement on the plan, including windows, doors, spigots, heat-pump fans, utility meters, and so forth. Mark which direction is north, and determine the area's sunlight. Mark existing plants that you intend to keep.

5. Compose a list of plants you'd like to use in the planned area. Make sure they're appropriate to the site. Jot down their sizes and bloom times.

6. Pencil in dots where each plant should go. Draw bubbles around each dot to represent the mature or planned widths of each plant. Pay attention to bloom times, heights, and forms and texture pairings as you go.

7. Look over the planting plan and picture what it will look like as the months change. Erase and make changes. (This is why you use a pencil; it's much easier to erase dots than to move plants later.)

It's best to prepare whole beds rather than digging and improving individual holes for each plant. When you improve a whole bed, the soil is uniform throughout. That gives plant roots free reign to spread unimpeded in all directions. When you're done, you'll have slightly raised beds that taper down to ground level around the edges.

If you're only planting a single tree or large shrub in a hole instead of planting a bed, the game plan is different. In this case, add no more than 10 percent organic matter. Why? If you greatly improve the soil in a small hole, tree and shrub roots will grow out until they hit the unimproved

"real-world" soil, then turn back inward where the going is easier.

Water also can back up into the improved hole when it hits the surrounding slower-draining, compacted soil. The effect is a lot like planting into an underground pot. If you must plant in a single hole, make the hole at least three times as wide as the root ball.

Once you've improved poor soil (assuming it needed improvement), follow the old gardening cliché: "Take care of the soil, and it will take care of the plants." Do that by keeping the soil's acidity and nutrition at optimal levels; not digging/ tilling soil when it's wet; regularly topping garden beds with mulch, compost, leaves or similar organic matter; and limiting use of herbicides, fungicides, insecticides, and other "cides" to what's absolutely necessary.

## WHEN TO DO DIRTY DEEDS

Removing turf and digging new beds can be done anytime the ground isn't frozen or wet enough that you'll ruin the soil structure. If it's sticky or muddy, don't dig. You'll squish the air spaces out of the soil and turn it into something akin to concrete when it dries.

One of the best times of year to dig a new bed is fall. The ground is typically warm and fairly dry then, plus it's more pleasant to be out working than in a 95-degree heat wave. Most plants do very well when planted September through the end of October, so it's a good time to get the whole project done at once.

If you dig but don't plant until the following spring, that's fine. Just cover the ground with 2 to 3 inches of wood or bark mulch to prevent winter erosion.

Spring is another good time to prepare a new bed. However, the soil might be colder and wet from snowmelt and spring rains.

Midsummer isn't an ideal time to plant because of the heat and usually drier conditions, but that doesn't mean you can't dig then. If you don't mind the heat, do your digging and soil work to get the beds ready in summer. Add your mulch, and walk away until the heat breaks in September. Then come back and plant later into the already-mulched bed.

That September/October time frame is one of two ideal planting windows in Pennsylvania. The other excellent time is early to mid-spring—from right after the ground thaws (typically late March) through May.

Plants grown in containers can be planted anytime from early spring through October—and maybe even a bit beyond if fall turns out to be long and warm. However, it's more of a shock to a plant

when it's transplanted in very hot weather, plus you'll have to be particularly careful about watering summer-planted plants. Those first six weeks after planting are critical for consistently damp soil.

If you *do* plant in summer, at least try to do it during a cooler spell, during cloudy weather, or ideally, right before a rain. Evening planting also is better than midday when a relocated plant will have to face the most brutal heat and sun right off the bat. Even then, plants transplanted into good soil and kept watered usually bounce back from wilting caused by heat shock.

Most plants do equally well whether planted in spring or fall. The exception is borderline-hardy plants that would rather not have to face a cold winter until their roots are more fully established. These include camellia, crape myrtle, nandina, cherry laurel, osmanthus, cedar, sweetbox, aucuba, and Japanese plum yew—or any plant with which you're pushing the winter-hardiness envelope. Spring planting is more ideal for those.

## WATCH THE SIZES

Don't space your plants based on how they look now. Consider their eventual sizes. Unlike sofas and tables in your indoor designing, a new plant doesn't stay that size for long.

Gauge plant spacing by the "mature" sizes listed on the plant tag. Keep in mind that these are sizing guides at a fixed point in time, often five or ten years down the road. The sizes aren't maximums but more of planning guidelines for how you intend to maintain the plant. Plants may slow in growth rates as they age, but they never really stop growing–until they're dead. A few spacing guidelines are:

1. When planting next to a wall or other barrier, take the mature width and divide in half. Plant no closer than that distance. (Example: A holly whose mature width is 8 feet around should be planted a minimum of 4 feet away from a wall.)

2. To determine how close to site plants to one another, space them the mature width apart. (Example: plant 4-foot-wide spireas no closer

than 4 feet apart.) If two plants of differing sizes are going next to one another, add the two mature widths together and divide in half to determine the minimum spacing. (Example: A 6-foot-wide viburnum and a 4-foot-wide spirea should be planted no closer than 5 feet apart. 6 + 4 = 10. Then 10 divided in half equals 5.)

3. Planning for height is easier. If your windowsill is 3 feet off the ground and you don't want to obstruct the view, look for plants that list out at 3 feet tall—unless you don't mind regular trimming.

In borders and foundation plantings, arrange your plants so that the tallest plants are in the back and the shorter ones in front. In an island bed in which you'll be able to view your plants from all angles, go with the tallest plants toward the middle and the shorter ones around the perimeter.

One last point on spacing is to be extra careful when planting along property lines. Plants hanging over neighboring properties are the source of numerous spats, not to mention district judge cases. To be on the safe side, use the same planting rule as when planting next to walls. Take the mature width of the plant, divide it in half, and plant no closer than that distance from the property line.

## PLANTING

Before diving into the hows, whats, and whens, it's helpful to understand some of the whys behind your gardening tasks. Take, for example,

When planting below a window, be sure the shrubs will not obscure the view.

planting. In recent years, technology has given us a new understanding of how roots function. This has changed some previously accepted planting practices—particularly involving trees and shrubs. Past advice often suggested heavily amending planting holes, adding a layer of stone "for drainage" under the rootballs, and immediately pruning top growth to "balance it out with the roots" lost in digging and transplanting.

Current tree-planting advice now suggests planting in unimproved soil (unless it's atrocious), digging holes no deeper than the rootball, planting on solid ground without stones underneath, and *not* pruning off any healthy, unbroken limbs. More emphasis is also being placed on way-too-common counterproductive practices, such as planting too deeply, failing to correct matted or circling roots before planting, failing to remove potentially strangulating ropes and strings, and packing mulch high up against trunks. (See March's "Here's How to Plant a Tree" for more tree-planting details.)

## WATERING

Watering plants is another issue that can go awry. Even though Pennsylvania usually receives adequate rainfall over the year, rain doesn't always fall at regular intervals. That means supplemental watering is often necessary.

Plants vary in their moisture needs, and soils vary in their ability to hold it. Changing weather is another variable. More water is needed during hot, dry, windy spells than during cool, cloudy spells. That's why the answer to the question, "How much should I water?" is, "It depends."

## FERTILIZE

The how and when of fertilizing plants is easy to determine. *Why* we fertilize is more complicated. Fertilizer is intended to feed the soil. Thus it feeds plants only indirectly. In situations where the soil has been depleted of certain nutrients and nature isn't replacing them via the decay of organic debris, the gardener must add them to the soil in the form of fertilizer.

The action of microbial life in the soil along with soil temperature and moisture help convert the nutrients in the fertilizer into a form that can be

## WATERING TIPS

- New plants need more frequent watering than mature ones because their root systems haven't yet spread to "mine" moisture efficiently.

- Water enough so that the soil is damp beyond the reach of the roots and to just below their depth. Young plants need less total water, and they need it fairly close to the plant's base. More developed plants need more total water and need it over a wider area. It does little good to wet just the mulch or top inch of soil. The idea is to encourage the roots to move out into the soil.

- Don't water at such a high rate that the water runs off instead of soaks in. Slow it to a trickle if necessary to keep it all on target.

- Don't overdo it. The goal is consistently damp soil, not soggy soil (unless you're growing bog plants).

- Water the soil rather than the plant. Wet leaves encourage disease.

- Sandy soil dries faster and requires more frequent watering. Clay soil holds water longer and requires less watering, but it's more at risk of leading to rotting roots.

- Water lawns deeply but not often, if you water them at all. Lawns often go brown and dormant in Pennsylvania summers, but established ones usually recover well even after a month of no water in a dormant state.

*Water directly onto the soil, not over the leaves.*

taken up by plant roots. Whether that happens rapidly or slowly depends on whether or not the fertilizer, especially nitrogen, is soluble in water.

Depending on what a soil test reveals, you may need fertilizer that is "complete" (has all three of the major nutrients of nitrogen, phosphorus, and potassium). Sometimes a soil test will show that all nutrients are present, but they are not in balance. Then the solution is to add a particular fertilizer that features a greater proportion of one or more nutrients.

Do-it-yourself soil test kits are available for about $10 through County Penn State Extension offices, many garden centers, or directly from Penn State's Agricultural Analytical Services Lab, online at http://agsci.psu.edu/aasl/soil-testing/soil-fertility-testing.

## PRUNING, PRIMPING, PROTECTING

Pruning is important to plant health. When done properly at the correct time, it fosters thick growth and prolific blooming and fruiting. It can bring back a plant from old age, forestall disease, or create a hedge or an espaliered work of art.

When done improperly or at the wrong time, pruning can ruin the next bloom season, or even kill a plant. Woody plants such as trees, shrubs, and vines are most often pruned to control their size, but the irony is that pruning incorrectly will actually stimulate plant growth.

## FERTILIZING TIPS

- Maintain the correct soil pH to ensure optimum effectiveness of fertilizer.

- Topdress your garden beds and lawns with organic material every year, such as bark mulch, compost, or leaves.

- Use slow-acting fertilizers for long-term, consistent nutrition over many weeks.

- Fertilize just before or during the growing season, not when plants are dormant.

- Pay particular attention to fertilizing in beds of plants that are heavy feeders.

## PRUNING TIPS

- Always have a pruning goal, and time the procedure correctly. The monthly pruning tips throughout this book will help you keep track of this.

- Keep your pruners, loppers, saws, and mower blades sharp.

- Promptly prune or pinch off injured and diseased plant parts.

- Disinfect pruning equipment used on diseased plants. A mix of 1 part bleach to 9 parts water is an effective homemade solution.

- Move plants that need constant pruning (to control size) to a larger space.

- Prune to maintain the natural shape of the plant. Reserve shearing for plants being used as formal hedges or topiary.

Besides pruning off or cutting back branches, landscapes can be kept in peak form by several other types of cuts.

One is the process of "deadheading," which involves snipping off spent flower heads. This not only neatens the look of the garden but can redirect plant energy from producing seeds to producing new flowers. One advantage of that is preventing unwanted seeding. Another is that deadheading may encourage repeat bloom. (See August's "Here's How to Deadhead Flowers," page 146.)

Picking or snipping off ratty leaves throughout the season is another good primping endeavor. In cases where the spotting or browning was caused by disease, removing the affected leaves can slow the spread of the disease without pesticides.

Most perennial flowers benefit from periodic division. This involves digging plant clumps that are dying in the center or spreading into unwanted areas. The dug clumps are divided into healthy, smaller clumps. These pieces can then be replanted to keep a perennial's spread in check or to expand a variety into a new area. (See April's "Here's How to Divide Perennials.")

And one other form of cutting is using a sharp tool to edge garden beds. This involves trimming off grass or weeds that are encroaching into mulched and planted beds. Long-handled, half-moon-shaped edging tools are available to do this deed, but a flat-edged spade also works well. Some gardeners even use axes to cut sharp edges along their beds. Others opt for gas- or electric-powered edgers.

Finally, think about protection for plants that might need a little extra TLC. Good plant selection will limit the need for much of this, but remember that even the toughest native plants aren't exactly "native" to the contrived environment that is now your yard. Sometimes plants need protection from the elements and their enemies. Examples:

- Stake plants that are vulnerable to injury by wind, rain, and people.

■ *Use your scissors, snips, or hand pruners to snip off dead flowers in a process called "deadheading."*

■ *Astilbe can be divided into smaller clumps and planted in other areas of your garden.*

- Know which potential pest problems affect your plants and be ready to use controls when necessary.

- Observe and inspect plants regularly for pest problems and signs of stress.

- Separate temporary or cosmetic plant problems from serious ones, and treat the serious ones as soon as possible.

- Shelter or spray antidesiccant products on the foliage of plants exposed to harsh winter wind and sun. (Antidesiccants, also called anti-transpirants, are oil-based sprays that slow the loss of moisture from plant leaves.)

- Fence out critters.

- Mulch plants to buffer soil-temperature extremes around their roots.

- Overwinter tender plants in frost-free areas.

- Acclimate plants gradually to indoor or outdoor sites rather than suddenly moving them.

That'll do it. Now you're ready to get out there and whack, deadhead, and dig with the best of them … but more important, enjoy what you (and Mother Nature) have created.

## HOW TO USE THIS BOOK

Try not to look at *Pennsylvania Month-by-Month Gardening* as a very fat to-do list. You don't have to do everything listed, and nothing disastrous will happen if you fail to carry out the exact details at the assigned timing. The idea is to help you garden more efficiently and become more confident in knowing your way around the yard. Rather than try to read this cover to cover, you'll get the best use by referring to each section as needed as the months go by.

Once you get through it two or three times, you'll likely need to refer to the book less and less. You'll just *know* what to do when, which is good because the book (we hope) will be dirty and dog-eared by then.

This book is laid out month-by-month so you can refer to it as the seasons progress. Under each month, there are six main categories:

**PLAN** covers the getting-ready or "cerebral" part, such as gathering supplies, prioritizing new projects, and deciding on plants to be added or moved.

**PLANT** gives you details on when to plant which plants and how to get the job done correctly.

**CARE** tells you what do to keep your yard and plants looking their best, including mulching, controlling weeds, and knowing when and how to prune what.

**WATER** is a rundown on how to deliver the right amount of moisture to each type of plant in the different seasons, both indoors and out.

**FERTILIZE** tells you when to fertilize which plants and how to know what kind and how much nutrition to deliver.

**PROBLEM-SOLVE** helps you figure out what might be going wrong, which problems you can ignore, what to do about ones you shouldn't ignore, and what early signs to look for before anything gets out of hand.

Under each of those six categories are nine subsections that break down the basic jobs for each plant type.

The **All** category covers the more general tasks, while the eight other categories cover **Annuals & Tropicals**; **Bulbs** (both winter-hardy and tender summer bloomers); **Lawns**; **Perennials & Groundcovers** (including ornamental grasses); **Roses**; **Shrubs** (both flowering and evergreen); **Trees** (both flowering and evergreen); and **Vines** (both woody perennials and tender annual ones).

We've devoted a separate section at the back of the book to maintaining water gardens throughout the season. Edibles aren't included because we're focusing on the ornamental plantings that most people have, and whole books are devoted to the specialized details involved in growing fruits, vegetables, and herbs.

The back of this book offers additional details and charts, including how to fine-tune your timing by watching what's going on around you, the pros and cons of different mulches, and how to determine the number of plants and how much soil or mulch you need. Now you're ready. Dig in. Just watch out for the buried cable TV line.

## USDA COLD HARDINESS ZONES

The U.S. Department of Agriculture divides the country into Cold Hardiness Zones based on each area's average lowest winter temperature.

Pennsylvania encompasses six zones, ranging from average lows of -15 to -20 degrees in the highest reaches of northern Pennsylvania (Zone 5a) to average lows of 5 to 10 degrees in the southeast corner around Philadelphia (Zone 7b).

Most of the state falls in the moderate Zones 6a and 6b, meaning lows bottom out no lower than 0 to -10 degrees.

Keep in mind those are *averages*. Many winters never hit zero, meaning it's possible to grow plants rated for warmer zones. But it's also possible for a rogue winter to go *below* the average, killing plants that normally survive.

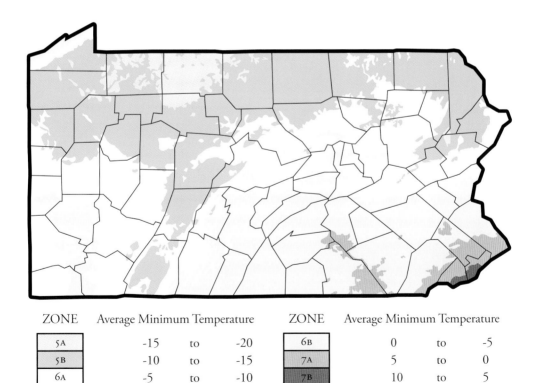

| ZONE | Average Minimum Temperature | | |
|---|---|---|---|
| 5A | -15 | to | -20 |
| 5B | -10 | to | -15 |
| 6A | -5 | to | -10 |

| ZONE | Average Minimum Temperature | | |
|---|---|---|---|
| 6B | 0 | to | -5 |
| 7A | 5 | to | 0 |
| 7B | 10 | to | 5 |

USDA Plant Hardiness Zone Map, 2012. Agricultural Research Service, U.S. Department of Agriculture. Accessed from http://planthardiness.ars.usda.gov.

# January

*January is down time in the Pennsylvania landscape … usually.*

Some years, when the heart of winter delivers a thaw and uncharacteristic 50ish spell, it's possible to get out and get a few "gardeny" things done. Winter weeds can be pulled. Broken branches and other debris can be whisked away. And edging the beds is a breeze in thawed, winter-softened turf.

But most years, it's either too cold to stay out for long, or our plants are buried under a layer of frigid, white "mulch." Though Keystone State gardeners might not always welcome it, snow is generally a *good* thing for plants—in reasonable amounts. Snow makes an excellent insulator to protect plant crowns, roots, and broadleaf evergreen foliage from the damaging blows of sub-zero polar intrusions. Obscene multi-foot dumpings of the Lake Erie kind, on the other hand, are *bad* news, causing our arborvitae to sag and our white pine branches to snap. Worse still are occasional ice storms that can bring down whole trees.

Trying to remove snowy and icy burdens not only is difficult or futile, the effort may do more harm than good. Whacking ice-laden junipers with a shovel (yeah, it's been done) is likely to snap off branches rather than rescue them.

That's why veteran gardeners usually figure that January is most productive when devoted to planning. It's a good month to curl up next to a fireplace with a how-to book or seed catalog and dream about the gardens-to-be.

Use this time to think back to last year's successes, failures, and postponements. Assess what worked, what didn't, and what you can (and should) do differently. Sketch out some ideas on paper. Make a to-do list that'll help you hit the ground running when the white mulch melts. Jot down plants you'd like to try.

Put this out-of-garden time to good use. Especially as you age, you might become grateful for a Pennsylvania January.

## PLAN

### ALL

Do you keep a garden journal? If not, this is a good time to start one. Journaling reminds us of past adventures (or misadventures!) in the garden, helping us avoid mistakes and become a better gardener each year. Among items to record: the weather; what blooms or leafs out, and when; new plants and their names; lessons learned; ideas to consider; and sketches of what's planted, where. A journal can range from a collection of note cards to a computer file to a lovely bound book. Whatever you use, keep it nearby so it's convenient to make regular entries.

Now's a good time to do jobs for which you won't have time once the gardening season begins. Clean and sharpen those tools. Catch up on that pile of gardening books and magazines. Clean your stored pots to get them ready for spring planting. Paint

■ *Even if snowy weather keeps you indoors, you can still work on getting ready for the spring.*

wooden handles of tools a bright color so you're less likely to lose them in the garden.

Study your winter landscape from windows throughout the house. What can you do to improve this overlooked fourth season of the landscape? How about winterberry hollies and red-twig dogwoods in front of that evergreen backdrop out the kitchen window? Maybe an arbor or bench could add hardscaped winter interest. Or maybe you just need a few more evergreens to add winter life to the now-dormant perennial gardens. How's your supply of seed and suet to feed the winter birds?

### ANNUALS & TROPICALS

Inventory leftover seeds and determine which ones are viable enough for another year. Most are good for two or three years if kept dry and out of extreme temperatures. If you're not sure, roll up a few in a damp paper towel, place the towel in a plastic bag, and set in a warm area for the prescribed germination time on the seed packet. Then unroll the towel and see how many sprouted. If it's few to none, toss the seed packet, and add seeds to your purchase list.

Check out the seed catalogs (paper or online), and order annuals that you plan to start from seed—both indoors over winter or ones to be direct-seeded in the garden in spring. The best selection and availability is *now*. Some of the easiest annual flowers to start from seed are marigolds, zinnias, sunflowers, bachelor buttons, nasturtium, cosmos, cleome, and hyacinth beans. Even if you don't buy seeds, catalogs offer a wealth of information on new varieties, cultural information, plant names (common and botanical), prices, and landscape design ideas.

It's a little early to start seeds, but you *can* get ready. Clean and sterilize used trays and seed-starting packs in a solution of 1 part bleach to 9 parts water. Or buy new ones. Are your lights in working order? Have enough seed-starting medium? Labels ready to go?

### BULBS

Those tulips, daffodils, hyacinths, and other spring-flowering bulbs that you planted back in fall are safely nestled underground—biological clocks ticking for when it's time to break dormancy and send up shoots. That's why they're planted in fall.

Summer-flowering bulbs, such as lilies, dahlias and cannas, operate on a different schedule. They're best planted in spring rather than fall. Check the catalogs for any of these you'd like to try this season.

## LAWNS

If you didn't already do it at the end of last season, clean your mower, sharpen the blades, change the oil, and get a new spark plug. The gas tank *was* drained, right? Or is it time to think about getting a new mulching mower or a rechargeable electric model this year?

Evaluate your lawn size. Are you tired of all of the mowing? Consider converting some lawn area into sites for trees for more shady sitting space, or into gardens for added wildlife interest, or into a vegetable garden for low-cost fresh food.

## PERENNIALS & GROUNDCOVERS

If you journaled or made notes from last season, get them out and nail down specifics of what perennial flowers and groundcovers will get this year's job done. Decide on which existing perennials need to be divided and/or moved. Make a list of new ones to look for at the garden center come spring. Catalogs can help here too.

## ROSES

It takes some imagination to visualize lovely roses out in the yard where now there are only humps of mulch and soil around stubby canes. Exercise your imagination by browsing the new varieties in garden catalogs and online.

Roses come in many different types, colors, sizes, and habits. Not all are high care. Consider where the beauty, long bloom, and fragrance of roses can add to your landscape, then scope out varieties that best fit your eye and maintenance levels. New varieties of hybrid teas are more disease-resistant than ever. Shrub types perform well on sunny banks and other hot spots. Climbers are naturals on arbors. And miniature roses are worthy choices for balconies and window boxes.

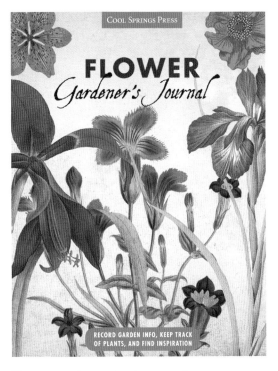

■ *Use a journal to record gardening notes from year to year.*

## SHRUBS

Evaluate your landscape's winter-interest shrubbery, both by taking a walk around the yard and looking out key windows. Can you even *see* shrubs out the windows, or are they all crowded up against the house?

Do your shrubs have ornamental features to relieve winter bleakness, such as berries, cones, interesting bark, and/or colorful evergreen foliage? Do you have a variety of sizes and shapes? Are there enough evergreens, or are you leaning too heavily on flowering shrubs that drop their leaves in winter?

If you're trying to be more wildlife-friendly, do you have enough shrubs that provide shelter and food in winter? Evergreens such as arborvitae, yew, and falsecypress offer protection, while fruit-producers such as holly, juniper, and chokeberry offer food.

Evergreen shrubs in particular are useful not only for screening out unwanted views in winter, but for blocking cold winter winds. The north and northwest exposures of your house are the best locations for blocking those arctic prevailing winds.

*Clematis can be grown to camouflage a plain brick wall.*

## TREES

Evergreen trees are bigger and more effective winter-wind barriers than evergreen shrubs. Spruce, fir, pine, arborvitae, holly, and Japanese red cedar are among the choices that can grow to give wind protection even to the second floor of your house. Evergreens provide wind protection for a distance of twice as far out as their height. For example, a line of 25-foot-tall spruces can protect areas up to 50 feet away on their down-wind side.

Do you have a few "specimen" evergreens to add winter interest and to make nice focal points out key windows? Good examples are weeping Alaska-cedar, Japanese umbrella pine, weeping Norway spruce, and golden Hinoki cypress.

Check out your flowering trees. Have you fallen completely for varieties that strut their glory in spring but offer little in winter? If so, consider adding species with interesting bark (stewartia, birch, crape myrtle, or paperbark maple, for example) or at least ones with interesting branching patterns when the tree is bare (such as Japanese maple, weeping beech, or Kousa dogwood).

Rather than throw it away, set your cut Christmas tree out in the yard and redecorate it with goodies for the birds. Adorn this repurposed feeder with pieces of citrus fruit, strings of cranberries and raisins, and pine cones stuffed with suet.

## VINES

Vines are the most overlooked and underused type of plant in most landscapes. These are excellent for adding life and eye-level color to all sorts of vertical structures around the yard, such as downspouts, porch columns, mailboxes, light posts, tree stumps, arbors, and pergolas. Do you have enough? Any?

Vines on a trellis are also a great choice for adding screening where you need height but don't have a lot of horizontal space to work with. Examples are narrow side yards between homes, between decks in condo and apartment complexes, in skinny beds along side-walks, and around heat pumps and trash cans. Do you have any of those spots where a trellis can be added?

A third good use for vines is softening bare walls. Again, add trellises, obelisks, teepees, or other vine supports to grow vining plants in front of windowless house walls, barn walls, brick buildings, or even the spaces between your home's windows to add vertical interest.

January is a good month to plan for which vines will suit which sites. Choices are available for sun to shade. Some flower, some are evergreen. Some climb by twining, others need tying, and still others stick onto surfaces by adhesive rootlets.

## TO START SEEDS INSIDE

You don't need a greenhouse, a fancy light contraption, or even special "grow lights" to start plants from seed. It's easier than you think:

■ *Start seeds in seed-starting medium.*

1. Clean and label used plastic containers, such as margarine tubs or cut-off milk containers. Drill eight or ten small holes in the bottom of each for drainage.

2. Fill each container two-thirds full with vermiculite (light, fluffy, water-holding stuff available at garden centers). Scatter seeds over the surface, and cover with a light layer of more vermiculite. Seed packets will tell you how much to cover each variety.

3. Place seeded containers on a clean foam meat tray from the grocery store or in a plastic seedling tray. Gently sprinkle the surface with water until the vermiculite is saturated and water is draining out the bottom.

4. Lay plastic wrap over the containers, and set the trays near a sunny window at room temperature. For varieties that prefer warmer temperatures to germinate, set those on a store-bought seedling heat mat or on top of a water heater or refrigerator. Within five to seven days, some seedlings will emerge; others may take up to three weeks. Check moisture every few days and lightly re-wet the surface if it's drying.

5. Once the first set of leaves unfurl, use a pencil or similar pointy object to lift each seedling out and into labeled, individual pots filled three-quarters full with moistened, lightweight potting mix from the garden center. For smaller plants, use recycled plastic 6-packs from past plant purchases. Clean and soak these in a 10-percent bleach solution for fifteen minutes before using. For bigger plants, use recycled 4-inch pots. (When moving seedlings, handle by their leaves, not their stems.)

6. Set the planted packs and pots in plastic seedling trays under ordinary fluorescent workshop lights for about fourteen hours per day. Use a timer to automate the process. A cool basement or room with temperatures in the 50s is ideal for most seedlings and promotes stocky growth. Hang lights from chains and hooks so you can suspend the lights 2 or 3 inches above the plants.

7. Add water with a balanced, water-soluble fertilizer mixed at quarter-strength to the *trays*, not over the top of the plants. Add enough so the plants soak up the water in fifteen or twenty minutes. This "bottom-watering" disturbs roots less and less likely to promote disease. Check every few days and add more water when the surface is drying and the tray's weight is noticeably lighter. Option: place a fan set on low to blow over the seedlings to further encourage stocky growth and to discourage disease.

8. Once the seedlings reach transplant size, take them outside to "harden off." Set them in shade for a couple of hours the first day, then gradually give more light and more time out until they're outside round the clock for two or three days before planting.

# JANUARY

## PLANT

### ALL

Other than burying those forgotten bulbs from last fall, January is not prime time for planting much of anything else. You *might* see landscapers installing trees or shrubs. Plants will do their best to survive this timing, but the survival odds are lower in winter than when the soil is warmer and when water (the unfrozen kind) is more available to plant roots.

### ANNUALS & TROPICALS

January is an excellent month to visit the houseplant section of your favorite garden center. Not only is it a warm, bright, and plant-filled getaway, but houseplant selections and sales are abundant this month. Many houseplants can serve double-duty by brightening your living room in winter and then becoming the centerpiece of an outdoor flowerpot in summer.

■ *Many houseplants like this peace lily, marble pothos, and peacock plant can be attractive combinations.*

### BULBS

Uh-oh! Found a few packs of spring-flowering bulbs that you bought but forgot to plant in fall? Better to get them in the ground *immediately* rather than wait until spring or next fall. They'll likely dry out and die by then. Plant them now, even if you have to hack through frozen ground to do it.

It's not too late to force amaryllis or paperwhite narcissus bulbs indoors. These need no chill period (as do the bulbs you planted outdoors in fall), and you might find some excellent post-holiday bargains on them at stores. (See December's "Here's How to Grow Amaryllis Inside," page 206.)

### LAWNS

Winter-sowing of cool-season grass seed (Kentucky bluegrass, perennial ryegrass, and tall or fine fescues) isn't optimal but it's possible if you need to get a jump on patching bare ground. First, the soil should be thawed. Seed scattered over the surface of frozen soil can wash away in a heavy January rain. Scratch the seed into the surface and top lightly with straw. The seed won't germinate until the soil warms to about 50 degrees Fahrenheit in spring, but at least it'll be in place.

September is the optimal month for seeding and overseeding lawns. (See September's "Here's How to Seed a New Lawn," page 162.)

### PERENNIALS & GROUNDCOVERS

Enjoy your perennials that stay evergreen most winters (hellebores, coralbells, and dianthus, for example), but don't think about transplanting or adding any now—even if you happen across refugees that weren't stored for winter at the garden center. Even perennials such as the Christmas rose (*Helleborus niger*), which has become a popular December potted plant, is best kept inside a sun room or protected garage until planting outside in spring.

### ROSES

Varieties that were forced into bloom for holiday sales shouldn't go in the ground yet. Grow them as houseplants next to a sunny window the remainder of winter, then plant outside in late April through mid-May after gradually acclimating them over a seven- to ten-day period.

## SHRUBS

Hydrangea is another flowering woody plant that you might find sold as a blooming December gift plant. As with forced-into-bloom roses, treat hydrangeas as houseplants by growing next to a sunny window over the rest of winter. Plant outside in late April to mid-May after acclimating them to outdoor temperatures seven to ten days. Some hydrangeas forced into bloom in winter are *not* flower-bud-hardy in Pennsylvania winters, meaning they may survive but never flower in your yard.

Cut branches taken late this month from early-blooming shrubs such as forsythia, fothergilla, witch hazel, and bridal wreath spirea can be "forced" into blooming in a vase inside for winter color. (See "Here's How to Force Shrub Cuttings to Bloom Inside," at right.)

## TREES

Cut branches from early-blooming trees such as cornelian cherry dogwood and filbert also can be forced to bloom in a vase inside.

April is a much better time to plant new trees outside. One exception is that live, balled-and-burlapped evergreen that you bought as a Christmas tree. Get that in the ground as soon as you can after Christmas. (See December's "Here's How to Plant a Live Christmas Tree," page 205.)

## VINES

It's okay to install trellises, arbors, and similar vine supports when the soil is thawed over winter, but wait until spring to plant the vines.

## CARE

## ALL

If you don't have at least an inch or two of mulch over your garden beds, and snow isn't insulating the ground for you, consider doing some January mulching (if you can get mulch now). Your neighbors will think you're nuts, but mulching frozen ground helps keep it frozen, which sidesteps the fluctuating temperatures that can cause plants to "heave" upward. That can expose roots and lead to them freeze-drying.

## HERE'S HOW

### TO FORCE SHRUB CUTTINGS TO BLOOM INSIDE

"Forcing" branches is the technique of cutting live branches from trees and shrubs and causing them to bloom inside in winter in a vase.

1. Plants that work best are those that naturally flower before May, such as fruit trees, dogwood, azalea, redbud, witch hazel, forsythia, and fothergilla. These species produce their flower buds the previous year.

2. On an above-freezing day, cut 1- to 3-foot sections off the ends of branches that are a ½-inch in diameter or less. Look for wood with plump buds, which are flowering buds. (Leaf buds are skinnier.)

3. Plunge the cut ends into a bucket with 6 to 8 inches of very warm water, 100 to 110 degrees Fahrenheit is ideal. Soak at least six hours.

4. After soaking, cut an inch off the bottoms at an angle and arrange the branches in a water-filled vase at room temperature. Maximize display life by adding floral preservative or antibacterial mouthwash (diluted to 1 tablespoon of mouthwash per quart of water).

5. Change water and preservative every three or four days. Most branches will bloom in two to four weeks, with the earliest natural bloomers taking the least amount of time to open.

■ *Cut a branch from a fruit tree or other spring flowering trees to bloom indoors.*

*Edge with a string trimmer by holding the head at a 90° angle to the ground. Carefully move along parallel to the line you are edging.*

Can't get mulch? January is a good month to chip your own yard trimmings if you've got a chipper-shredder.

Take advantage of thaws to edge your garden beds. Turf cuts easily when it's soft and damp over the winter.

Go easy on rock salt used to melt ice. The salty runoff can end up in lawns and planted beds where excess sodium impedes water uptake. That can lead to brown leaf tips and edges, especially in hot, dry weather. Instead of rock salt, consider manually removing ice or improving traction by scattering gritty material, such as sand or wood ashes. If you use a melter, look for more plant-friendly calcium magnesium acetate, calcium chloride, or potassium chloride.

## ANNUALS & TROPICALS

Rooted cuttings that you're growing indoors benefit from your brightest windows. Or better yet, set them under grow lights or fluorescent workshop lights.

Pinch back any annuals you've potted for overwintering indoors if they're getting spindly ("leggy"). These also appreciate bright windows or supplemental light.

## BULBS

If you notice crocus or daffodil foliage emerging outside already during a winter thaw, don't panic. In fact, don't do anything. There's no need to pile more mulch on the foliage for protection. At worst, freezing temperatures might brown the foliage tips a bit, but the bulbs will develop additional leaves and bloom just fine. Hardy bulbs have a lot of experience with winter weather.

When your amaryllis bulb finishes blooming, cut off the flower stalks. Treat it as a houseplant the rest of winter—watering when the soil goes dry, displaying it next to a sunny window, and fertilizing monthly with a balanced houseplant fertilizer (something similar to 10-10-10). After danger of frost passes, gradually acclimate the plant to outside conditions over seven to ten days, then either grow it as a potted plant outside or plant it in the ground over summer. If you *don't* plan to keep your amaryllis for another year, just toss the bulb when the flower show ends.

Improve the appearance of blooming potted bulbs by mulching their soil surface lightly with decorative gravel, colorful pebbles, sphagnum moss, nut shells, or some other attractive material. Trim off any withered foliage tips or blooms.

## LAWNS

Other than preventing rock salt runoff that can exacerbate drought stress in summer, there's not much to do to the lawn this month. It's normal even for cool-season turfgrasses to lose their rich green color in winter. They'll green up fine when warm weather returns.

One thing that's helpful is to avoid walking on frozen grass. Even though the grass is dormant, crushing ice crystals can damage the plant crowns (the point from which new blades emerge).

Don't worry if your zoysia grass lawn looks dead. It's a warm-season grass and can spend five or six months of the year dormant and looking straw brown in Pennsylvania's climate. That's why cool-season grasses are preferred here. They don't look quite as brown in the dead of winter, they hold their color later in fall, and they green up faster in spring.

## PERENNIALS & GROUNDCOVERS

Newly planted perennials and groundcovers are particularly prone to heaving during alternating winter freezes and thaws. They're not yet fully rooted. Check your garden beds during January thaws to make sure none of your perennial clumps are sporting exposed roots that winter winds can harm. Tamp clumps back down. If you can, add an inch or two of mulch (leaves are fine) to lessen a repeat of this problem.

Let perennials and ornamental grasses stand for another month or two. Seedheads offer a food source for overwintering birds, while dried grass stems are a favorite nest-building material. Dead vegetative parts can also help insulate plant crowns (especially mums) during winters in which snow insulation isn't happening. If things are blowing around and driving you crazy, go ahead and cut whatever's dead and brown.

## ROSES

Low light and dry air are stressful to potted indoor miniature roses. Stress increases their vulnerability to pest and disease problems; fluorescent lights help. Pinch off spent flowers and yellowed leaves.

Outdoors, interweave needled branches cut from your Christmas tree around the base of roses as extra insulation. Prune off any broken or winter-injured canes as soon as you notice them.

Climbing roses can be pruned this month.

## SHRUBS

If you're using anti-desiccant sprays on evergreen shrubs in sites exposed to harsh winter sun and wind, re-apply them this month. These sprays can slow moisture loss from the leaves and are mostly used on broadleaf evergreens, such as cherry laurel, osmanthus, holly, hardy camellia, and nandina. Apply only on relatively mild days (over 40 degrees Fahrenheit), and follow the directions on the product label.

Limit pruning to cutting off damaged and broken branches. Make clean cuts back to where the branch joins a larger branch or a main stem. Take care not to gouge into wood on the main branch or trunk. Leave the wound as is to heal in the air; there's no need to paint or apply tar to wounds.

If heavy snow is weighing down your yews, boxwoods, rhododendrons, hollies, and other evergreens, it's usually best to do nothing. Most plants will spring back from moderate snow-load pressure when the snow melts and the weather warms. If it looks like you're crossing the line from sagging to snapping, use a soft implement such as a broom to *gently* release the snow with an upward motion.

## TREES

Trees can suffer their worst winter beatings this month. Evergreens may brown around their leaf edges in our coldest-of-the-year temperatures, while wind gusts that follow ice storms can rip off limbs, especially from brittle-wooded species such as white pine, birch, flowering pear, Chinese elm, poplar, willow, and locust. There's not much you can do about any of that, other than possibly removing some of the low-hanging snow loads that you can reach from the ground (with that same upward motion of a broom that you used on the shrubs).

■ *The weight of snow is enough to weigh heavily on shrub and tree branches and can break them if you don't gently push them up to shake off the snow.*

Cut off broken branches that you can reach from the ground back to healthy joints. No ladder-and-chainsaw attempts! Call a trained, insured pro to handle any higher-hanging limbs (*immediately* for ones over traffic areas) and ragged stubs.

Spray evergreen trees that are vulnerable to winter drying with an anti-desiccant spray—to the extent you can reach. Remember, apply it only when daytime temperatures are above 40 degrees Fahrenheit, and follow all label instructions—especially before applying it to blue-needled trees. (These sprays may discolor those.)

January is a good month to prune deciduous trees that get "sappy" when you cut them while temperatures are warmer in spring. Three that fall into this category: maple, birch and dogwood. It's also a good month to prune fruiting apple trees. (See February's "Here's How to Prune a Tree," page 43.)

## VINES

Clip off broken branches of your woody vines anytime you discover them. Clean cuts prevent further tears on the bark and will heal faster. Also cut back branches that are whipping around in winter wind because they are too long or have come unattached from their support.

Annual vines (hyacinth beans, morning glory, black-eyed Susan vine, and so forth) can be pulled if you didn't already do that.

## WATER

### ALL

Hoses can be safely packed away most winters. The exception is an unusually dry, windy winter with little to no snow. In that case, some landscape plants benefit from a good soaking or two during thaws. Tops on the list are broadleaf evergreens (which lose more moisture in winter than any other plant), followed by needled evergreens and also any trees, shrubs, vines and perennials that you've planted in the last year or two.

Gauge water needs by inserting a water meter probe into the soil, about 6 inches deep. Or get an idea by inserting your index finger into the thawed ground.

Indoors, dry air from our heating systems can be eased by using a room humidifier, clustering plants closer together, setting dry-sensitive plants in the kitchen or bathroom, or setting plants on shallow trays of damp gravel.

## ANNUALS & TROPICALS

Water houseplants, overwintering tropicals, and potted annuals when the soil surface dries and your pots feel noticeably lighter. Once a week usually does it. Don't overwater. Water demands go down in the low-light, slow-growing conditions of winter. Soggy soil is the leading cause of houseplant death.

Misting plants doesn't do much to counteract dry indoor air. It might keep them clean (or encourage leaf disease), but research has found it has little to no useful benefit when it comes to a plant's humidity needs.

## BULBS

Water potted bulbs such as amaryllis, paperwhites, and hyacinths when the soil surface dries and the pots become noticeably lighter—assuming you plan to keep them going. If not, toss the bulbs when the flowers finish. Avoid soggy soil, which is a good way to rot bulbs.

## LAWNS

No water is needed, even in a dry January. Turfgrass is dormant now. Besides, the soil is frozen most or much of the time in January anyway.

## PERENNIALS & GROUNDCOVERS

Newly planted ones might benefit from a soaking or two during January thaws if the soil is unusually dry and snowless.

## ROSES

Miniature roses being grown indoors in heated homes can dry out quickly, so monitor the soil moisture regularly. You may need to water these twice a week. As with houseplants and potted bulbs, though, never water so much that the soil is soggy.

## SHRUBS, TREES & VINES

Newly planted ones might benefit from a soaking or two during January thaws if the soil is unusually dry and snowless. That's especially true of broadleaf evergreens, such as cherry laurel, nandina, osmanthus, holly, hardy camellia, sweetbox, rhododendron, azalea, and euonymus.

## FERTILIZE

### ALL

Put away the fertilizer for your outside plants until at least the end of winter. It's wasteful to your wallet and harmful to our waterways to apply fertilizer over frozen ground, only to have it carried away by winter rains or melting snow.

Indoors, fertilizer needs are low during this limited-light, slow-growing time. Overfertilizing plants that don't need it also is wasteful and potentially counterproductive to healthy growth.

### ANNUALS & TROPICALS

A balanced fertilizer once a month is typically adequate for your houseplants and overwintering tropicals. This includes poinsettias, which should hold their color all month.

If you added slow-acting, granular fertilizer to cuttings that you potted in fall, there's no need to fertilize again. Otherwise, add a balanced, water-soluble fertilizer diluted to half-strength about every three or four weeks. Plants that are not blooming do not need much fertilizer.

Fertilizing ailing indoor plants is usually counterproductive. *Plant food is not medicine.* Plants won't take in more nutrients than they need, and adding more than needed won't cure problems. In fact, too much can burn roots or discolor leaves. A better course of action is to figure out what's causing the plant to lose vigor, then address that.

### BULBS

Bulbs come packaged with their own "fertilizer" in the form of stored energy. Those that are potted for forced bloom will have enough to produce lovely blooms this season. If you plan to keep potted bulbs for another season or plan to plant hardy ones outside in spring, fertilize monthly with a balanced, water-soluble fertilizer formulated for bulbs.

### LAWNS

No lawn fertilizer is needed now. Wait until the ground thaws in late March to apply the season's first potential treatment. Snow actually has light levels of nitrogen that can naturally fertilize lawns as it melts.

### PERENNIALS, GROUNDCOVERS, SHRUBS, TREES & VINES

Wait until end of winter to fertilize.

### ROSES

If you added slow-acting fertilizer to your potted miniature roses when you potted them last fall, that'll suffice. Otherwise, add a balanced, water-soluble fertilizer diluted to half-strength about every three or four weeks.

Wait until end of winter to fertilize your outdoor roses.

## PROBLEM-SOLVE

### ALL

January is one the worst months for deer browsing—especially in years when snow cover takes away alternate food sources and makes your landscape plants the main dish on the menu. If you're depending on repellents to keep hungry deer from eating favorites such as arborvitae, yew, azalea, rhododendron, and even jaggy holly and rose, reapply your product of choice this month according to label directions.

### ANNUALS & TROPICALS

Stressed indoor plants are more vulnerable to bug damage. New seedlings and young plants are especially at risk if pest insects have managed to ride inside over winter. Cold drafts, insufficient light, and dry air from hot-air heat are three key indoor plant stressors.

*An easy way to clean houseplants that have been inside for a year is to put them in the shower. Let the water run over all of the plant leaves, into the pot, and down the drain.*

Whiteflies, aphids, scale, mites, and mealybugs are the five main threats. Try controlling them by rinsing infested foliage and stems under the faucet or under the shower. (Yes, some gardeners regularly give their houseplants showers—although body wash and deodorant afterward are carrying it too far.) Water can wash away bugs and their waste as well as interrupt the insects' life cycle.

If you catch a problem early, try pinching off infested or diseased leaves. Or try wiping away pests with a soft rag slightly dampened with rubbing alcohol.

To handle major infestations, take plants outside on above-freezing days long enough to spray them with insecticidal soap, horticultural oil, or other insecticide labeled for houseplant use. Get them back inside as soon as the spray dries. Follow all label directions.

## BULBS

Rot is sometimes a problem with bulbs potted for forcing. It's a particular threat in cool, soggy soil. If you find this destruction has occurred, throw away the bulbs. Examine bulbs regularly for discolored, soft spots before planting them, and do not overwater.

Check stored dahlias, callas, cannas, gladioli, and such to make sure they're not too damp and rotting as well. If your storage medium feels wet, replace it with drier sawdust, peat moss, or sand, and toss any bulbs that already are showing signs of rot. Look for a drier spot to store them for the rest of winter. If the medium is so dry that the bulbs are shriveling, slightly dampen the medium and look for a storage spot with higher humidity.

## LAWNS

Voles could be doing surface-tunnel damage under a snow cover, but spring is the time to patch that with new seed. Set out cage traps or snap traps baited with peanut butter near fresh surface tunnels to capture or kill them.

Soil compaction can happen anytime. January is no exception, especially during thaws when snow is melting or when winter rains are falling. Foot traffic compresses the tiny air spaces among soil particles, making it more difficult for grass roots to penetrate. Stay off soggy or wet lawns in winter to the extent possible, and encourage others to do the same.

## PERENNIALS & GROUNDCOVERS

Herbaceous perennials and groundcovers (ones that die back to the ground and go dormant in winter) have the good fortune to sidestep winter deer and rabbit damage with this trait. But some species are both evergreen *and* tasty to animals. Damage can happen when there's little to no snow cover (plants are unprotected) and little else for deer and rabbits to eat. Particular favorites are wintercreeper euonymus, strawberry, hardy geranium, spurge, and sometimes, even ivy.

Guard against deer and rabbit damage by fencing (either the whole yard or by spot-fencing vulnerable plants) or by spraying repellents around favored plants. Alternating products that repel by smell or by taste is more effective than using the same one repeatedly.

## ROSES

Spider mites and aphids are problems for many indoor plants but especially for miniature roses. Mites are tiny, spiderlike pests that cause pale stippling on foliage. Sometimes their fine webbing is visible among the stems. Aphids are about the size of pinheads, emit a telltale sticky waste, and cause leaf curling and stunting. The simplest solution is to wash the plants thoroughly in tepid water from the kitchen faucet every couple of days for two weeks. Persistent infestations may need a spray of insecticidal soap.

Powdery mildew appears on foliage of miniature roses as a gray or whitish coating. There is no cure for already infected leaves, but you can spray uninfected foliage and new foliage with horticultural oil or a garden fungicide listed for this use. Follow the label directions. Promote better air circulation around your roses with a small fan.

## SHRUBS

Check the winter mulch under shrubs for signs of rodent nests. Stamp snow down around the base of shrub stems to collapse any vole burrows.

If some of the lower branches are buried in deep snow or bent over with ice, leave them as is to prevent injury to brittle stems. The snow will protect them, and gradual melting will release them gently.

Deer get bolder about venturing into your yard as they get hungrier from reduced food choices in winter. You may see damage to shrubs that weren't bothered before. Deer are creatures of habit and will return to eat more if it seemed like a safe-enough proposition. Break that habit by either spot-fencing any newfound favorites or spraying with repellents.

Winter damage to evergreen shrubs isn't limited just to bitter cold, frozen ground, or lots of snow. Especially in species that are borderline hardy to a region or improperly sited, damage also can come from bright, glaring sun that reflects off snow or glossy evergreen leaf surfaces, drying foliage, and tender bark.

Strong winds also can break shrub branches over winter, causing broadleaf evergreen foliage to puncture itself and lose additional moisture. Frozen soil prevents shrub roots from drawing replacement moisture from the soil, leading to browning around the leaf margins. Make clean cuts to remove broken branches, and soak soil during a winter thaw if the ground is dry.

## TREES

If you haven't already done so, wrap tree trunks with plastic spiral wraps or hardware cloth to keep rodents from chewing the bark. Make sure it is high enough to account for snow that may give rodents an extra foot or two of lift.

Signs that deer are browsing (or may soon browse) your trees:

1.  Tender new growth at the branch tips is being nibbled, leaving slightly ragged as opposed to sharply cut ends.

2.  The lower stems of shrubs and trees are stripped of foliage, up to about the height of, say, an adult deer with its neck extended.

3.  The presence of small piles or clumps of bullet-shaped dark-brown pellets ("deer poop").

4.  Tall weeds flattened where the deer are bedding down. If you see these, it's time to think about barriers or repellents.

## VINES

Deer damage is about the only worry this time of year. Virginia creeper, trumpet creeper, and many clematis varieties rank fairly high on the deer-tastiness list. Either protect these with fencing or spray with a deer repellent.

# February

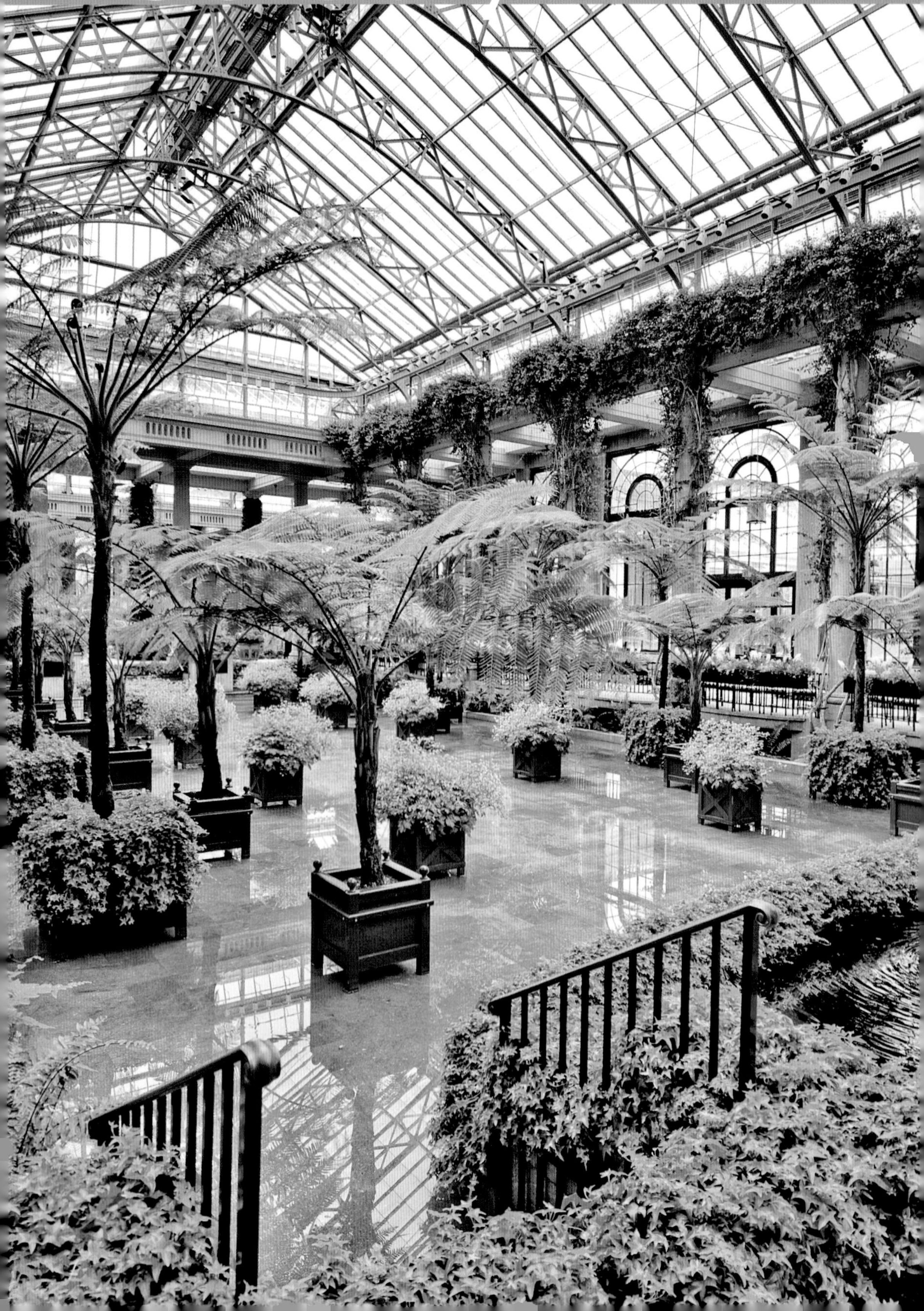

*February is when stir-crazy Pennsylvania gardeners can be found wandering aimlessly around the houseplant section of garden centers, trying to fend off chlorophyll deprivation. It's going on four months now since fall frost ended the growing season. Depending on your location and winter's mercy, figure on another month until botanical life returns. That doesn't mean gardeners are reduced to twiddling their catalog-ink-stained thumbs all month. Thaws can lead to pockets of outdoor opportunity, such as pruning, bed-edging, and cleaning up dead perennial foliage.*

Even when we're stuck inside, February is a time for getting ready. Once the weather warms enough to go outside, a flurry of job demands hit at once. Are your tools ready for it? Are you stocked up on fertilizer, crabgrass preventer, plant protectors, and other early-season supplies? Have you nailed down plans on what plants you're going to move, remove, or add? Seed-starting is one actual hands-on gardening activity that gets underway this month.

Home and garden shows start popping up toward the end of the month, offering more chlorophyll-deprivation therapy. These are like horticultural robins—the first sign that spring is close. And while you're waiting for the snow to melt and the deer to find lunch elsewhere, think about public gardens you'd like to visit this year.

Choices for these inspiring, plant-idea places abound near and far, from gems such as our own Longwood Gardens (shown in the photo to the left) and Chanticleer to world-class eye-poppers like Canada's Butchart Gardens and England's RHS Garden Wisley.

If you visit a lot of them, consider buying a membership that includes the American Horticultural Society Reciprocal Admissions Program. Becoming a member at one site gets you in free at scores of other participating gardens. See more details at www.ahs.org or at your favorite public garden.

Finally, be patient. Rest a spell. We're getting there. One day soon we'll be outside again in our own little Longwood.

## PLAN

### ALL

Thinking of calling on professional help this season? Whether you're looking for a design, planning to turn over a big planting job, or pondering a new paver patio, make your calls now. Set up planning visits, hash out ideas, get bids, and get on your landscaper's calendar. If you wait to call in April or May like everybody else, you'll likely have to wait weeks or months. You may even get a better bid price as the early bird.

Every yard has multiple "microclimates"—specific areas that are warmer, colder, drier, wetter, windier, and so forth than other parts of the yard. February is a good month to assess those. For example, masonry walls absorb heat and reflect light to warmer, brighter spots; fences and shrub hedges shelter harsh winds; and low-lying areas tend to trap frost. Especially pay attention to what happens with snow. Pile-ups give you a clue about prevailing wind. Spots where the snow melts first give you a clue about your sunniest, warmest spots.

### ANNUALS & TROPICALS

Decide which annuals you're going to start from seed and which you're going to buy in plant form in spring. Buy or order your seed now. Late February through March is time to get most seedlings started inside. Even for species that

### SEEDING VS. TRANSPLANTS

Advantages to growing annuals from seed indoors: 1. It's less expensive than plants. 2. You control the timing of when they're ready for planting. 3. The expanded choice of varieties. 4. It's a way to enjoy gardening in winter.

Advantages to buying transplants instead of starting your own from seed: 1. It saves time and energy. 2. Professionally raised plants are dependably sturdy. 3. You choose just the number of plants you want. 4. It's easier to select for color since most annual transplants are blooming at purchase time.

■ *Seed packet displays will be up at garden centers and home-improvement stores soon if they are not already.*

you plan to direct-seed outside in April or May, get them now before retailers sell out of what you want.

Many mail-order seed vendors now offer live plants. It's not too early to order these either. They'll be shipped at the correct planting time (in theory).

### BULBS

Look for snowdrops and winter aconite poking up anytime now. They're the first bulbs out of the gate, often blooming amid melting snow. What? You don't have any? Make a note to add a patch or two of these winter beauties in October.

If you don't have a sketch or map of where hardy bulbs are planted in the yard, plan to make one this spring as their bloom season unfolds. It'll be useful next fall when you're deciding where to plant new bulbs.

Plan where you'll site tender, summer-blooming bulbs later this spring, such as dahlias, gladioli, and callas. You can order these now in addition to seeds.

## LAWNS

Take the lawn mower and other lawn-care equipment to the shop for servicing while it's a slow period. When grass-cutting season starts, *everybody* will be there and you'll wait longer.

One good trait of cool-season grasses such as Kentucky bluegrass and perennial ryegrass is that they often hold some green color during winter dormancy. In a season with little snow cover, the green redeems an otherwise bleak landscape. Warm-season grasses—zoysia is the main one that some Pennsylvanians grow—go straw brown with fall frost and stay that way until mid-spring. Zoysia grass also can invade neighbors' lawns—and those folks may not be as okay with six months of straw-brown lawns as zoysia fans are.

## PERENNIALS & GROUNDCOVERS

Local garden centers generally carry only species that are reliably cold-hardy to their area. Pay attention to that if you're ordering perennials or groundcovers by mail order. Know your USDA Hardiness Zone (it ranges from Zone 5A in northwestern Pennsylvania to Zone 7B in the Philadelphia area, based on average winter low temperatures; see page 19).

The perennial border is the classic perennial garden. Potentially stunning but also fairly high-maintenance, it features wall-to-wall perennials of numerous varieties planted in a long, narrow bed along a fence, hedge, property line, walkway, or building. More common is the mixed border,

■ *Snowdrops* (Galanthus nivalis) *aren't called that for nothing!*

which features flowering perennials and foliage plants, shrubs, and maybe small trees. Other kinds of perennial gardens to consider include an island bed that's viewed from all sides; a naturalistic woodland/shade garden; a rock garden; a meadow; and a cutting garden for producing flowers, foliage, and dried pods for bouquets.

## ROSES

Both cut roses and potted ones are popular sellers this month because of Valentine's Day. The gift of a garden rose is an even more enduring expression of affection—doable in the form of a gift card to a garden center or favorite mail-order rose supplier tucked in a Valentine card.

Now that you've perused last month's catalogs, think about where you want to add roses to the landscape. They're not limited just to a dedicated rose garden. Different types make roses versatile in a variety of settings. Among these are colorful hedges, screening unwanted views, anchoring a mixed flower border, covering an arbor or pergola, controlling erosion on a slope, replacing a lawn as a sunny groundcover, adding color to sunny foundations, and accenting island or border beds.

## SHRUBS

As planting time approaches, think about the shrubs on your property. Are some getting too big or in the wrong place? Plan to move them when the ground thaws.

Do you have some shrubs that are perfectly healthy, but you just don't like them? Instead of cutting them down, try contacting landscapers or garden centers to see if they'd be interested in buying yours. Mature plants can sell for hundreds of dollars. Even if they don't pay you, they may dig them for free, saving you the cost or work of removal.

Other shrubby points to ponder: Is this the year to throw in the trowel on species the deer keep eating? Is it time to gain privacy with a new hedge? What shrubs will encourage more birds? Do some of those new colorful-leafed beauties deserve a spot in the yard? And how about some summer and fall bloomers to pick up the slack after the spring bloomers are done?

■ *Tree roots are powerful and can push sidewalks and pavement out of place.*

## TREES

One of a gardener's toughest decisions involves cutting down mature trees. In snowy, icy and/or windy winters, the weather may do the deciding for you by bringing down large limbs or entire trees. But winter is also a good time to evaluate tree health because trunks and limbs are easier to see with the leaves off. Remove any that are showing signs of failure, such as leaning, expanding cracks (especially at the juncture of large limbs or V-shaped double leaders), and rotting or sunken wood. Hire a certified arborist or experienced tree professional if you're not sure.

Is it time to remove street trees that are pushing up sidewalks, driveways, curbs, and even the streets themselves? Simply sawing off big roots and replacing the concrete is bad for tree health and may compromise the tree's stability. Those skinny "tree lawns" between curbs and sidewalks just aren't big enough to support most tree species. Before removing, check your municipality's rules about street trees. Some require approval to remove and/or replace, and many have strict rules now on exactly which species are allowed in curbside tree lawns (if any).

Check your pruning equipment, and sharpen loppers and saws for the new season.

## VINES

Think about whether you want a vine that climbs by twining or by sucking itself onto surfaces via rootlets. Twiners need a trellis, lattice, or similar support and maybe a little guidance to get going. Clingers usually need little help, and can pull themselves up solid walls (and up and up and up). An important consideration: twiners are easier to bring down for pruning or painting the supports in the off-season; clingers are harder to pull off, they let rootlets behind when they're removed, and they may accelerate the demise of aging wooden walls or stone or brick walls that have failing mortar.

Examples of perennial/woody twiners that do well in Pennsylvania are clematis, trumpet honeysuckle, American bittersweet, hardy kiwi, and native Kentucky wisteria. (Climbing roses are more "ramblers" than twiners.)

Perennial/woody vines that cling or have adhesive disks and do well in Pennsylvania are climbing hydrangea, Japanese hydrangea vine, Boston and English ivies, climbing forms of euonymus, cross vine, trumpet creeper, and trumpet vine.

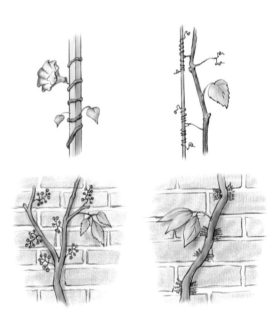

■ *Vines cling to supports in one of three ways: wrapping tendrils, twining around, or clinging with holdfasts or aerial roots. Be sure you know what type of method a vine needs before you bring it home from the nursery.*

## PLANT

### ALL

Scrap the idea of going outside with a blowtorch to thaw and plant. Wait until at least next month to get into planting gear.

### ANNUALS & TROPICALS

If you feel the urge to plant something now, take cuttings from last year's overwintering annuals or tropicals. Clip 3- to 4-inch stems with at least two sets of leaves. Strip off all but the top set of leaves, dip the bottom in rooting powder (available at garden and home-improvement centers), and plant them in a lightweight, soilless mix with the top set of leaves sticking out. Keep the mix damp, and you should have rooted "babies" in a few weeks.

It's time to set up a light stand if you're starting seeds indoors. Seeds of cool-season annuals and annuals that need a long head start can be sown indoors by the end of February. Pansies, calendulas, and snapdragons are three examples. Read the seed-packet instructions for timing advice. Most annuals will not go out into the garden until May and need only about eight weeks of grow time, so wait until March to start most of them.

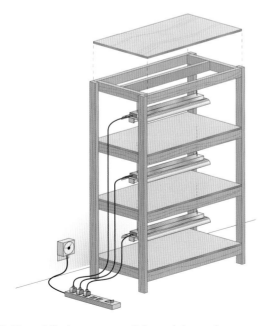

*It's not difficult to construct a light stand that can be adjusted as seedlings grow.*

## HERE'S HOW

### TO WINTER-SOW SEEDS

Some seeds can be started outside in small containers, sidestepping the need for lighting equipment inside. It's a technique known as "winter-sowing."

1. Save gallon or half-gallon clear-plastic jugs, cut in half horizontally, except at the handles to create "flip-top" containers.

2. Cut small holes or slits at the base of each corner with an X-Acto knife for drainage.

3. Add about 4 inches of seed-starting mix to each container. Dampen the mix with water, and scatter seeds on the surface. Lightly cover with the amount of mix recommended on the seed packet for each variety. Label which seed you've planted.

4. Use pieces of duct tape, placed vertically on two of the sides, to secure the container and create a mini-greenhouse. Set outside with the caps off.

5. Open to sprinkle with water every few days if it's dry. As the weather warms, the seeds will sprout, and young plants will grow that can be planted in the garden.

**Good annual flowers for winter sowing are** ageratum, sweet alyssum, snapdragon, calendula, celosia, cosmos, diascia, sunflower, nicotiana, cosmos, cornflower, browallia, larkspur, nigella, Joseph's coat, and tithonia.

**Good perennial flowers for winter sowing are** aster, astilbe, babys breath, gaillardia, liatris, coreopsis, gaura, penstemon, phlox, black-eyed Susan, coneflower, Shasta daisy, yarrow, carnation, coralbells, baptisia, hollyhock, salvia, and veronica.

Dress up your green houseplants by adding a few blooming potted plants from the garden center or florist around the edges of your pots. If you can't get these small plants through the surface roots of your bigger potted plants, set the pots on top of the soil and add Spanish or sphagnum moss to hide the plastic pot.

## BULBS

Transplant or thin snowdrops and winter aconite once they're done blooming. Or make a note to do this next month if the ground is frozen now.

## LAWNS

You can scratch seed into the soil if the ground is not frozen, but it's not going to germinate until soil temperatures reach around 50 degrees Fahrenheit. Late March or April is better.

## PERENNIALS & GROUNDCOVERS

Most people buy their perennials as plants at the garden centers, but many can be started from seed—either directly in the garden in spring or ahead of time inside. Many perennials take longer to germinate and/or need a longer growing time than annuals, so February isn't too early to start them. Among the easier perennials to start from seed: rudbeckia, columbine, balloon flower, purple coneflower, statice, yarrow, dianthus, and Shasta daisies. (See January's "Here's How to Start Seeds Inside," page 25.)

## ROSES

Although it's too early to plant roses outside, it *is* time to get your rose order in. Suppliers will be shipping bare-root roses starting in March.

## SHRUBS & TREES

Cut branches taken in early February from early-blooming woody species can be "forced" into blooming in a vase for winter color indoors. Examples include apple, cherry, crabapple, ornamental pear, azalea, PJM rhododendron, dogwood, and redbud. Cuttings from beech, birch, Japanese maple, lilac, magnolia, quince, red maple, serviceberry, mock orange, and willow can be taken from mid-February on to add flower and leaf color to vase arrangements. (See January's "Here's How to Force Shrub Cuttings to Bloom Inside," page 27.)

One clue that it's time to start planting shrubs and trees is when local garden centers and nurseries begin receiving their new stock. That's usually not until March, so don't get antsy—even if the soil is thawed and you're seeing a string of warm days. Winter isn't over yet.

## VINES

Sweet peas are cool-season annual vines that often peter out when the weather gets hot. Maximize their life by starting seeds inside this month, then planting them outside in April. Nick their hard, brown, outer seed coat with nail clippers or a file to aid germination. Plant them an inch deep in pre-moistened potting mix, then grow them as described in January's "Here's How to Start Seeds Inside," page 25. Be gentle transplanting the seedlings outside because sweet pea roots resent being disturbed.

## CARE

### ALL

Weeds aren't just tenacious growers in summer. Winter annual weeds—including chickweed, henbit, purple deadnettle, speedwell, and prickly lettuce—germinate in the cold of fall and even winter. These are ones you might see looking hale and green already during snow melts. If you're up for the cold and the ground is thawed enough to release these weeds, use a weeding tool to dig them.

Thawed winter soil also is soft, making it easy to edge your garden beds. If you weren't able to tackle that in January, try again this month.

Also during a thaw, pick up twigs on the lawn and debris in the garden beds. Check for the first bulbs while you're out there. Avoid walking on the beds and lawn if they're wet or soggy, though. That compacts the soil, which impedes root growth.

### ANNUALS & TROPICALS

Keep houseplants blooming as long as possible by displaying them away from hot spots like heater vents, TVs, and computer monitors. Also, don't display them near the fruit bowl. Ripening apples and other fruits give off ethylene, a natural gas that growers use to accelerate flower development.

If you're buying new bloomers, pick a plant that's in full bud or at the beginning of bloom rather than one in peak bloom. And if you're buying a blooming plant at a grocery store, pick one as far away from the produce section as you can (again because of those ethylene-spewing fruits).

To promote sturdy stems and a compact habit of cuttings taken from annuals and tropicals, pinch the stems of any that are getting leggy. These pinchings can be rooted for even more plants.

## BULBS

Don't worry if a sudden cold snap or snowstorm comes along after you've noticed bulb tips emerging. They'll be fine. Even early bloomers such as snowdrops and winter aconite are adapted to surviving typical Pennsylvania weather in February. The worst thing that will happen is the foliage tips will brown. Bulbs that aren't adapted to flowering this early keep their flowering stalks safely underground until the time is right.

Check to make sure excessive amounts of leaves, mulch, discarded trimmings, or other debris aren't covering bulb beds. Bulbs can easily poke up through 2 or 3 inches of leaves or mulch, but when it piles up much more than that, blooming and even shoot emergence may be hindered.

Check stored tender bulbs such as cannas, dahlias, and gladiolas from last year. Discard any that are mushy or dried out. Make sure the room temperature doesn't dip below freezing. In another month or so, it'll be time to bring them out of storage to plant in pots for an early indoor start. Wait until at least mid-May and even early June to put tender bulbs in the ground.

Cut the spent flower stalks off your amaryllis as soon as it's done flowering—if you didn't already do that last month. Wait until frost threats finish in May to move the pot outside or plant in the ground.

Colchicum foliage (fall crocus) usually appears this month. The bright green leaves will soak up the sun all spring, then gradually yellow and die back by June. Do not cut them off until they have collapsed. Colchicum flowers will poke up in September.

## LAWNS

One of the best ways to keep grass healthy is to make sure your mower blade is sharp. Sharp blades cut grass foliage cleanly rather than bludgeon its tips. Ragged tips turn brown, increase moisture loss,

■ *To sharpen a lawn mower blade, secure the blade in a vise and inspect the entire blade for damage. File along the cutting edge, using smooth, even strokes at an angle that matches the existing bevel. Use the same number of strokes on each edge.*

and make grass more prone to disease. Use February downtime to sharpen your mower blade so it'll be ready when the grass starts growing. Resharpen after every twenty-five hours of cutting time.

Continue to go easy on rock-salt ice-melters that can end up on your lawn when they run off. Better choices include traction-improving gritty materials, such as sand or wood ashes, or more plant-friendly ice-melters, such as calcium magnesium acetate, calcium chloride, or potassium chloride.

## PERENNIALS & GROUNDCOVERS

Check those recently planted perennials again to make sure the rootballs haven't "heaved" partly out of the ground due to alternate freezing and thawing. Tamp them back down if you see it. Add more mulch around heaving plants if you don't have about 2 inches over the soil already.

Another good reason to mulch 2 inches over perennial beds is to prevent them from appearing prematurely during a sunny, relatively warm period over winter. Mulch moderates these confusing temperature swings and keeps the soil more consistently cool until spring warmth arrives for good.

If you haven't cut back your ornamental grasses yet, now's when the blades often start breaking and blowing around the yard. Consider letting one or two clumps standing as nest-building material for the birds. (See "Here's How to Cut Ornamental Grasses," right.)

## ROSES

Check to make sure sufficient insulating mulch is piled around the crowns of outdoor roses. Hybrid tea roses are at risk for winter damage because they are typically grafted—an attractive stem variety attached to a sturdy root system of a second variety. The bud union (graft) is a small knob low on the stem near or under the soil. If it's not well protected against winter cold, the top part of the rose shrub may die, and the new growth will come from the rootstock. That explains why a rose suddenly looks different from the season before. Pull back the extra mulch when warm weather arrives in April or May.

Climbing roses can be pruned this month if you didn't do it in January.

Indoors, prune off bare stems from the potted miniature roses. Also thin out excess twigginess from the plant centers to encourage good air circulation.

## SHRUBS

If heavy snow is threatening to snap shrub branches, use a broom and gentle, upward motions to release snow from them. No whacking down on them with a shovel or you'll do more harm than good. Start removing the snow from the lower branches first so you don't overburden them by dropping more snow from the upper branches.

Removing ice from shrub branches is much more difficult. You're better off letting them alone and hoping the ice doesn't build up enough to cause snapping. Ice-laden shrubs may surprise you. They may look threateningly saggy when the ice is piling up, but they usually spring back soon after the ice melts.

It's often still cold enough in February that some plants will benefit from one more anti-desiccant spray. These are oils that slow moisture loss

1. First, tightly bundle the grass clump about halfway up with jute, rope, or similar strong ties.

2. Use gas-, electric-, or hand-powered shears to cut the bundle to a stub about 2 or 3 inches high. For big or tough grasses, you may need to use a chainsaw. For smaller ones, pruners are fine.

3. Bundling causes the clump to drop like a tree, keeping the blades from blowing around. Discard the bundles, or better yet, run the blades through a chipper-shredder to use as compost or mulch.

from leaves. Consider them mainly for broadleaf evergreens that are somewhat cold-sensitive, such as cherry laurel, osmanthus, holly, hardy camellia, and nandina. Apply only on mild days, over 40 degrees Fahrenheit, and follow the precautions on the product label.

## TREES

Check trees that were staked when planted last year. Sometimes alternate freezing and thawing loosens the soil and the supporting stakes. Pound the stakes back down if they're coming up. And while you're looking, make sure the ties aren't rubbing the tender young bark. Loosen them if they are—or replace them with the wider bands you should've used in the first place.

Shade trees and species that don't flower in spring are candidates for dormant-season pruning. The branches are easier to see before the leaves appear. If a young tree has a double trunk, cut away the less dominant one, creating a single strong trunk that also avoids the likelihood of splitting later. (See "Here's How To Prune a Tree," below.)

## HERE'S HOW

### TO PRUNE A TREE

1. First, remove any dead, broken, or rotting wood back to live, healthy branches or buds.

2. Look for branches that are crossing one another, and remove the one heading in the least desirable direction. Do the same for multiple branches coming out of the same area. Keep the best one.

3. Remove other branches heading in the wrong direction, including "water sprouts" growing straight upward. Make all cuts to just outside the small rings that can be seen where a smaller branch attaches to a larger one or to the trunk.

4. Remove any additional branches if growth is still overly dense, but limit total wood removal to one-third of the original amount.

5. If necessary, shorten the "keeper" branches back to the desired length, ideally cutting just outside a bud facing the direction you'd like the branch to grow.

6. For large branches 2 inches in diameter and greater, make a three-step cut to prevent branches from ripping bark as they fall. The first cut is from underneath, starting 12 inches out from the final cut and going about one-quarter through. The second cut is from the top, about an inch out from the first partial cut. Cut until the branch falls off. The third cut removes the stub, close to the trunk and just outside the rings where the branch attaches.

7. There's no need to treat the wounds with tar, paint, or goo. Let the cuts air-dry.

## VINES

If the weather's decent, February is a good time to prune woody vines that bloom on new wood in summer. That includes summer-flowering clematis (as well as the fall-blooming sweet autumn clematis), climbing hydrangea, Japanese hydrangea vine, ornamental (hardy) kiwi vine, trumpet vine, and American bittersweet.

A few wisteria varieties also bloom on new wood and are best pruned in winter. Some bloom on old and new wood. And some gardeners like to prune any wisteria both in July and over winter to limit size. For winter wisteria pruning, correct denseness by thinning excess branches back to the main stem. Then shorten each "keeper" stem to 2 or 3 inches so it has two to four buds.

Passion vines are annuals in much of Pennsylvania, which means dead ones are yanked and new ones planted each spring. In warm winters or protected spots, though, some of these beauties overwinter some years. Don't automatically yank them at the end of the growing season. Wait until late spring to see if any growth emerges. Then prune off just the dead wood or buy new ones.

## WATER

### ALL

Most watering this month will involve houseplants, overwintering potted annuals, and the first few "babies" you've started from seed. Consistently damp is good. Don't overdo it and rot roots. Remember, growth is slow over winter, and water demands are low.

Outside, the only time you'll have to think about watering is in an unusually dry winter with no snow cover. Then a soaking or two might benefit newly planted trees and shrubs, especially broadleaf evergreens.

### ANNUALS & TROPICALS

Water houseplants, tropicals that you're over-wintering inside, and any young plants you've rooted from cuttings when the soil feels dry about 1 inch down. Water until drainage comes out the

■ *Easily feed African violets and other indoor plants by adding fertilizer to the water in a self-watering container. Follow the instructions on the fertilizer label when adding fertilizer to make sure that you don't add too much.*

holes in the bottom of the pots. Then pour off any standing water.

Another good way to water seedlings and rooted cuttings is by setting the pots in a tray and adding water to the tray when the soil is getting dry and noticeably lighter in weight. Add enough water so that the soil soaks it up within fifteen or twenty minutes. This "bottom-watering" is less disturbing to young roots and less likely to foster leaf disease than watering over the top.

Give an occasional small drink to any semi-hardy plants you're overwintering in pots in the garage. The roots can use just enough moisture to keep them from totally drying but not enough that they attempt to push new growth yet.

### BULBS

Hardy bulbs (daffodils, hyacinths, crocuses, and so forth) planted out in the yard in mulched beds will not need supplemental water even if winter rain and snow is limited. Those planted in window boxes and aboveground outdoor planters are a different story. Moisture evaporates faster from those. Soak when the soil is thawed and dry. Make sure containers have drainage holes so excess water or melting snow can drain away.

## PERENNIALS & GROUNDCOVERS

Dormant perennials use very little water. Most years, melting snow or winter rain does the deed.

## ROSES

Continue to check soil moisture in your indoor potted miniature roses. Soak them when the soil goes dry and is noticeably lighter in weight until water runs out the bottom. Pour off excess water.

Outdoor roses are dormant and shouldn't need any winter watering, except possibly for first-year plantings in an abnormally dry winter when the soil isn't frozen.

## SHRUBS & TREES

Mulched and established flowering trees and shrubs should need no water while dormant over winter. The only exception for leaf-dropping species (lilac, weigela, hydrangea, dogwood, for example) is first-year plantings in an unusually dry winter when the soil isn't frozen.

Evergreens, particularly broadleaf types such as cherry laurel, hardy camellia, and holly, continue to lose moisture through their needles and leaves all winter. They're more susceptible to dry winter soil. If the soil is dry during thawed periods, give these a good soaking or two. Newly planted broadleaf evergreens and those in windy sites are most susceptible to dry-soil trouble over winter.

## VINES

Rarely, a dry and windy winter will come along and brown out species such as ivy and vining evergreen euonymus. A soaking during a thaw can help, but more often it's the combination of cold wind and frozen soil that leads to this browning. Even when there's moisture in the soil, the roots can't take it up when it's frozen. On the bright side, these vines are hardy enough to survive and push out new growth in spring while shedding the browned-out foliage.

## FERTILIZE

### ALL

It's still too early to fertilize landscape plants. Definitely do *not* apply fertilizer to frozen ground.

If a winter rain comes along while the product is sitting on the icy surface, it'll wash away into the sewer system, creeks, rivers, and so forth.

Inside, it's still slow-growth time, so go easy with the fertilizer on houseplants or other tender species that you're overwintering in pots.

## ANNUALS & TROPICALS

If you did not add slow-acting fertilizer to your pots of rooted cuttings, mix a liquid, balanced fertilizer into the water every other watering. Half-strength is usually plenty at this time of year.

Seeds carry their own energy for early development. Sprouts need no fertilizer until new sets of leaves are growing and your seedlings are in their individual containers or pack. Then, a half- or quarter-strength dose of balanced liquid fertilizer is fine to add to the trays of seedlings every watering or two when you're bottom-watering (that is, adding water to the trays and letting the soil take it up from the bottom).

Another fertilizer option for seedlings is to use a seed-starter potting mix that already comes with fertilizer or to work a small amount of gradual-release fertilizer into your mix before planting. A pale green or yellowish color to the leaves is usually a sign that fertilizer is needed.

## BULBS

For amaryllis and any other potted bulbs that you plan to continue growing for additional seasons, apply a half- or quarter-strength dose of balanced liquid fertilizer every other watering.

## LAWNS

Do you burn wood in a fireplace or woodstove? Wood ashes are a good source of potassium—one of the three main nutrients that lawns (and other plants) need. Save them for scattering over the lawn in March or April, especially if your soil is acidic. Ashes make soil more alkaline (raises the pH).

## PERENNIALS & GROUNDCOVERS

It's still too early to fertilize your perennial garden outside. Next month is better. Groundcovers seldom ever need fertilizer.

Inside, start using a dilute fertilizer on perennials you're starting from seed as soon as the second set of leaves starts growing. Add a dose of half-strength to quarter-strength liquid, balanced fertilizer to your water every other time you water.

## ROSES

Indoor miniatures like an occasional boost from kelp (an organic seaweed product). Mix it in water as directed, and give your minis a dose or two of it this month. The trace minerals are thought to boost plant resistance to insects and diseases as opposed to stimulating bloom.

## SHRUBS, TREES & VINES

Save fertilizing outdoor woody plants for March or April, if it's even needed then.

## PROBLEM-SOLVE

### ALL

Planning to spray dormant oil this month to smother insect eggs on the leafless trees, shrubs, and roses? Be sure you're using a sprayer just for oil and pesticides and *not* the same one you used to spray weeds last season. Herbicide residue that isn't thoroughly cleaned out can be enough to harm sprayed plants—and not just now but anytime you use a herbicide-contaminated sprayer. If you spray for weeds, keep a sprayer for that use only.

Most bugs are still inactive outside, but many pest animals (deer, rabbits, voles and, as winter winds down, groundhogs) are active and getting hungrier in a diminished food environment. Check to be sure your fencing and plant wraps are still in place and not being violated. The sooner you discover that and fix it, the better you'll limit damage. Keep in mind that groundhogs climb as well as they dig, and deer can outperform Olympic high-jumpers (8 feet up and higher isn't unusual).

### ANNUALS & TROPICALS

A common indoor bug this month is the fungus gnat. The adults are mostly just annoying, but the soilborne larvae can cause wilting and leaf-yellowing that results from root feeding, especially in seedlings and other young, tender plants. New generations can occur every two to three weeks through winter. Since this bug thrives in damp soil, water infrequently (soakings as needed instead of daily sprinklings), and cover the soil with an inch of sand to keep the surface dry, scratchy, and less hospitable to egg-laying. Fabric softener sheets laid over the soil seem to repel them. Yellow cards coated with a sticky substance (petroleum jelly is cheap and effective) works like a flytrap. Commercial traps also are sold at garden centers. Or kill the larvae by drenching the soil with a product containing B.t.i. (*Bacillus thuringiensis* var. *israelensis*) or one of several insecticides labeled for fungus gnat control on houseplants.

Aphids and whiteflies are other indoor pests that often reach a crescendo in February. Controls include rinsing infested foliage and stems under the faucet or under a shower; wiping away bugs and eggs with a soft rag dampened with rubbing alcohol, and spraying with insecticidal soap, horticultural oil, or other insecticide labeled for houseplant use. Ideally, spray outside on an

■ *To catch whiteflies and other flying insects, use sticky traps; small pieces of paper that are coated with a sticky substance.*

above-freezing day, and get plants back inside as soon as the spray dries.

## BULBS

Squirrels *love* early crocuses. Discourage them by laying chicken wire over the beds before the shoots emerge.

Deer also browse on most crocuses, but they love tulips even more. They'll often nibble the buds off tulip flower stalks even before the flowers open. The earliest tulips will be budding soon, so get repellent sprays ready and spray the plants ahead of time.

Continue checking your stored dahlias, callas, cannas, gladioli, and so forth to make sure they're not rotting or drying.

## LAWNS

Voles are still the biggest threat this month as they tunnel out into areas where they normally wouldn't risk venturing without cover of snow. Set out cage traps or snap traps baited with peanut butter near where you're seeing fresh surface tunnels. Deal with the existing damage by seeding killed areas next month.

## PERENNIALS & GROUNDCOVERS

Those sneaky voles will also eat the roots out from underneath selected perennials, sometimes killing them. Some of their favorites are foamflowers, coralbells, foamybells, dianthus, hosta, and lilies. Set out cage traps or snap traps baited with peanut butter to try and capture them. Or turn a cat loose. Tamp down and firm soil around any plants you've discovered that are partially eaten; if enough roots are left, they may reroot.

## ROSES

You wouldn't think animals would eat anything with thorns, but rabbits and deer are notorious for nibbling roses in winter when other food is scarce. To protect branches, surround them with wire cages tall enough so deer can't reach inside and/or spray stems with a critter repellent. Remember, if snow gets deep, animals can reach higher than usual.

Mice and voles also find rose roots to be tasty. They may chew on the bark as well. To prevent this in the future, delay mulching until after the ground freezes so the rodents seek another place to nest. For now, spray stems with a critter repellent. If you can identify the nest site, pull the mulch away and destroy it.

February is a good month to spray egg-smothering horticultural oil on the bare, stubby stems of roses that have a history of insect problems. Follow the directions on the product label. Spray heavier dormant oil only before leaves appear. Spray light, or superior, oil at other times of the year.

Indoors, check potted miniatures for insects and diseases. Remove and discard any dropped, discolored leaves that could harbor blackspot fungal spores or insect eggs.

## SHRUBS

Deer continue to be a potential problem. Erect tall cages around plants they're attacking (or around vulnerable ones you really don't want to see eaten). Renew your deer-repellent spray.

## TREES

Heavier dormant oil can be sprayed this month on fruit trees and other leafless trees that are subject to scale and other insect pests with overwintering eggs or larvae on the bare branches. Use dormant oil only before foliage and flower buds emerge. Use light (superior) horticultural oil on leafed-out or budding trees.

## VINES

Woody vines aren't particular deer favorites. Established ones often have enough wood that losing some of it to deer isn't a big problem. Many get pruned at winter's end anyway, so deer may reduce your work. (If only you could teach them which branches to take and how much.) Spring-blooming clematis is the main exception, so you might want to cage these or spray with a deer-and/or rabbit-repellent. Spring bloomers flower on last year's wood, so animal browsing over winter can reduce this year's show.

March

*It's here! A new gardening season semi-officially gets under way this month as the snow retreats and the first new leaves appear on landscape shrubs.*

March is a changeable month in Pennsylvania. It can bring 70-degree days, but it also can bring some of the state's heaviest snowfalls. Occasionally, it's 70 degrees Fahrenheit one day and snowing the next.

Erratic though it is, March isn't too daunting for a smattering of stoic bloomers. Most years, Pennsylvanians will start to see color other than white this month on Lenten roses, witch hazel, star magnolias, forsythia and, of course, early bulbs such as snowdrops, winter aconite, and crocuses.

Aren't you glad you planted all of those bulbs back in October? If you didn't, now you're stuck with buying more expensive potted bulbs for your winter-ending hurrah.

On days when you don't risk getting blown away in a March gale, you'll be able to get outside and start spring cleanup. This involves removing last year's dead perennial foliage, clearing out any leaf excesses, raking debris off the lawn, and yanking weeds that laughed off winter. While you're down on the ground, pay attention to what's coming up. You'll likely see all kinds of little shoots poking up and tiny buds poking out, making it a favorite time of hope and optimism for many a soil jockey. Take some time to admire these demure pleasures.

Toward the end of March, it's usually warm and dry enough—at least in the state's warmer regions—to start planting. Vegetable gardeners often go by St. Patrick's Day as their cue to plant peas.

Stick with planting only the hardier landscape fare in early spring—winter-tough trees, shrubs, evergreens, and perennials. Wait until all danger of frost is past in May to plant those tender annual flowers and to move your houseplants and tropicals outside.

We're not quite there yet … but at least things are looking better than they did in mid-January.

## PLAN

### ALL

Know your USDA Hardiness Zone before deciding which plants to add. The U.S. Department of Agriculture divides the country into cold hardiness zones based on each area's average lowest winter temperature. Pennsylvania encompasses six zones, ranging from average lows of -15 to -20 degrees in the highest reaches of northern Pennsylvania (Zone 5a) to average lows of 5 to 10 degrees in the southeast corner around Philadelphia (Zone 7b). Check plant labels and listings to make sure the ratings are within your hardiness zone.

Most indoor home and garden shows happen in March. They're good resources for getting ideas, seeing what's new, touching base with landscapers, and generally being around blooming plants after way too long without them. The granddaddy is Pennsylvania's own Philadelphia Flower Show—the world's biggest and oldest indoor flower show. It traditionally runs the first week of March.

Get organized before things get too crazy. Locate trowels, shovels, and rakes. Sharpen pruners and garden scissors. Check your supply of stakes, wire cages, garden twine, plant labels, fertilizer, potting mix, and whatever else you regularly use. It won't hurt to start doing some stretching exercises either.

### ANNUALS & TROPICALS

Annuals, by definition, live their entire lives in one season. That means each spring brings an opportunity to try something new or different. Finish inspecting plant catalogs to order annual seeds (the option that gives the greatest choice) or to plan what varieties to seek out in plant form at the garden center in spring.

### BULBS

The spring bulb-bloom show gets under way in earnest this month. Bulbs can be tricky to use well because they flower at one time of year but get planted at another. Jot down successes and deficiencies this spring so you'll have something to jog your memory come bulb-planting time in fall.

■ *If you have a greenhouse or shed that's dedicated to gardening and has adequate structural integrity, a built-in potting bench is a good way to create a sturdy work surface that is efficient in its usage of materials and floor area.*

### LAWNS

Hiring out lawn care or mowing work? Decide what you'd like someone else to do and get bids now so you've got an action plan in place at the end of March or early April when the work should begin.

If you didn't do it at the end of last season, get your mower ready. Replace the spark plug. Clean gunk and grass clippings from the engine, fan, and undercarriage. Clean and sharpen the blade. Replace the fuel filter and clean or replace the air filter. Change the oil. Drain old gas, and add fresh gas right before cutting for the first time.

### PERENNIALS & GROUNDCOVERS

See "Peak Perennial Bloom Times," on the facing page.

### ROSES

You'll need your pruning tools shortly, so either clean and sharpen the ones you've got or buy new ones.

## PEAK PERENNIAL BLOOM TIMES

The season's first perennials begin blooming as winter winds down. Since perennials typically only bloom for several weeks out of the year, the best way to get season-long color is to pick varieties that bloom at different times throughout the season. Here's a guide to peak-bloom times:

**March:** Lenten rose

**April:** Barrenwort, bergenia, bleeding heart, bloodroot, brunnera, columbine, creeping phlox, euphorbia, foamflower, lamium, primrose, pulmonaria, rock cress, Virginia bluebell

**May:** Amsonia, bachelor button, baptisia, candytuft, catmint, creeping veronica, dianthus, foamybell, forget-me-knot, fringe-leaf bleeding heart, geum, goat's beard, hardy geranium, Jacob's ladder, lamium, lily-of-the-valley, meadow rue, iris, peony, poppy, salvia, snow-in-summer, sweet woodruff, Solomon's seal, thrift, trillium

**June:** Astilbe, bellflower, catmint, coralbell, coreopsis, daylily, delphinium, evening primrose, yarrow, foxglove, gaillardia, gaura, hardy geranium, hosta, knautia, lady's mantle, lamium, lavender, lupine, penstemon, red hot poker, rodgersia, rose mallow, scabiosa, Shasta daisy, shooting star, silene, spiderwort, tiger lily, verbascum, veronica, yarrow, yellow corydalis, yucca

**July:** Agastache, Asiatic and Oriental lilies, baby's breath, balloon flower, beebalm, black-eyed Susan, blackberry lily, butterfly weed, cimicifuga, coreopsis, crocosmia, garden phlox, heliopsis, hollyhock, hosta, Jupiter's beard, liatris, obedient plant, purple coneflower, Russian sage, sea holly, soapwort, stokesia, veronica

**August:** Aster, cardinal flower, goldenrod, Japanese anemone, Joe-pye weed, leadwort, ligularia, liriope, monkshood, perennial sunflower, purple coneflower, reblooming daylily, Russian sage, sedum, sneezeweed, turtlehead

**September:** Aster, boltonia, catmint, gaillardia, goldenrod, Japanese anemone, mum, salvia, sedum, toad lily, turtlehead

**October:** Aster, goldenrod, mum, Nippon daisy

Stock up on rose fertilizer and bug and disease controls for the season. Are your thorn-tough rose gloves still in good shape or do you need new ones?

## SHRUBS

Shrubs will start showing up at the garden center late this month, so finalize plans for those you plan to add. Some of their key uses are color for house foundations; focal points in garden beds; softening house corners; hedging to mark off property lines or different parts of your yard; flanking doorways; food and shelter for wildlife; flowers in three potential seasons; fall foliage; screening for heat pumps, trash cans, and other "uglies"; and enclosures around patios.

Do your homework to be sure the shrub you're considering will match the light, size, soil type, and moisture levels of the site you're considering. You'll save money in plant deaths by taking the time to get this right up front.

## TREES

With the rise of the native-plant movement, many original tree species are being used again in home landscapes. Some of the more "yard-worthy" tree species native to Pennsylvania include American fringe tree, American hornbeam, American and pagoda dogwoods, American beech, American larch, American linden, blackgum, chokecherry, hop hornbeam, red maple, redbud, red and white oaks, river birch, sassafras, serviceberry, sweetbay magnolia, witch hazel, and sweetgum (if you don't mind the spiky seedballs).

Match your tree choices to the size and site conditions you've got, and lean toward bug- and disease-resistant species. Among useful purposes besides just the sheer beauty of the flowers, leaves, and bark: shade for a patio; blocking noise from a nearby road; screening unwanted views; marking property lines; creating a future shady get-away area; and in the case of a line of tall evergreens along the north or northwest exposure, blocking cold winter wind.

## VINES

Now—while the landscape is at one of its barest points—is a good time to look for big, bare walls that could be dressed up with the addition of vine-covered trellises. Even if you're planting leaf-dropping vines, the trellises themselves can add wintertime interest.

## PLANT

### ALL

The end of March is the beginning of planting season, especially in the warmer south-central and southeastern parts of the state. Container-grown and field-dug, balled-and-burlapped trees, shrubs, and evergreens start showing up at the garden center, and mail-order vendors begin shipping their bare-root stock. You'll also find the first greenhouse-grown perennials, already leafed out.

Traditionally, March is mud month. Melting snow and early spring rains conspire to turn even great garden soil into sticky slop. Don't ruin your soil structure by digging too soon. Working wet soil forces out air particles and leaves you with something akin to concrete.

## ANNUALS & TROPICALS

Pansies and their Johnny-jump-up and viola cousins show up at the garden center this month and can be planted in the garden as soon as the soil thaws. Plant them 6 to 8 inches apart in a sunny area for fullest coverage. Or plant some in pots and window boxes for early-season color.

Sow seeds indoors for warm-weather annuals that need six to eight weeks' lead time before they're ready to go in the garden. Determine the expected last spring frost date for your area, and count back the number of weeks of grow time indicated on the seed packet. Add two to three weeks for seed-germination time at the front end and for "hardening-off" time at the back end (the process of gradually getting indoor-grown seedlings acclimated to the outside before planting). All-time late frost dates range from end of April in the Philadelphia area to around Memorial Day in the northwestern mountains.

Some biennials—plants that sprouted and developed leaves last season and that will flower this season—may start popping up in March. If they are bunched together, transplant them to where you'd like them once the soil can be dug.

■ *Trees (and shrubs) can be sold bare root, balled and burlapped, and container grown.*

Transplant cool-season annuals that you started from seed last month (pansies, calendula, snapdragons, and so forth) into compartments of 4-packs or 6-packs or into their own larger individual pots. Continue to grow them under lights inside or next to a sunny window until planting out next month.

Retrieve geraniums that you stored bare root over the winter in the basement or attic. Examine them and pot them up in a soilless potting mix if they're in good condition. Their stems should be green, even though the leaves are dried out.

## BULBS

If you didn't plant your own hardy bulbs last fall, buy already-blooming potted tulips, daffodils, and hyacinths from the garden centers. Either remove the bulbs from the pots and plant them in the ground, or plant them next month after you've displayed the flowering bulbs in the pots.

Snowdrops, winter aconite, and any other early bulbs that have finished blooming can be dug, divided, and transplanted late this month or in April. Gently dig up masses, and shake away excess soil. Tease apart individual bulbs, taking care not to tear the roots or break off the foliage.

Discard any bulbs that are damaged or diseased. Replant some of the bulbs in the original spot, and plant the rest where you'd like to spread the colony.

## LAWNS

If temperatures are mild and the soil is not too wet, patch bare spots in the lawn with either pieces of sod cut to fit or with grass seed. Loosen the bare soil, and scratch in some granular, slow-acting fertilizer before seeding or sodding. Water daily if spring rains are insufficient to keep the patched areas constantly moist.

## PERENNIALS & GROUNDCOVERS

Hardy perennials are adapted to Pennsylvania's climate, and unlike most annuals, they can tolerate spring frosts. That means they can be planted in late March and throughout April.

It's best to plant new perennials on a cloudy day, in the evening, or when rain is in the forecast. Those conditions reduce the shock of transplanting.

Give store-bought perennials a few days outside in their pots before planting to make sure they're acclimated. Most perennials are grown in greenhouses, and when you buy at the very beginning of the season, the plants may not have been displayed for very long outside at the garden center yet. This also gives you the option of moving the plants inside briefly in case a very cold and windy spell pops up in the forecast.

## ROSES

Late March is the beginning of prime time for planting bare-root roses—ones that are dug dormant with the soil removed. A bare-root rose typically comes with three or four leafless, stubby brown stems joined at the plant crown (where the emerging stems transform into the roots). The roots are temporarily covered with moist sawdust, sphagnum moss, or shredded paper, all covered by a plastic bag with air holes. Some bare-root roses are packaged in boxes.

Store bare-root roses in a cool (above freezing), dark place so they remain dormant. Make sure the material around their roots stays moist until planting, and plant as soon as you can. (See "Here's How to Plant a Bare-Root Rose," page 54.)

## SHRUBS

Most flowering and evergreen shrubs can be planted starting late this month—as soon as the ground thaws and dries enough that it's no longer soggy. (See "Here's How to Plant a Shrub," page 55.)

Mail-order vendors also sell and ship many bare-root shrubs beginning this month. These are

## TO PLANT A BARE-ROOT ROSE

1. Set the plant in a pail of water so its roots are immersed for at least eight hours prior to planting but no more than three days. (Change water daily if you soak roots for more than one day.) Clip off any damaged or broken roots.

2. Dig a hole about as deep as the roots are long, and at least 2 feet wide.

3. Form a mound in the middle of the hole so you can set the rose on it with its roots draping down the sides. Use a yardstick or flat board to determine the height of the mound. With grafted roses, the bud union (the knobby joint where the stem meets the roots) should be planted 2 to 4 inches below ground level. With roses growing on their own roots, the point where the stem splays out into the roots should go at ground level.

4. Mix compost or similar organic matter into the removed soil (about 1 part compost per 4 parts existing soil). Also mix in a scattering of slow-acting, granular fertilizer formulated for roses. Use this to backfill the hole, firming it gently around and over the roots.

5. Soak well to settle the soil around the roots. Cover ground with 2 inches of bark mulch.

similar to bare-root roses—dug when dormant and sold with roots devoid of soil. Garden centers occasionally sell some varieties of bare-root shrubs, although most now have gone strictly with container-grown and field-dug, balled-and-burlapped options.

Bare-root shrub planting is similar to planting a bare-root rose. Dig the hole and improve the soil in the same manner. (See "Here's How to Plant a Bare-Root Rose," left.) If your soil is reasonably good and not compacted clay, use less or no compost. A key exception is that since almost all flowering and evergreen shrubs are grown on their own roots, the planting depth should be so that the crown (where the emerging stems transform into the roots) is at or slightly above ground level. Do *not* plant shrubs with the crown below grade. Soak well after planting, and cover the soil surface with 2 to 3 inches of bark mulch or wood chips, kept a few inches back away from the stem.

Once the soil thaws, it's also a good time to *transplant* most shrubs that you'd like to move to a new location. Early spring is good for moving shrubs because the plants are still dormant and leafless but the soil is warming enough to encourage root growth. Early spring also is usually damp and cool—ideal for giving a transplanted plant time to recover from the root loss and damage that's inevitable anytime you dig and move an established shrub. (See May's "Here's How to Transplant a Tree or Shrub," page 105.)

## TREES

Most trees also can be planted toward the end of the month or when the soil has thawed and isn't soggy. As with shrubs, trees are now primarily grown in containers or field-dug and wrapped in burlapped balls.

Mail-ordered trees, on the other hand, are almost always sold as bare-root varieties to hold down shipping costs. Bare-root tree planting is similar to the bare-root planting of roses and shrubs. (See "Here's How to Plant a Bare-Root Rose," left.)

## VINES

Woody vines such as clematis, climbing hydrangea, and Virginia creeper begin appearing late this

## HERE'S HOW

### TO PLANT A SHRUB

1. Dig a hole at least three to five times as wide as the rootball but no deeper than the rootball's height.

2. Mix the excavated soil with 10 to 20 percent compost or similar organic matter. If your soil is reasonably good and not compacted clay or subsoil, skip this.

3. For container-grown plants, remove the plant from the pot and fray out the roots, especially if they are circling. It's okay to disturb or remove some of the soil to do this. If you can't free the roots by gently pulling them, make three or four vertical cuts in the rootball to break up the tight mat.

4. For balled-and-burlapped plants, set the shrub in the hole and cut off and remove as much of the burlap as you can. Also cut apart or remove wire baskets and any rope or strings tied around the trunk or roots.

5. Set the shrub on solid ground so that the crown of the plant (where the emerging stems transform into the roots) is sitting an inch or two *above* grade. Remove or add soil to adjust to this planting depth. Do not plant with the crown below grade.

6. Adjust the plant so the "good" side (if there is one) is facing the way you want. Check the plant from all angles to make sure it's in the ground straight. Backfill halfway with soil, tamp, recheck for straightness, water, then finish backfilling and tamp again.

7. Cover the ground with 2 to 3 inches of bark mulch or wood chips and then water again.

month at garden centers and can be planted outside once the soil thaws and dries. The planting technique for container-grown and balled-and-burlapped varieties is the same as for shrubs (see "Here's How to Plant a Shrub," above).

Planting bare-root woody vines is similar to planting bare-root roses (see "Here's How to Plant a Bare-Root Rose," left.) The exception is that if your soil is reasonably good, use less compost than the 20 percent recommended for roses—or none. Plant so that the crown (where the emerging stems

■ *Planting clematis below ground level helps keep the roots cool.*

## HERE'S HOW

### TO PLANT A TREE

1. Dig a hole three to five times as wide as the rootball but no deeper than the rootball's height. Planting on solid ground will ensure the soil doesn't settle and cause the tree to end up too deep in the ground (one of the leading causes of tree death).

2. Mix the excavated soil with 10 percent compost or similar organic matter (i.e. 1 part compost to 9 parts existing soil). If your soil is reasonably good and not compacted clay or subsoil, skip this.

3. For trees grown in containers, remove the tree from the pot, and fray out the roots, especially if they are circling. It's okay to disturb or remove some of the soil to do this. Make a few cuts if necessary to free circling roots if you can't tease them apart with your fingers.

4. For field-dug, balled-and-burlapped trees, set the tree in the hole, and cut off and remove as much of the burlap as you can. Also cut apart or remove wire baskets and any rope or strings tied around the trunk or roots.

5. Set the tree so that its crown (where the trunk flares at the base to transform into the roots) is sitting about 2 inches *above* grade. Remove or add soil to adjust to this planting depth. Never plant with the crown below grade. There's no need to line the bottom with stones as once was recommended.

6. Check the plant from all angles to make sure it's in the ground straight and situated as you like. Backfill halfway with soil, tamp, recheck for straightness, water, then finish backfilling, and tamp again.

7. Cover the ground with 2 to 3 inches of bark mulch or wood chips, and then water again.

8. Staking is *not* necessary unless you've planted a rather large tree with a comparatively small rootball, or if you've planted on a slope or in a windy area. If staking is needed, hammer two or three stakes in the ground, and secure the tree with a wide band or strap at chest to shoulder level. Tie securely but not so tight that the tree can't move at all. Don't use wire or rope, which can cut into the bark. After no more than one year, the staking should come off.

transform into the roots) is at or slightly above ground level. The *exception* to that is clematis, which does better planted at grade or an inch or two *below* ground level.

Sweet peas prefer chilly weather, just as their edible cousins do. Plant seeds of these annual flowering vines outside as early as mid-month in warm parts of the state and near the end of March elsewhere.

## CARE

### ALL

For roadside plants that got blasted with salty snow-plowings or salt runoff this winter, give them a good soaking with a hose if spring rains didn't help do that. Sodium in road salt can "burn" foliage, but more insidiously, it impedes water uptake by the plant's roots, leading to symptoms of brown leaf tips and margins during hot, dry spells in summer. Ample rain flushes soils better than anything, but scratching a layer of gypsum (calcium sulfate) into the soil surface can counteract the effects of sodium overload in the ground.

Weeds increasingly appear now anywhere there's bare soil. Not only do perennial weeds begin to emerge from their roots, but annual weeds that germinate in cool weather also pop up this month. Pull them, dig them, or spray them *immediately*. It'll only get worse if you don't.

Another weed-fighting strategy is weed preventers, also called "pre-emergent herbicides." These are granular products that don't kill existing weeds but that do stop many new weeds from sprouting. Ones with corn gluten meal offer a marginally effective alternative to synthetic chemicals, although it's likely the product was made from genetically modified (GMO) corn, rendering it technically *not* "organic."

Weed preventers don't harm most existing plants and can be applied over top of perennials and underneath shrubs and trees. Check the label for species that are susceptible to damage by weed preventers. Most are effective for eight to ten weeks. Ideal timing for applying weed preventers is when forsythia has reached peak bloom. That's late March to early April most years.

### ANNUALS & TROPICALS

Transfer annuals being grown inside from rooted cuttings into larger pots if they're outgrowing their original containers.

Adjust fluorescent lights over young annuals being grown indoors from seed to within 2 or 3 inches of the tops of the plants as they grow. This will

■ *Before planting or adding mulch to your garden bed, spread a pre-emergent herbicide. Pre-emergents work by preventing weed seeds from sprouting.*

keep the stems sturdy. One method is to hang your lights on chains, allowing you to raise the lights gradually as needed. Another method is to set seedling trays on blocks or scrap wood, then remove the blocks as needed.

Rotate seedlings growing on a windowsill every few days so that light falls on every side. This keeps them from leaning in one direction.

Research suggests that gently brushing tender tops of seedlings a couple of times a day with your fingertips or open hand helps them develop sturdy stems. Annual seedlings also grow fuller and bushier by pinching the tips of their stems periodically.

### BULBS

Do *not* cut back, tie, or otherwise disturb bulb foliage while it is still green! This interferes with its job of collecting sun for energy for next year.

There's no need to pinch off the faded flowers of small bulbs, such as Siberian squill, anemone, and snowdrops. Spent flowers of larger bulbs, such as daffodils, early tulips, and hyacinths, are more noticeable, so it helps to neaten the garden by snipping off their entire flower stalks. Eliminating flower stalks prevents bulbs from wasting energy trying to produce seeds.

Allow the foliage of potted bulbs to mature in a sunny window. Then plant them outdoors either late this month or in April.

Check stored tender bulbs (dahlias, callas, gladioli, and so forth) one more time this month to be sure they haven't dried or rotted. You'll be able to start them inside in April or plant outside in May.

## LAWNS

If your lawn has a chronic crabgrass problem, consider using a crabgrass preventer this year. These products kill crabgrass as the seeds germinate, stopping it before it gets started. Most crabgrass preventers should be applied to lawns before crabgrass hits peak germination, meaning late March to early April most years. When forsythia hits peak bloom is a good indicator. Most preventers work for only eight to ten weeks, so in cool, damp springs, a second application might be needed in June to prevent later-germinating crabgrass.

A few crabgrass preventers, such as ones containing dithiopyr (Dimension), both prevent and kill young crabgrass, so they can go down as late as May to control crabgrass. Most crabgrass preventers also stop several other annual weeds from sprouting in lawns, including foxtail, barnyard grass, and spurge. Products with corn gluten meal offer a marginally effective alternative to synthetic-based chemical crabgrass preventers.

If your soil is acidic and you forgot to lime the lawn last fall, early spring is also a good time to do it.

## PERENNIALS & GROUNDCOVERS

Don't fret if a sudden and unusually cold spell browns the tips and edges of newly emerged perennial foliage. The plants almost always will grow new leaves to replace the cold-zapped ones. Pick or snip off the brown leaves as that happens.

Take advantage of nice days to get outside and start cleaning up the perennial beds. Rake out debris and excess leaves. Cut back browned-out ornamental grasses if you haven't already done that. And remove the browned-out foliage from last year's perennials, except for those that are "evergreen perennials" (ones that keep their foliage all year

long). (See April's "When to Cut Perennials," page 78, for a plant-by-plant rundown.)

One plant that might fake you out is liriope. This grassy-looking perennial often comes through winter looking green, leading many gardeners to avoid cutting it. However, last year's foliage will turn brown as this year's new foliage emerges, making it much tougher to remove when the two are intertwined. Clip off old liriope foliage before new growth emerges down to ½-inch stubs. Use a mower set on high or a string trimmer to cut back groundcover beds of liriope.

## ROSES

When leaf buds start to swell, begin gently removing the piled protective soil or mulch from around the canes of both established and newly planted rose shrubs. Wait until temperatures are consistently above freezing at night and at least 45 degrees Fahrenheit during the day. That's usually late March in warmer parts of the state and early April in the coldest parts.

Also as the buds swell and are just about ready to open, begin pruning roses. First, remove any damaged, broken, or winter-killed wood. Then thin out and shorten canes to get them ready for the season's new growth. Early April is the best time most years in most of the state, but rose pruning can be done as early as late March in the state's warmest south-central and southeastern sections. (See April's "Here's How to Prune Roses," page 79.)

For climbing roses, this is your last, best shot at pruning them if you didn't do it in January or February. New growth will take off shortly.

## SHRUBS

End of winter is a good time to start cutting back overgrown shrubs. Species that flower before mid-June are almost all ones that form their flower buds the season before, and so they should be left to flower first before pruning. Species that flower after mid-June generally produce their flower buds on that season's new growth, and so they're best pruned heading into a new season (that is, now). (See "Here's How to Prune Flowering Shrubs," at right and April's "Pruning Timing of Shrubs, Trees, & Vines," page 80.)

Sometimes a big or neglected shrub benefits from something more radical than a run-of-the-mill, once-a-year trim. "Coppicing" involves cutting back an entire shrub to within a few inches of the ground. Not all species tolerate that, but many respond by pushing out a new array of fresh, healthy growth from the stubs or roots. Butterfly bush, spirea, redtwig dogwood, forsythia, beautyberry, burning bush, caryopteris, ninebark, summersweet, and Virginia sweetspire are among those that accept coppicing without complaint. As the plants regrow, it's also fine to remove some of the weakest or "directionally challenged" shoots.

A third shrub-pruning option is rejuvenation. This involves bringing an overgrown shrub back under control over a three-year period and then keeping it that way. Old-fashioned French lilacs are best pruned this way, but it's also a good way to maintain mock orange, bridalwreath spirea, forsythia, sweetshrub, weigela, chokeberry, beautybush, and most viburnums. With rejuvenation, identify and cut back the oldest, thickest, woodiest stems to 3 or 4 inches above the ground. Do this to about one-third of the total number of stems. Do the same the following year and the same the following year. By the fourth year, you've got a whole new shrub. Keep doing the one-third thinning each year to constantly encourage young wood, which flowers better and often has better disease-resistance than old wood.

■ *Use a tree pruner to cut woody brush that has a diameter of less than 1½".*

## TO PRUNE FLOWERING SHRUBS

Summer-flowering shrubs (ones that bloom after mid-June) are best pruned at the end of winter. Spring-flowering shrubs (ones that bloom before mid-June) are best pruned immediately *after* they flower to avoid cutting off that season's flower buds that formed the fall before.

1. First, remove any dead, broken, or rotting wood back to live, healthy branches or buds.

2. With loppers or a handsaw, thin out up to one-third of the biggest, oldest stems. Cut as close to the ground as you can. Skip or reduce this if the shrub has been flowering well, hasn't been suffering from disease, and you prefer maximum denseness.

3. If necessary for size control, shorten "keeper" branches back to branches or buds facing the desired direction. Make angled cuts facing down and away from the branches or buds. For most shrubs, remove no more one-third of the total wood.

4. Shrubs being grown in a hedge setting or in cases where dense growth is desired (abelia, boxwood, yew, or spirea, for example) can be sheared instead of hand-pruned. Limit removed wood to one-third in most cases.

For evergreen shrubs, late March to early April is a good time to thin out, cut back, or shear holly, boxwood, euonymus, nandina, cherry laurel, yew, and Japanese plum yew. For size control, do your cutting before new growth occurs. These can even be cut back into where the inner stems are leafless, and they'll fill back in.

Several other evergreens also can be pruned heading into a new season, but they *don't* push new growth very well when cut back severely. Juniper, globe arborvitae, bird's nest spruce, and dwarf cryptomeria are examples of species that should never be cut back beyond green growth on the branch ends.

Remove winter protection from shrubs by mid- to late March. Most years, tender broad-leaf evergreens will be fine by this time, but if you're stretching the cold-hardiness range in your zone, you might keep the protection on until early April for varieties such as fig, bay laurel, osmanthus, aucuba, skimmia, and red, yaupon, and Chinese hollies.

## TREES

March is a good month to prune most deciduous (leaf-dropping) trees. They're still dormant and leafless—much easier to see the branches and less messy than pruning with leaves in the equation. One thing to keep in mind—if you prune spring-flowering trees such as dogwood, redbud, and cherry now, you'll reduce the number of this season's flowers. Prune spring bloomers right *after* they flower if you want to maximize flowers. This isn't a concern for shade trees or summer-flowering trees that bloom on this year's wood (crape myrtle, *Hydrangea paniculata,* and seven-son flower, for example).

Some evergreen trees can be pruned or sheared for size control starting this month, so long as you don't cut back so severely that you're into the bare inner wood. Examples are arborvitae, Leyland cypress, cryptomeria, Hinoki cypress, cedar, and falsecypress. American holly trees also can be pruned in March, including back into bare wood, if necessary. Wait until June after new growth finishes to prune fir, spruce, and pine.

## HERE'S HOW
## TO PRUNE EVERGREENS

1. First, remove any dead or snapped limbs. Make a clean cut back to live growth or back to just outside the branch collar (the ringed area where a branch attaches to the trunk) in the case of a whole lost limb.

2. Pine, spruce, and fir grow in clusters of shoots called "whorls." When the size reaches the desired maintenance level, these are best maintained by letting the new season's shoots grow and then snipping all or most of it off. The best timing is mid- to late spring.

3. Arborvitae, yew, cedar, falsecypress, juniper, hemlock, holly, cryptomeria, Hinoki cypress, and Douglas fir are best pruned at the end of winter, just before new growth begins. Avoid cutting back so far, though, that you're into the bare inner part of the branches. This timing lets new growth quickly hide your pruning cuts. Lighter maintenance trims also can be done again in early to midsummer.

4. Species that tolerate shearing and even harder cutbacks into bare wood include holly, boxwood, yew, hemlock, nandina, and euonymus. Still, it's best to cut back no farther than where green growth intersects bare wood. The best timing is end of winter through midsummer.

5. Avoid pruning evergreens from late summer through early fall. That's when dormancy is beginning. Late-season pruning can encourage new growth that won't "harden off" before winter, making it more susceptible to cold kill.

Branches of leaf-dropping conifers such as dawn redwood, larch, and baldcypress can be thinned out or shortened now before new growth begins.

The lowest limbs of all trees can be removed this month if you need more space to sit or walk under—or if you just want to expose more of the trunk. You might also find that the lower limbs of aging evergreens are dying; these can come off now too. Rule of thumb: never remove branches more than one-third of the way up.

For trees you've been staking since last spring, remove the stakes late this month or next. One year is long enough.

## VINES

Summer-blooming vines such as climbing hydrangea, Japanese hydrangea vine, ornamental kiwi, trumpet vine, American bittersweet, and some clematis can be pruned this month before new growth begins, if you didn't get to it in February.

Perennial vines wake up from dormancy soon. Check trellises and other supports to be sure they're ready to meet the challenge of vigorous vines. Now's your last chance to paint or stain wooden supports before new growth starts covering them again in April.

## WATER

### ALL

Winter-ending snowmelt and/or cold, early-spring rain means soil is usually wet enough this time of year. Occasionally, though, a dry spell following a snowless late winter might mean a soaking is needed for newly planted pansies, sweet peas, or anything that's less than a year old and not yet well rooted.

### ANNUALS & TROPICALS

Use a water meter or your finger to keep tabs on the soil moisture of potted cuttings—especially in terra cotta pots. Indoor air is dry so long as the central heating is still on.

Keep seedlings moist, but don't cross over into sogginess. It's okay if the soil dries out slightly between waterings. Many annuals are adapted to a wet/dry cycle. If seedlings are drying very quickly, that's a sign they need to be repotted into a larger pot. Water seedlings with tepid water, not water directly from the cold-water faucet.

### BULBS

Normal rain or melting snow is usually plenty of moisture for bulbs. In a rare end-of-winter dry spell, soak bulb beds after the ground has thawed. Then water is needed only if that rare spring dryness continues.

### LAWNS

Lawns need no water so long as they're still dormant in winter. You'll only need to think about a watering if it's unusually dry and warm once the grass starts to green—if even then. Newly seeded or newly sodded lawns are more in need of early-season water than established lawns.

### PERENNIALS, ROSES, SHRUBS, TREES & VINES

None of these should need March watering in a typical year. The exception is a dry spell following a snowless late winter, and in particular, plants that are less than a year old. Your 2- to 3-inch layer of mulch around these plants is usually enough to maintain adequate soil moisture.

## FERTILIZE

### ALL

Wood ashes from the fireplace or woodstove are a good source of potassium – one of the three main nutrients that plants and lawns need. Wood ashes also increase soil alkalinity (raise the pH), which is a second benefit when the soil is leaning overly acidic. Test your soil pH to determine whether applying wood ashes is a good idea or not. Most of the time, it's a benefit to lawns but not a good idea around hollies, azaleas, dogwoods, blueberries, and other plants that prefer acidic soil.

### ANNUALS & TROPICALS

Continue adding a half- to quarter-strength dose of balanced liquid fertilizer to the trays of your annual seedlings every watering or two.

■ *A soil pH that's too high can lead to poor leaf color, such as this case of iron chlorosis on a maple tree.*

The brightening days of March signal the beginning of a new growing season for houseplants and overwintering tropicals. Increased growth means it's time to ramp up fertilizing. Use a balanced fertilizer at about half-strength every other time you water.

## BULBS

If you're planning to yank your tulips after their first year (many of them go downhill in ensuing years), there's no need to fertilize them. But for spring bulbs you'd like to keep going for years, lightly scratch a granular fertilizer into the soil surface sometime this month or next. Use a product with a balanced nutrient breakdown or one slightly higher in phosphorus and potassium (the last two numbers on the fertilizer bag) instead of one high in nitrogen (the first number). Something with a 5-10-10 to 10-10-10 breakdown is ideal.

## LAWNS

The three optimal times to fertilize a lawn, according to Penn State University's Center for Turfgrass, are mid- to late spring, end of summer, and late fall.

If you're going with a commercial "four-step" lawn-fertilizer plan, the four times are early spring, late spring, late summer, and late fall. That means late this month or early April is time for step one.

March is a good month to apply either wood ash or pelleted lime to the lawn if a soil test indicates your soil is too acidic (low on the pH scale). Wait until the ground has thawed to apply it. A pH reading of 7.0, which is neutral, is ideal. Mildly alkaline, or slightly above 7.0, also is fine. No ash or lime application is needed in that case.

If you didn't spread fertilizer on the lawn last fall, spread a quarter-inch layer of compost or a granular, slow-acting lawn fertilizer late this month after the ground has thawed. Depending on the number of weeks listed on the fertilizer label, this application might last through summer.

If you *did* spread slow-acting fertilizer last fall or winter, it will begin to kick in this month and last until late spring to early summer. There's no need to apply another dose now.

## PERENNIALS & GROUNDCOVERS

Late March through April is the best time to scatter a dose of organic or slow-acting granular fertilizer over the beds of blooming perennial flowers. Lightly scratch it into the soil or mulch for best results. Spring rains will dissolve and carry the nutrition to the roots just as nutrient demands go up at the beginning of peak growth time.

Groundcovers and perennials being grown for their foliage instead of their blooms usually don't need supplemental fertilizer. Fertilize these only

■ *Granular fertilizer is easy to spread evenly with a spreader, so many homeowners choose it over liquid fertilizer.*

■ *March is a good month to broadcast granular fertilizer over both new and existing beds.*

## SHRUBS & TREES

Established trees and shrubs that are growing well usually need no supplemental fertilizer, especially if the lawn around the plantings is being fertilized.

If the growth rate is not up to par or the leaf color and size is not normal, it's best to first test the soil. The result not only will tell whether a nutrient deficiency is a problem, it'll spell out exactly what breakdown of fertilizer is needed and at what rate. Otherwise, you're just guessing.

If fertilizer is needed, early spring is an ideal time to add it. Rain will dissolve it and carry it into the root zone just as the shrub or tree's increased growth rate demands the extra nutrition.

A soil test will indicate whether the soil's acidity level (pH) should be adjusted. Lime or wood ash will raise the pH (make the soil more alkaline). Sulfur will lower the pH (make it more acidic). Most shrubs and trees prefer neutral to mildly acidic soil. Holly, camellia, mountain laurel, azalea, rhododendron, blueberry, dogwood, birch, and most needled evergreens prefer moderately acidic soil.

## VINES

Do *not* encourage large, fast-growing vines such as wisteria or trumpet vine by fertilizing! These hardly ever need any nutrition help.

Most other woody vines (climbing hydrangea, clematis, honeysuckle, and so forth.) also usually get the nutrition they need from average soil. If poor growth, poor color, or a soil test indicates a particular nutrient is needed in any of these, late March is a good time to apply it.

## PROBLEM-SOLVE

### ALL

Rabbits are active all winter and usually turn their attention then to young bark, low-to-the-ground twigs, bulbs (especially tulips), and selected plants that hold their leaves in winter. Imagine what a treat it is when all kinds of new, tender, tasty, young shoots begin appearing this time of year! Fencing works best for vegetables and gardens

if the growth rate or color is poor, or if a soil test indicates a nutrient deficiency.

## ROSES

Roses are heavy feeders and perform best when fertilized regularly throughout the growing season. End of winter is the time to get started.

For organic leaners, a layer of compost, a granular organic fertilizer formulated for roses, and/or a scattering of aged manure is the recipe, starting around the end of March. Many a rosarian swears by banana peels as a good recycling strategy to add the potassium that roses crave; they simply bury their peels in and around the roses. Many also scatter a half-cup of Epsom salts around each plant this month to supply magnesium.

For chemical gardeners, scatter granular rose fertilizer according to label directions, or water in the season's first application of liquid rose fertilizer, also starting in late March.

in which you don't mind the Fort Knox look. Otherwise, spot-protect young trees, shrubs, and perennials by surrounding them with wire fence or hardware-cloth cylinders. Or regularly apply one of the many commercially available rabbit repellents.

## ANNUALS & TROPICALS

Rabbits are particular fans of pansies and violas— the cold-hardiest annual flowers that can go in the ground as soon as the soil thaws. These are some of the first plants you might want to spot-fence or treat with repellents.

Are you seeing a thin white crust growing over the soil surface of your houseplants or overwintering tropicals? This is fertilizer salt or minerals left behind by evaporated water. It's harmless to plants in small amounts and can be scraped off if it bothers you. To head off buildups, some gardeners give their houseplants periodic showers (yes, in the tub) to wash out salts being left on the surface by fertilizer. Another option is to simply repot your plants in fresh potting mix at winter's end—a good idea anyway if it's been a couple of years since you've done that.

"Damping off" is the bane of seedlings. It's caused by a soilborne pathogen and is aggravated by an overly wet medium. The telltale symptom

■ *Damping off is a disease that causes young plants to keel over at the soil line.*

is a stem that darkens near the soil surface and then keels over. To prevent damping off, use a sterile, soilless planting medium and add water to the tray, not over the top of plants. Dump any water that's left standing in the tray after about fifteen minutes.

If your seedlings are getting "leggy" (long and skinny instead of stocky), that's usually due to insufficient light. Move your lights closer. Growing in cooler conditions instead of room-temperature 70 degrees Fahrenheit also helps.

If indoor leaves look mottled or speckled with yellow dots, inspect closely for tiny bugs called spider mites. Another sign is fine webbing on the stems and leaves. Spider mites are almost too small to see without a magnifying glass. If you have them, spray or wash the foliage with tepid water several times a week to remove and disrupt the mites. Use insecticidal soap on stubborn infestations, following label directions.

## BULBS

Both deer and rabbits are fond of tulips and some crocuses and will nibble the flower buds before they open—if not the emerging shoots even before that happens. Fence your beds of vulnerable bulbs or apply deer and/or rabbit repellent. Or switch to daffodils, hyacinths, Siberian squill, glory-of-the-snow, and other bulbs that are less tasty to four-legged pests.

■ *To protect young trees from rabbits and rodents, place a cylinder of one-quarter-inch mesh hardware cloth around the trunk. The cylinder should extend 18 to 24 inches above the soil and 2 to 3 inches below ground.*

Mice and voles are threats to eat bulbs (especially tulips) by tunneling underground. Cover the bed with chicken wire and a light layer of mulch to prevent tunneling. Or try trapping rodents with snap traps or cage traps baited with peanut butter.

## LAWNS

Snow mold is a term for two fungal diseases that occur in turfgrass that suffers prolonged cold, wet conditions or compacted snow cover in winter. After spring thaw, patches up to 2 feet in diameter may be covered with a white or gray fungus or with matted, dead grass that is pink in color. To prevent it, avoid overdosing the grass on nitrogen late in the season, and remove thatch if it's more than a ½-inch thick. Cut the grass short (about 2 inches) for the last cut of the season. Avoid piling shoveled snow into large mountains on the lawn. If you get snow mold anyway, rake off the dead grass and wait for warmer, drier weather to solve the problem for you. There's no need to treat with a fungicide or other product.

## PERENNIALS & GROUNDCOVERS

Slugs—those slimy snail relatives without the shell—often become active before we expect. They overwinter in moist, acidic, organic debris in shady areas in the yard and especially favor hostas. Set out traps now to catch the first arrivals. Use a shallow pie plate or a commercial slug "bar" trap filled with beer (they are attracted by the yeast) near vulnerable plants. Check it daily for slug bodies to pinpoint when they start feeding. Set out more traps (at a slight distance from vulnerable

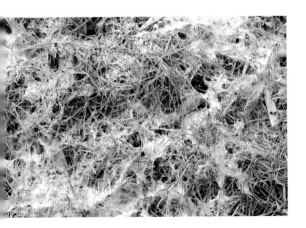

■ *Snow mold is a common end-of-winter lawn disease.*

plants) to lure more slugs once you know they are active.

Watch for rot diseases that can cause some low-growing groundcovers to mysteriously "melt away." Bugleweed (*Ajuga*) is especially prone to this in cold, wet winter soil. Add compost or similar organic matter to improve drainage in the bare areas, then either transplant living groundcover plants or add new ones.

## ROSES

Proper pruning is a good early-season, first-line bug- and disease-prevention strategy that removes dead and diseased tissues and overwintering insect eggs. It also establishes good air access to prevent fungal disease on foliage. (See April's "Here's How to Prune Roses," page 79.)

## SHRUBS

Brown needles on Hinoki cypress, dwarf pines, arborvitae, and other evergreens are not necessarily cause for alarm. So long as the browning is limited to the inner needles, this is aged foliage that is giving way to new replacement foliage farther out on the branches. It's normal but can be more pronounced following dry years, extra-cold winters, and similar stresses. If the tips are green and growing, don't worry.

## TREES

Birds are allies in the campaign against pest insects in trees. Woodpeckers, flickers, and others dig borers and beetles from tree bark. Robins enjoy tent caterpillars. Wrens favor tiny insects. Even seed-eating birds hunt for bugs to feed their babies in the spring. Invite birds to set up housekeeping in your yard by putting up birdhouses (nesting boxes) for species that prefer houses. Those that prefer open-air living will build nests in the branches of your trees, and will be on the job when the pest insects begin to appear.

## VINES

Young clematis is a rabbit favorite—some varieties more so than others. Surround plants with wire cylinders or 2-liter plastic soda bottles, cut vertically to wrap them around the clematis shoots. You may not need to do this after three or four years when the shoots have thickened.

April

*Blooming glory emerges from the erratic cold and wind this month in the Pennsylvania landscape. Lengthening days and warmer weather trigger a symphony of color, ranging from the familiar dogwood and redbud show overhead to a stream of bulb blooms and early-season perennials underneath.*

Color is everywhere—or at least it *should* be if you've planted some of the many species that flower in April. Flowering pear, flowering cherry, and those dogwoods and redbuds are trees that peak this month. Forsythia, fothergilla, and some spirea are among the first shrubs to color. Barrenwort, brunnera, candytuft, bleeding heart, and foamflower are perennials that bloom almost as soon as they leaf out. And, of course, spring bulbs hit full stride, especially daffodils, early tulips, and one of spring's most fragrant flowers: the Dutch hyacinth.

Frost comes to an end late this month most years in the warmer south-central and southeastern parts of the state, opening the door to the season's first annual flowers for those willing to chance the odds. Days typically start to reach into the 60s and even the 70s. Evenings are cool but pleasant. Showers come regularly enough to water the new plantings and green the lawn.

Overall, it's one of the best months of the year, both for plants and the gardeners tending them.

Speaking of that, April is a busy time in the garden. It's time to finish winter cleanup and weed the beds in preparation for new mulch. It's time to cut back roses, summer-blooming shrubs, and some of those overgrown evergreens. It's time to plant those new trees, shrubs, and perennials you've been drooling over in the catalogs all winter.

But most of all, it's time to look around, sniff, admire, and otherwise enjoy all of the fresh beauty that verifies that winter is now officially gone.

## PLAN

### ALL

Turn your landscape's winter plans into reality this month. It's time to transfer your ideas and sketches to the ground outside. Use a hose or rope to mark off new or changed garden beds. Then dig and improve the soil in advance of your future beautiful new planting. (See "Here's How to Turn Lawn into a New Garden Bed," right.)

Acquire your season's supplies if you didn't already do that. You'll need them *very* soon now—potting mix, slow-acting flower fertilizer, stakes, string, plant labels, sprays, gloves without holes, and so on.

Clean your stored garden accessories (birdbaths, birdhouses, feeders, statues, fountains), and return them to the outside. Make repairs to anything that got banged up in the move. Also clean your pots and get your hanging baskets ready for a new season of duty.

Reset and secure stones in walls, walks, and terraces that may have been moved by freeze-and-thaw cycles in the soil over the winter.

Hang onto your plant receipts for anything new you buy. Sellers often guarantee plants for a year—sometimes more. A receipt is your proof in case the plant doesn't make it.

■ *A natural stone retaining wall not only adds a stunning framework to your landscape, but it also lends a practical hand to prevent hillsides and slopes from deteriorating over time.*

### ANNUALS & TROPICALS

Frost-hardy annual flowers are available at the garden center now, and the full lineup will show up toward the end of the month in the state's warmer regions. Decide which varieties you'd like to try—or at least which colors and light conditions you need—so you're not wandering aimlessly around the garden center among the endless choices.

Fewer people are planting massed beds of annuals these days. Reason: the replanting work, the expense, and the watering. The trend lately is using annuals for *spots* of color, especially in pots and baskets. Annuals offer multiple benefits: they bloom all season; they come in almost every imaginable color; they're perfect for tucking among perennials and shrubs to ensure season-long color; they're versatile (choices for sun, shade, wet, dry, even climbing up supports); most make good cut flowers; many are attractive to birds, butterflies, bees and other pollinators, and some are fragrant.

Get combination ideas for this season's pots and hanging baskets by thumbing through garden magazines and online gardening sites. Planting time is getting close.

### BULBS

While fall is the time to plant spring bulbs, now's the time to assess your current efforts. Look around as the different varieties bloom and make notes on which ones need to be "beefed up" with additional bulbs, which ones need partners, which ones need to be moved, and which bare areas would benefit from some daffodils, snowdrops, or glory-of-the-snow.

One overlooked spot for spring bulbs is in plantings of low groundcovers, such as pachysandra, creeping sedum, sweet woodruff, leadwort, and hardy ginger. Larger bulbs, such as daffodils, tulips, hyacinths, alliums, Spanish bluebells, and crown imperials, will push up through the groundcover and bloom over its top.

Another good area is among perennials that are either just emerging or that haven't yet come up. Bulbs poke up and bloom while the perennials are just getting started. Then the perennials hide the bulb foliage as it fades, and take over the space

## HERE'S HOW

### TO TURN LAWN INTO A NEW GARDEN BED

1.  Use a hose or rope to mark the boundaries of the new bed. Then spray paint the outline on the grass.

2.  Use an edger, spade, or ice-chopper to cut along the line. Be sure there are no buried utility lines nearby before digging. Call Pennsylvania One Call at 811 or 1-800-242-1776 to have lines located at no charge. Or visit the service online at http://www.pa1call.org/PA811/Public.

3.  Remove turfgrass. Option 1 is to manually strip off the grass with a spade. Use the stripped-off patches to replace bare spots in the lawn. This is free sod! Or compost it. Or save the pieces to flip over—roots up—on top of the soil and under the mulch later.

4.  Option 2 is to kill the grass with a non-selective herbicide, such as one containing glyphosate (Roundup® is the best known brand), or with vinegar, or a similar organic herbicide. Be careful not to let the spray drift onto anything that you *don't* want to kill. Once the grass is dead (usually ten to fourteen days), it can be tilled in.

5.  Option 3 is to smother the grass with black plastic, a tarp, cardboard, sections of newspaper, or similar covering that shuts out light. Keep the covering in place for at least six weeks to be sure the grass is dead, then remove it or dig it in.

6.  If your soil is good, loosen it to a depth of 10 to 12 inches. If it's compacted or poorly drained, work 1 to 2 inches of compost or similar organic matter into the loosened top 10 or 12 inches. Incorporate it well.

7.  Top the improved bed with 2 to 3 inches of bark mulch. When you're ready to plant, just pull back the mulch, open your holes, plant, and push the mulch back into place as you go.

when the bulbs go dormant in summer. Good perennial bulb partners are hosta, daylily, liriope, coneflower, sedum, and black-eyed Susan.

Some other potential bulb areas to scope out are along a fence, around a light post, around a water garden, under trees, and along bare walls.

Not sure what some spring bulbs look like? Pay a visit to one of the many Pennsylvania public gardens that have excellent spring bulb displays, such as Chester County's Longwood Gardens and Dauphin County's Hershey Gardens. Public gardens label the varieties, and give you a better read on what you'll like than relying only on catalog pictures.

## LAWNS

Get the mower ready (sharp blade, new spark plug, fresh gas), and get your fertilizer, crabgrass preventer and other supplies on hand. The lawn will green up quickly now.

All grass is *not* the same. It may all *look* green and bladed, but five distinct turfgrass types make up most Pennsylvania lawns. Four are "cool-season" grasses—ones that grow best in spring and fall, go dormant in winter, and often go temporarily dormant in a hot, dry summer. The fifth is zoysia, a "warm-season" grass and the only one of this type that's cold-hardy enough to reliably survive Pennsylvania winters, and even then only in the more southern parts.

To plan what's best for your yard, here's a rundown on each:

**Kentucky bluegrass**—It has medium-textured blades and dark green color. *Pluses*: spreads well; recuperates quickly from drought and injury; good tolerance to cold, heat, and drought; takes foot traffic well. *Minuses*: not good in shade or wet soil; fairly heavy feeder; prone to thatch (spongy buildup underneath); slow to germinate; moderate risk of bugs and disease.

**Perennial ryegrass**—It's finer textured than Kentucky bluegrass and slightly darker green. *Pluses*: germinates and establishes quickly; tolerates foot traffic, heat and cold well; less prone to thatch than Kentucky bluegrass. *Minuses*: doesn't recuperate as quickly from drought and injury as Kentucky bluegrass; only moderate shade- and drought-tolerance; somewhat prone to bugs and disease.

**Fine fescue**—Includes chewings, hard, creeping red, and sheep fescues. It has the finest texture and medium green color. *Pluses*: best shade tolerance; light fertilizer demand; recovers quickly from drought or injury; does well in drought and acidic soil. *Minuses*: doesn't appreciate heavy foot traffic; fairly prone to thatch.

**Turf-type tall fescue**—Has the coarsest foliage, to the point of looking too rough sometimes when used with the previous three finer-bladed grasses. *Pluses*: excellent heat, drought and foot-traffic tolerance; more shade-tolerant than Kentucky bluegrass or perennial ryegrass; minimal thatch problems. *Minuses*: slow to establish and recover from injury; not as attractive as narrow-bladed types.

**Zoysia**—Medium to fine texture and medium green summer color. *Pluses*: very thick grower, making it excellent for choking out weeds; recuperates quickly from injury; good drought-tolerance; light feeder. *Minuses*: overtakes other grasses, including into the neighbor's yard; turns brown at first frost and stays brown until May; expensive to establish (planted by plugs, not seed); prone to thatch.

## PERENNIALS & GROUNDCOVERS

Many new introductions really are improvements, but just because something is new doesn't mean it's better. Traits that a breeder or plant-seller might consider a plus might not matter to you, so start by assessing what's most important to you. Long bloom time? A certain color? Something that doesn't need spraying or staking? Or maybe plants that aren't on the deer-favorite list. Compare your "wish traits" against the characteristics of plants you're considering.

Not only do some perennials do better in some parts of the state than others (State College's weather is not the same as Philadelphia's), but where you plant them in your own yard can make a big difference too. Pay attention to your yard's microclimates. An astilbe may do fine in the damp shade along your eastern foundation, but it may fry by your sunny driveway. If you guess wrong and find that a new perennial suffers, don't hesitate to move it to a more suitable spot.

The trees are leafing out, making this a good time to evaluate sites for a shade garden. Other shady possibilities around the yard include the north foundation and any area to the east or north of a fence, building, or screening of tall evergreens. Shade-tolerant perennials include astilbe, Japanese anemone, woods aster, barrenwort, bleeding heart, brunnera, cimicifuga, coralbell, foamflower, foamybell, hosta, Japanese forestgrass, lamium, ferns, Lenten rose, variegated liriope, lungwort, woodland phlox, variegated Solomon's seal, turtlehead, and Virginia bluebells.

## ROSES

Roses show up at the garden center this month, so get there early for the best selection. Favorites can go quickly.

Did you identify any new opportunities for using roses in the landscape? If not, here's one: how about near where you sit or near a kitchen window so you can take maximum advantage of the fragrance?

## SHRUBS

How's the shrub show going? You should be seeing a nice selection of color by now. If not, you're missing the boat on early-spring-flowering shrubs. Varieties to consider adding: forsythia, fothergilla, viburnum, early types of spirea (especially bridalwreath and 'Ogon'), spicebush, sweetbox, mahonia, PJM rhododendron, and winter hazel.

## TREES

Pennsylvania celebrates Arbor Day this month for good reason. For one thing, it's an ideal month to plant new trees. But April is the month when more trees flower than any other. If you're not cashing in on this color show, consider adding species that bloom in early spring, including many magnolias and dogwoods, flowering cherry, flowering pear, flowering plum, redbud, serviceberry, and maybe even crabapple in a warm season.

Pay attention to ultimate sizes when picking your new tree. They might all look fairly small at the nursery, but some get much bigger than others. Stick with small species in small yards, and make sure you're planting far enough away from buildings and power lines that you don't set up future trouble.

## VINES

Vines are good choices to hide "uglies" around the yard—crumbling walls, radon pipes, down spouts, heat pumps, the neighbor's junk pile, and so forth. Either buy a trellis, or build your own support so it's in place for prime time planting of vines this month and next.

Some of the better-behaved vines are good choices to ramble up a tree. Clematis is ideal for this use. So are shade-preferring and semi-shade annual vines, such as black-eyed Susan vine, Rex begonia vine, and moonflower. Climbing hydrangea and Japanese hydrangea vine are two other good shade-tolerant, woody, perennial vines for growing up trees; just keep them pruned enough that the vine

leaves don't cover too many of the tree leaves and shut off sunlight to them.

As the songbird nesting season approaches, hang a house from your arbor or pergola before the vines leaf out and access becomes difficult.

## PLANT

### ALL

Are you planting on a slope? The trick is to create a level platform for anything you plant there. Instead of planting on a downward angle along the original grade, loosen the soil and level it to a "terrace" of about 1 foot across for a perennial or about 2 feet across for a larger tree or shrub. Then taper the bed down in the front, and finish it off with mulch, making sure the roots are covered. These little terraces will catch rainwater, allowing it to soak into the roots instead of running straight down the hill.

### ANNUALS & TROPICALS

Finally! It's time to plant some annual flowers. Varieties that can take a frost (pansy, viola, dusty miller, snapdragon, and annual dianthus) can be planted statewide this month. Most annuals, though, should wait until after danger of frost. In an *average* year it ranges from mid-April in the warmer Philadelphia area to almost mid-May in the coldest regions. Most gardeners prefer to play it safe and go by the all-time *latest* killing frost dates, which range from late April in the Philadelphia area to the end of May in the coldest regions.

Use those same temperature guides to determine when to start annuals from seed directly in the ground outside. This is less expensive than buying transplants. Loosen the soil, scatter the seed, and follow the packet label to determine how deeply to cover the seeds with soil. Keep the soil damp to aid germination. Hardier annuals that can be planted slightly before the anticipated last frost date include larkspur, annual poppies, cleome, and sweet alyssum. Annuals that can be direct-seeded at or soon after the last frost date are cosmos, four-o'-clocks, portulaca, bachelor's buttons, marigold, calendula, flax, nasturtium, sunflower, nigella (love-in-a-mist), nicotiana, and zinnia.

attached, unless it's already started to yellow. In that case, cut it off and replant. The correct depth is about three times as deep as the bulb is tall. Good spacing is three times apart as the bulb's width.

Before starting bulbs such as a caladium indoors in pots, trim off any rotten or diseased sections.

Remove hardy bulbs growing inside from their pots, and plant outside this month. Cut off the foliage after it yellows.

Get a jump on dahlias, cannas, calla lilies, tuberous begonias, and other tender bulbs by starting them in pots inside this month rather than waiting to plant directly in the ground outside next month. First cull out bulbs that are injured, diseased, or shriveled. Divide ones that have formed clusters. Plant in a soilless potting medium with a bit of granular, slow-acting fertilizer mixed in. Water them, and set the pots in a bright room for a few weeks. By the time planting time arrives in May, they'll be sprouted and growing.

■ *Sprinkle seeds from a packet in a row according to spacing instructions on the seed package*

It's too early yet to plant out most annual seedlings you've been growing inside (except for the frost-hardy ones mentioned). You may be able to move them to a "halfway house" or cold frame outdoors to help with the transition, though. This protection is usually enough to nurse young plants through cold nights while giving them improved outdoor light during the day. Since they're not planted yet, you can bring your trays inside if a really cold night threatens. Vent the cold frame on sunny days so plants don't cook.

## BULBS

Bulbs that are done blooming can be dug, divided, and transplanted. Division usually improves the performance of too-crowded bulb plantings. Now is a good time to do this because you can see where the bulbs are; the foliage is still attached. Gently dig up masses, shake away the soil, and tease apart individual bulbs. Toss bulbs that are damaged or diseased. Replant immediately with the foliage

■ *Dahlias can be started inside in pots to get a jump on the season.*

## LAWNS

To plant a new lawn, Penn State University's Center for Turfgrass recommends these mixes:

**Sunny, open area**: Use either all Kentucky bluegrass or all turf-type tall fescue. Or use a mix that's 80 percent Kentucky bluegrass and 20 percent perennial ryegrass, or a mix that's 40 to 60 percent Kentucky bluegrass, 30 to 40 percent fine fescue, and 10 to 20 percent perennial ryegrass.

**Partly shaded area**: Use a mix of 40 to 50 percent Kentucky bluegrass, 40 to 50 percent fine fescue, and 10 to 20 percent perennial ryegrass.

**Shady area**: Use all fine fescues.

**Sunny area that gets a lot of foot traffic**: Use all turf-type tall fescue, or a mix of 80 to 90 percent Kentucky bluegrass and 10 to 20 percent perennial ryegrass.

Just as with flowers and vegetables, grass comes in an array of varieties within each grass species. Some varieties perform markedly better than others, especially in drought tolerance, bug and disease resistance, and color. Penn State performs annual turf trials, and the results are posted on the National Turfgrass Evaluation Program website at www.ntep.org. Select the State Data button, then hit Pennsylvania on the map. You'll get a list of top-rated varieties in each species that you can use when scouring garden centers and online vendors for seed.

April is one of the best months to seed a new lawn as well as patch bare spots in a thin lawn. Two important steps: loosen the soil so you have good seed-to-soil contact (don't scatter seed over a compacted surface), and keep the seed and young grass consistently moist to help it germinate and establish. (See September's "Here's How to Seed a New Lawn," page 162 and "Here's How to Overseed a Thin Lawn," page 164 for step-by-step tips.)

## PERENNIALS & GROUNDCOVERS

April is prime time for planting almost all new perennials, groundcovers, and ornamental grasses. It's also when you'll find the best selection in garden centers. (See "Here's How to Plant Perennials," page 74.)

Perennial spacing varies depending on the size of the plant, how fast each variety spreads, and your patience. A good general rule is somewhere between 18 to 24 inches apart. Larger perennials, such as Russian sage, hardy hibiscus, baptisia, ornamental grasses, and large-leafed hostas, can go 3 to 4 feet apart.

When you're planting a new bed, it's best to space the pots over the ground before planting anything. This gives you a chance to make minor adjustments to the spacing without having to go back and dig anything up. An alternate plan is to use sticks or bamboo stakes to mark planting spots ahead of time.

If your existing perennial beds are getting crowded, weedy, or generally going downhill, it's time for a renovation. This involves digging the plants, removing weeds, improving the soil with compost, dividing large clumps, and replanting. Most perennial plantings benefit from this every five to ten years. April is a good month to do it, especially for perennials that aren't yet in bloom.

If you bought Lenten or Christmas rose (*Helleborus*) as a potted holiday plant, gradually acclimate it to the outside over seven to ten days and plant it in the ground.

## ROSES

April is an ideal month to plant container-grown roses. The process is similar to planting any other shrub. (See March's "Here's How to Plant a Shrub," page 55.) One exception is that in the colder regions of Pennsylvania, instead of planting at the same depth as the container, locate the bud union (the knob where the top part of most roses have been grafted to the rootstock), and set the plant so that the union is 2 to 4 inches below ground.

It's also still fine to plant bare-root roses this month. Some rosarians even prefer to treat container-grown roses like bare-root roses by removing all of the container soil before planting their new rose. (See March's "Here's How to Plant a Bare-Root Rose," page 54.)

## HERE'S HOW

### TO PLANT PERENNIALS

1. Perennials perform best in soil that has been loosened to 10 or 12 inches deep and improved by incorporating an inch or two of compost, rotted leaves, mushroom soil, or similar organic matter into it. If you're planting in individual holes, loosen as deep as the rootball and at least two to three times as wide. Work in a handful or two of the above organic matter.

2. Remove the plant from the pot. Fray out the roots, including cutting three or four vertical slits if necessary to free a badly circled root mass. It's okay to remove most of the soil in the process.

3. Open a hole and set the plant so that it's at the same level as in the pot. Be careful not to bury the crown of the plant—the point from which the stems emerge.

4. Tamp soil firmly all around the plant and cover the ground with an inch or two of bark mulch. Keep the mulch from touching the base of the plant.

5. Water well and keep the soil consistently damp through the first season via soakings once or twice a week when it doesn't rain.

Miniature roses that have been growing as potted plants inside over winter can be gradually acclimated to the outside over seven to ten days and then planted in the ground. Early to mid-April is good in the warmer parts of the state; mid to late April is better in the colder parts.

## SHRUBS

April is an excellent month to plant new shrubs—including widely available container-grown ones as well as larger-sized, field-dug, balled-and-burlapped types. (See March's "Here's How to Plant a Shrub," page 55.)

Potted hydrangeas or azaleas that were holiday gift plants can be planted in the ground outside this month. Gradually get them used to the outside by giving them more sunlight and wind exposure each day over a seven- to ten-day period. Then plant.

## TREES

*Warning:* Sometimes new trees and shrubs are already buried too deeply in their pots or burlap bags. Check for that by looking for a slight widening where the trunk turns into the roots (a point known as the "root flare" or the "root-shoot interface"). When the tree is planted, this flare should be slightly *above* grade. If you can't locate it, gently remove soil until you find this flare. That's your guide point for gauging tree depth in the hole. (See March's "Here's How to Plant a Tree," page 56.)

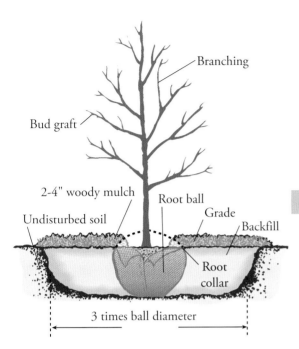

Branching

Bud graft

2-4" woody mulch

Undisturbed soil

Root ball

Grade

Backfill

Root collar

3 times ball diameter

■ *Plant a tree so it's on solid ground with the root flare slightly above grade. Burlap should be removed from the rootball before backfilling the hole with soil.*

You may have heard you should add a layer of stone "for drainage" at the bottom of your planting hole. That's not necessary, and according to current research, is actually counterproductive, leading to poorer drainage. Skip the rocks when planting.

Remove burlap, cages, and any other protective material from around a tree's roots once the tree is in the hole. Those materials are used to secure trees in transport. Once the rootball is safely in the ground, they're no longer necessary. Burlap eventually will decay, but in the short term can impede root spread. Burlap or fiber pots left above ground can wick moisture out of a rootball. Ropes and ties can be slow to decay and can constrict roots and the trunk. The worst case is that rope will grow into the bark and cause a weak spot that's prone to snapping. Bottom line: remove anything that goes between a plant's roots and the soil or that could constrict roots and shoots.

## VINES
Woody vines such as clematis, honeysuckle, and climbing hydrangea can be planted this month. Just keep them damp after planting if it's not raining.

If you're trying sweet peas, get the seeds in the ground by early April. These need an early start and fizzle out when summer heat arrives.

In warm-weather parts of the state, summer vining annuals can be direct-seeded in the ground late in the month. These include black-eyed Susan vines, climbing nasturtium, purple hyacinth beans, and moonflowers.

## CARE

### ALL
Weeds love this warming weather and plentiful rain as much as the desirables do. Pull them when they're young, especially after a rain moistens the soil. Dig weeds such as dandelions and thistle that have deep taproots. Or spot-treat weeds with a herbicide. A little tenacity now will save a lot of work later.

April is a good month for adding new mulch. Don't be too quick to put it down, though. Let the soil warm and dry out a bit. Mulching too soon can trap moisture and keep the soil colder longer, slowing the start of growth.

■ *Use a sprayer with liquid herbicide to spot-treat for weeds.*

## ANNUALS & TROPICALS

Get your beds ready for planting by clearing out weeds, any remaining dead plants from last year, and any debris from winter. You could even dig in a light layer of compost and rake the beds smooth so you'll be ready to plant once frost is done.

Do *not* dig the soil in areas that you're devoting to self-sowing annuals, such as cleome (spider flower), nigella (love-in-a-mist), larkspur, snapdragons, four-o'-clocks, calendula, cosmos, and sometimes even gloriosa daisy, zinnias, marigolds, and petunias. Don't mulch over the top of these areas either. The seeds will be popping up shortly, if not already.

Pinch back stems of maturing seedlings and plants grown from rooted cuttings if they're getting overly long and "leggy." This will make their stems sturdier and their foliage denser.

## BULBS

You may be tempted to cut off the leaves of bulbs that already have bloomed. Resist the urge, even if the foliage is getting floppy. It's fine to snip off faded flowers and spent flower stalks, but let the leaves continue to soak in sunlight to recharge the bulbs for next year's flowering. Wait at least until the leaves yellow to get rid of them.

No braiding or tying the bulb foliage either. That cuts down the surface area of leaves available to soak up sunlight. There's plenty else to do this time of year besides giving your bulbs a hairdo.

## LAWNS

Grass growth kicks into high gear this month, and so will your mower. Don't scalp your grass this year. Keep the blades 2½ to 3 inches tall. Taller grass retains soil moisture, chokes out sunlight to weeds, and provides more chlorophyll for stronger grass-root growth. Try mowing on the highest (or a higher) setting and see if it's the levelness that you like, not necessarily the shortness.

Sharpen the mower blade if you didn't do it over winter. Sharp blades make clean cuts instead of the ragged, brown tips left behind by dull mower blades. Ragged tips also lose more moisture and

A simple weed puller can make extracting even deep-rooted weeds such as these dandelions a fairly easy chore. The tool also helps ensure that you pull as much of the root system as possible so the plant is less likely to grow back.

are more prone to disease. Resharpen blades every twenty-five hours of cutting.

Mow only when the grass is dry to minimize compaction and fungal disease.

As for frequency, mow often enough that you're never removing more than one-third of the grass blade at a time. Example: to maintain grass at 3 inches tall, mow when it reaches about 4 inches tall. If it gets *really* long, do two cuts several days apart. Cut as high as you can to bring it down to 4 inches, then mow a few days later down to 3 inches.

If you get behind with mowing due to unrelenting rain or being away, grass clips may pile up enough to make mats or channels. Those can smother grass underneath and should be raked and removed. Add them to the compost pile or use them as mulch (after they brown if you're using them around plants)—but only if you haven't treated the grass with weed-killers.

It's not too late to apply crabgrass preventer if you've had a problem with this weed in the past.

It's also not too early to begin killing off weeds in the lawn by applying a broadleaf weed-killer formulated for lawns. These kill non-grassy plants only. Spot-spray a liquid broadleaf weed-killer to control occasional weeds, or apply a granular broadleaf weed-killer if you've got them everywhere.

Handpick or dig larger lawn weeds. Dandelions are edible and nutritious, assuming you haven't treated them with a herbicide.

## PERENNIALS & GROUNDCOVERS

April is a good month to dig and divide most perennials and groundcovers that are getting too crowded or outgrowing their allotted space. The exception is plants that are blooming this month, or in bud and about the bloom. A good rule of thumb is to divide species in the opposite season from which they bloom (spring bloomers in fall and fall bloomers in spring, with most summer bloomers tolerating either spring or fall). (See "Here's How to Divide Perennials," below.)

Once the soil has warmed and dried a bit, mulch the perennial beds. It's easier to get good coverage before the perennials grow and spread in the coming weeks.

Cut back any remaining dead foliage from last season if you haven't already done it. (See "When to Cut Perennials," page 78, for a list of what gets cut, how, and when.)

Some perennials hold their leaves all year and just need some neatening snips to get rid of winter-injured or ratty leaves. In most parts of the state, these include Lenten rose, coralbells, ajuga, dianthus, and bergenia.

(See "Here's How to Divide Perennials," below.)

## HERE'S HOW

### TO DIVIDE PERENNIALS

1. In spring, first cut back last year's dead foliage if you haven't done so already, except for species that hold their leaves all year long. In fall, green growth should be left intact so long as it's healthy and alive.

2. Dig down in the soil and around the clump until it dislodges. Lift the entire rootball out of the ground.

3. Using a spade, ax, or similar sharp tool, cut the clump into pieces at least the size of a fist. Some species, such as daylilies and garden phlox, have roots that can be pulled apart into smaller clusters. Discard any dead sections, and make sure each piece has roots of its own.

4. Replant one of the pieces at the same depth as before, and water well. Use the remaining pieces to expand your planting elsewhere, or give them away.

5. An alternate option for most plants (and ones that aren't dying out in the center) is to use a spade to cut, separate, and remove pieces from the perimeter of the mother plant without digging up the whole thing.

Established evergreen groundcover plantings of ivy, pachysandra, and vinca need very little routine care, but if they're getting overcrowded, diseased, or losing vigor, an April mowing can rejuvenate the planting. Mow or cut the planting down to about 2 to 3 inches. Remove large or excess cuttings. Then scatter a light, ½-inch layer of compost over the bed. You might also sprinkle a small amount of granular, slow-acting, all-purpose fertilizer over the area. Water if it does not rain within a day or two. In a few weeks, the groundcover will generate fresh new foliage.

## ROSES

Roses wake up this month and start elongating their leaf buds from the canes. That's your cue to get busy pruning. Different types of roses require different techniques. (See "Here's How to Prune Roses," page 79 for a rundown.)

The return to growth also signals it's time to remove winter protection, and pull back any extra mulch you've added around the stems. If an overnight frost threatens to harm tender new growth in exposed spots, cover the plant overnight with floating row cover or a light blanket or sheet.

Once the soil warms and dries, add a fresh topping of mulch over the rose beds. Bark mulch is ideal. Add just enough to provide 2 to 3 inches total, and do not allow it to touch shrub crowns or stems. Mulch discourages weeds, and helps control leaf disease by reducing the splashing of fungal spores from the soil onto the leaves.

## SHRUBS

Prune early-spring-flowering shrubs right after they finish blooming. This includes witch hazel, forsythia, bridalwreath spirea, and fothergilla. Do not prune flowering shrubs now that will bloom later this spring, or else you'll cut off the flower buds before they open (azalea, lilac, weigela, bigleaf hydrangea). (See "Pruning Timing of Shrubs, Trees, & Vines," page 80.)

Summer-blooming shrubs, such as butterfly bush, rose-of-Sharon, and caryopteris, are best pruned at the end of winter. But if you didn't get to it then, these can still be clipped if they need it. Do it as soon as you can this month. You're wasting the plant's energy by letting growth happen and then cutting it off. Plus, if you wait too long into the season to prune summer bloomers, they may not flower at all.

## WHEN TO CUT PERENNIALS

Perennials fall into one of four categories when it comes to when and how to cut them back each year:

- **Cut to the ground after frost browns foliage in fall:** anemone, armeria, aster, balloon flower, baptisia, beebalm, bleeding heart, boltonia, brunnera, catmint, centaurea, cimicifuga, columbine, corydalis, coreopsis, crocosmia, daylily, filipendula, garden phlox, goat's beard, goldenrod, hardy hibiscus, helianthus, hosta, iris, lily, lysimachia, obedient plant, penstemon, peony, salvia, sneezeweed, spiderwort, verbascum, veronica

- **Cut to the ground in early spring before new growth begins:** acanthus, amsonia, asclepias, astilbe, black-eyed Susan, campanula, coneflower, creeping phlox, delphinium, echinops, epimedium, eupatorium, ferns, foamflower, Frikart's aster, gaillardia, geum, heliopsis, hollyhock, Jacob's ladder, lamb's ears, leadwort, liatris, ligularia, liriope, lobelia, lupine, lychnis, monkshood, mum, poppy, rose mallow, sea holly, sedum, sundrops, stokesia, turtlehead, yarrow

- **Cut back to 2 or 3 inches in early spring before new growth begins:** artemisia, baby's breath, candytuft (right after blooming), gaura, hardy geranium, Jupiter's beard, lady's mantle, ornamental grasses, red hot poker, Russian sage, scabiosa, thyme

- **Don't cut, just trim off ratty foliage as needed:** ajuga, bergenia, coralbells, dianthus, evergreen ferns, foamybells, lamium, Lenten rose, ornamental strawberry, pulmonaria, snow-in-summer, verbena

## HERE'S HOW

### TO PRUNE ROSES

1. Cut out all dead and damaged canes on all types of roses as soon as you notice it. Cut back to live wood or back to the main stem if the whole branch is dead.

2. Use sharp pruners, loppers, and pruning saw blades for a clean cut. Disinfect pruner blades between plants and cuts by spraying the blades with rubbing alcohol or household disinfectant.

3. Make cuts about ¼ inch above buds or shoots pointing in the desired direction (usually outward-facing). Make cuts at a 45-degree angle downward. Some rosarians recommend sealing cuts with a dab of white glue.

4. For hybrid teas, floribundas, and grandifloras, select three to six healthy, finger-sized canes evenly spaced around the bush. Cut them back to 12 to 18 inches tall. Cut off all other canes at the base. Make the cuts about ¼ inch above an outward-facing leaf bud, angled so that rainwater will drip away from it.

5. Long-armed landscape roses benefit from renovation pruning. At the end of winter to early spring, thin out about one-third of older canes and weak branches. Reduce the length of remaining canes by one-third of their length.

6. Polyanthas and miniature roses need more of a grooming. At winter's end to early spring, prune back stems to 3 to 5 inches. Clip off twiggy growth, especially from the center.

7. Groundcover and shrub roses can be sheared, also ideally at the end of winter to early spring. Cut all canes to about 6 inches.

8. Climbers are best pruned over winter but can be cut in early spring before new growth begins. Train new climbers by loosely tying main stems to supports. Since flowering is best on horizontal branches, tie them within a 45-degree angle of the ground. Starting the third year, thin out excess shoots and shorten the remaining side branches by two-thirds of their length. Over time, cut back some of the oldest shoots back to the base and select younger ones to replace them.

9. Ramblers also are best pruned over winter when the leaves are off. Prune off all canes that are two years or older back to the base (about one-third of the total wood). Shorten the remaining side branches by two-thirds of their length. Select and tie new young main shoots to replace the ones you've removed.

When mulching around shrubs, keep the mulch a few inches back away from their trunks. Mulch can trap moisture against the bark and encourage rotting.

For evergreen shrubs such as holly, boxwood, globe arborvitae, euonymus, nandina, cherry laurel, yew, and Japanese plum yew, early April is still a good time to prune or shear. Wait to cut spruce, fir, and pine until spring growth finishes.

### TREES

Now that grass and weeds are growing fast, you'll likely be spending much time with the

## PRUNING TIMING OF SHRUBS, TREES, & VINES

- **Shrubs and trees that are best pruned in late winter to early spring (that is, heading *into* the growing season):** abelia, arborvitae, aucuba, barberry, beautyberry, boxwood, burning bush, butterfly bush, caryopteris, cherry laurel, clematis (summer bloomers), coralberry, crape myrtle, dogwood (shrub types), euonymus, falsecypress, heather, hemlock, holly, juniper, nandina, oak, panicle hydrangea, potentilla, privet, most roses, rose-of-sharon, St. Johnswort, seven-son flower, smooth hydrangea, spirea (most), summersweet, snowberry, vitex, yew

- **Shrubs and trees that are best pruned right *after* they bloom:** azalea, beautybush, bigleaf hydrangea, bittersweet, bridalwreath spirea, chokeberry, flowering cherry, clematis (spring bloomers), cotoneaster, daphne, deutzia, dogwood (tree types), enkianthus, flowering almond, fothergilla, forsythia, fringe tree, heath, honeysuckle, kerria, lavender, lilac, magnolia (most), mahonia, mock orange, mountain laurel, ninebark, oakleaf hydrangea, pieris, flowering plum, pyracantha, quince, redbud, rhododendron, Scotch broom, serviceberry, smokebush, snowbell, spicebush, sweetshrub, viburnum, weigela, witch hazel

weed-whacker. Be careful that you don't whack the tree's bark! Also don't run into tree trunks with mowers. Both can open wounds and lead to infection. This is one of the many reasons why it's good to maintain mulched circles around the base of trees.

Remove staking from trees planted last spring. One year is enough. While you're at it, check other more recently staked trees to make sure the ties aren't too tight.

Early spring-flowering trees (star magnolia, redbud, and cornelian cherry dogwood, for example) can be pruned right after they're done flowering. Wait a bit longer to prune late-spring bloomers so you don't cut off this year's flower buds that haven't yet opened.

April also is fine to prune most evergreen trees, including arborvitae, Leyland cypress, cryptomeria, Hinoki cypress, cedar, holly, and falsecypress. Wait until June after new growth finishes to prune fir, spruce, and pine. Dead wood can be cut off anytime from any species.

## VINES

This is last call to cut back or shape summer-blooming woody vines such as climbing hydrangea, Japanese hydrangea vine, ornamental kiwi, trumpet vine, American bittersweet, and summer- or fall-flowering clematis if you didn't already do it.

Leaves emerge this month on all clematis vines, giving you a chance to assess what's alive and what might've died over winter. Dead wood comes off first. Then shorten and shape the "keeper" shoots to stimulate vigorous new growth and flowering. Wait until after bloom to shorten the keepers on spring bloomers.

## WATER

### ALL

Watering usually is one of the last things you'll need to worry about in April. The soil usually starts out moist from winter snowmelt, then frequent showers make this month largely hoseless.

It's always a good idea to "water-in" anything newly planted to help the soil settle around the roots, though. Then just watch to make sure rain keeps the soil consistently damp in the early going.

### ANNUALS & TROPICALS

Newly planted cold-hardy annuals benefit from watering two to three times a week (whenever it doesn't rain) to help them establish. The roots of new annuals are small and shallow, so they're more prone to drying when the soil surface goes dry. This is a case where frequent shallow waterings are called for instead of infrequent deeper ones, as with trees and shrubs.

### BULBS

Unless it's unusually dry, you won't need to water spring bulbs. Bulbs in pots dry faster, though, so you may need to water those every day or two.

### LAWNS

Established lawns almost never need any water in a Pennsylvania April.

Newly seeded lawns are a different story. Keep seed continually moist with frequent (even daily) light sprinklings until it sprouts. Then water the young growth a little deeper every two to three days in the absence of rain. The goal is consistently damp soil in the top 4 to 6 inches to encourage the young grass roots to penetrate downward.

Newly sodded lawns also need regular water. Soak well after planting, then water every two to three days in the absence of rain to keep the soil consistently damp in the top 4 to 6 inches. Be sure to apply enough water that it's soaking through the sod layer and down into the soil.

### PERENNIALS & GROUNDCOVERS

April showers are usually enough to satisfy established perennials and groundcovers. Give them a weekly soaking if it's unusually dry. Newly planted perennials and groundcovers should be soaked about twice a week if rain doesn't do the deed for you.

### ROSES, SHRUBS, TREES & VINES

Established woody plants seldom need any April watering, especially if you've maintained a 2- to 3-inch mulch layer around their base. The exceptions are ones less than two years in the ground. The roots of these are still young enough that a deep soaking once or twice a week is beneficial if rain isn't watering for you. The goal is to keep the soil consistently damp all around the growing rootball and just under it.

## FERTILIZE

### ALL

The beginning of a new growing season is prime time for giving the soil new nutrition. However, the idea of fertilizing is to supply the soil with *adequate* amounts of each of the nutrients the plants in that bed need. *More isn't better.* Plants will take up what they need, and the rest either goes unused or leaches out or runs off.

The only sure way to determine your soil's nutrition status is to do a soil test. Do-it-yourself kits from Penn State University's soil testing lab

■ *In addition to measuring the relative levels of different nutrients in the soil, a soil test should accurately depict the pH level. When reading your results keep in mind that the scale is exponential: a one-point difference in the scale—say, from 6 to 5—represents a tenfold increase in acidity or alkalinity.*

are available at all county Extension offices, most garden centers, and online at http://agsci.psu.edu/aasl/soil-testing/soil-fertility-testing. Send in your soil sample, and the lab returns a report on key nutrient levels, the soil's pH (acidity level) and recommendations on the type and amount of fertilizer needed (if any).

If your plants are growing well and showing no signs of poor color, stunted growth, or other symptoms related to a nutrition deficiency, you probably don't need fertilizer.

Organic gardeners often top their soil each spring and/or fall with a light layer of compost, mushroom soil, or similar organic matter to add nutrition.

## ANNUALS & TROPICALS

Annuals are relatively heavy feeders and benefit from rich, loose soil. Work compost into the soil before planting each year, and consider adding a small amount of granular, organic flower fertilizer or a granular, slow-acting flower fertilizer to gradually release nutrients through summer. You can do this "bed-prep" work this month (once the soil dries adequately) in advance of next month's annual-planting prime time.

## BULBS

If you're planning to yank the tulips after their first-season performance (many of them go downhill in ensuing years), there's no need to fertilize them. But for daffodils, hyacinths, crocuses, and other spring bulbs you'd like to keep going, lightly scratch a granular fertilizer into the soil surface if you didn't already do that in March. Use a product with a balanced nutrient breakdown or one slightly higher in phosphorus and potassium (the last two numbers on the fertilizer bag) instead of one high in nitrogen (the first number). Something with a breakdown close to 5-10-10 or 10-10-10 is ideal.

## LAWNS

If you already spread a slow-acting granular fertilizer in late fall, there's no need to do so again until May or early June.

If you *didn't* spread fertilizer on the lawn last fall and didn't get to it in March either, it's not too late

to do it in April. A soil test will tell you the exact analysis your lawn needs if you haven't checked that in a few years. Generally, a granular organic lawn fertilizer or one that's high in slow-release nitrogen and low in phosphorus is ideal. Lawns often need no phosphorus at all (the middle number of the three-digit reading you'll find on the label).

Another fertilizer option for organic gardeners is to spread a light layer of compost over the soil surface in spring and/or fall.

Avoid overdoing it with fertilizers high in fast-release nitrogen. They're quick to green up the lawn, but they also increase the growth rate to undesirable levels. That means more mowing and energy that's going into excessive blade growth instead of strong root growth. Excess nitrogen also can increase the likelihood of some lawn diseases. The labels of chemical lawn fertilizer will tell you what percentage of its nitrogen, if any, comes from slow-release nitrogen.

## PERENNIALS & GROUNDCOVERS

Groundcovers seldom need supplemental fertilizer. Fertilize those beds only if poor growth or a soil test indicates a deficiency.

Many established perennials also do fine with existing soil nutrition, boosted by nutrients coming from each season's topping of mulch and/or compost that's breaking down. Some gardeners like the "insurance" of adding a scattering of granular organic or slow-acting flower fertilizer over the perennial beds each April, just as new growth is taking off.

## ROSES

Roses are *heavy* feeders and benefit from a scattering of granular, organic, or slow-acting rose fertilizer as growth begins in a new season. Apply that now if you didn't already do it in March.

## SHRUBS, TREES & VINES

Most of these don't need routine fertilizer. Especially for woody plants growing in or near lawns, their roots will grab some of the fertilizer being applied to the lawn. Mulch that's breaking down also supplies nutrition.

A good rule of thumb is to skip fertilizer unless poor growth or a soil test indicates it. Yellowish or smaller-than-normal leaves, for example, may be a sign that the soil is too alkaline or lacks nitrogen. Rather than guess and buy something unnecessary or even counterproductive, it's best to test the soil and act based on the report.

## PROBLEM-SOLVE

### ALL

The key to healthy plants is keeping them stress-free. That starts with getting the right plant in the right location—one that provides the preferred soil type, adequate moisture, correct light, and room to grow. Plants that are growing as stress-free as possible have well-functioning immune systems that defend against insect and disease attacks. Even if a problem strikes, a healthy, well-placed plant will recover faster than a stressed one in a poorly chosen site.

Don't guess about perceived problems and wing it with a treatment. It's best to identify a problem first and target your response—if one is even needed. Routinely spraying the entire yard for insects and diseases "just in case" is wasteful, polluting, and harmful to beneficial or harmless organisms, which make up the majority of landscape life.

A problem-solving game plan is to ask yourself: Does your plant really have a problem, or are those yellowing, dropping needles and flaking bark normal? If it is a bug, disease, or other insult, is it a threat to the plant's health and life, or is it just a cosmetic issue that'll resolve on its own? If it *is* a serious threat, exactly what's causing it? What can be used to solve the problem without causing collateral damage to off-target organisms or the environment? And when is the correct time to apply it?

### ANNUALS & TROPICALS

Deer and rabbits are big fans of those tender, newly planted annuals. Fencing defeats the purpose of ornamental plants, so your best bet is applying scent or taste repellents. Reapply them as frequent spring rains wash them off.

Spot-fencing young plants being targeted by marauding animals works well—if you don't mind looking at the fence.

### BULBS

Deer and rabbits also like the flower buds of some spring-blooming bulbs, *especially* tulips. Keep a repellent spray on them if you're running into trouble. Or consider a fence around them.

Tulip fire (*Botrytis tulipae*) is a disease that attacks tulips growing in the same place for several years, deforming their flowers. If that's happening, dig up and discard affected bulbs, and avoid tulips in that soil for at least four years. The disease will die out on its own.

### LAWNS

That zoysia grass that's still brown isn't dead or diseased. It's still waking up. Your neighbors might not like how it's creeping into their now-green cool-season lawn. (Zoysia elbows out most other grasses.) To keep zoysia within your borders, sink a plastic, metal, or concrete barrier down at least 3 or 4 inches deep and also 2 or 3 inches above grade to keep runners from spreading. Anything that's already spread has to be dug out or sprayed with a non-selective, kill-everything herbicide such as glyphosate. Then the cleared-out soil should be seeded or sodded with species similar to what's adjacent.

Thatch is a normal component of all lawns. This is the spongy layer of decomposing organic matter (mostly dead grass roots) at the soil surface. A

■ *Determine the extent of thatch buildup by digging out a small section of lawn.*

½-inch layer or less is fine, but some grass types and some practices encourage it to thicken to levels that impede oxygen, moisture, and nutrition to the roots. Leaving grass clippings on the lawn *does not* cause this problem. To deal with excess thatch, use a power rake or dethatching attachment to the mower to rip up this mat. Rake the removed thatch, and compost it.

Red thread is one of the first lawn-disease threats out the gate. It's caused by a fungus that prefers cool, damp conditions, and it shows up as a pinkish, thready look at the tips of grass blades. Fertilizing usually fixes it, as does warmer, drier weather.

## PERENNIALS & GROUNDCOVERS

Slugs are often a problem this month. These slimy crawlers prefer shady areas and are especially fond of hosta. Set out homemade traps, such as a shallow pie pan filled with beer. Or buy commercial slug traps or repellents.

Other ways to deter slugs: go out at night when they're most active and sprinkle them with salt; scatter sand, gravel, or a similar scratchy material over the ground (their soft bodies are sensitive); set boards or cantaloupe half-shells over the ground at night and check underneath in the morning for hiding slugs; or surround the bed with copper wire or strips (which apparently give off enough of an electric charge to make sensitive-skinned slugs uncomfortable).

Deer, rabbits, groundhogs, and voles may nibble the tender foliage of emerging perennials. They

■ *Large holes in leaves indicate a slug problem.*

■ *To make a beer trap, put a shallow jar or butter lid on the ground next to the afflicted plant. Fill the trap with beer to catch the slugs.*

each have particular favorites. Watch for chewing damage, and either spot-fence the plants or use repellents. Once the growth thickens, this early damage often dwindles.

On the bug front, one of the season's first pests is aphids, which are small, pear-shaped green or black bugs sometimes called "plant lice." Lady beetles and other predator bugs often clean up aphid infestations without you doing anything. But if it's getting out of hand, and you're not seeing beneficials, sprays of insecticidal soap or neem oil control aphids.

## ROSES

Watch out for a fairly new and deadly rose disease called "rose rosette disease." It's caused by a virus that's thought to be spread by a mite. Symptoms include elongated canes that are thicker than usual, deformed flowers, mutated new growth that's often red in color, and excessive thorns. Have a sample diagnosed by your Extension office or a trusted garden center to rule out bugs, herbicide injury, or other possibilities. If you've got rosette disease, there's no effective cure. The recommended treatment is to remove the diseased rose. Almost all roses are at least moderately susceptible. Fortunately, it's not terribly common. Yet.

Canker is a fungal disease that shows up as dark splotches on the canes. It's most noticeable in colder weather, and is sometimes mistaken for

■ *Groundhogs are voracious eaters with a taste for numerous landscape plants.*

winter injury. Remove cankered canes by cutting them off well below the infection. Improve air circulation by thinning overly dense growth, and sterilize pruners between cuts with a household disinfectant.

Aphids may cluster on tender new rose foliage and buds. Squishing them with your fingers is a quick, effective "organic" control. Or spray aphids with insecticidal soap or neem oil if they're getting out of control and beneficial insects aren't coming to the rescue.

## SHRUBS

If you're seeing brown tips and edges on your broadleaf evergreen leaves, especially marginally winter-hardy ones such as cherry laurel, nandina, sweetbox, and aucuba, it's most likely "windburn" from cold winter winds. Wind and frozen soil team up to dry these leaves over winter, and the first tissue to go brown is the extremities (tips and edges). Assuming the branches are alive, the brown leaves will drop, and fresh growth will fill in. Dead branches and branch tips should be pruned back to live growth once you're sure they're dead and not just not in the process of re-leafing.

Some shrubs are also prone to aphids, which tend to cluster on tender new tip growth and suck the chlorophyll out of the leaves and needles. You may see ants running along stems because they like the sweet "honeydew" that aphids secrete. If aphids

are out of control and causing noticeable damage, try blasting them out with a stiff spray of water, or spray them with insecticidal soap or neem oil.

## TREES

Aphids may cluster at the tips of some tree branches too. Use the same strategy as with shrubs.

Tent caterpillar nests are visible in tree branches around the end of April. Either cut off the branches they are attached to and put them in the trash, or poke the tents open with a long stick so birds can eat the eggs and young caterpillars.

Woolly adelgids are a serious bug pest of hemlock, Pennsylvania's official state tree. These aphid-like bugs suck the chlorophyll out of hemlock needles under the protection of little, white, cotton-like balls. This cottony growth can be seen forming at the base of hemlock needles now. You have two treatment options: apply a liquid adelgid-killer, such as imidacloprid, to the soil in late March or April for season-long control, or spray the foliage twice two weeks apart in April and again in September to early October with a chemical adelgid-killer or with horticultural oil or insecticidal soap.

## VINES

Honeysuckle is particularly prone to aphids in April. Lady beetles usually clean up the problem, but if you're impatient or seeing unacceptable damage, spray with a blast of hose water or with insecticidal soap or neem oil.

■ *White cottony masses on hemlock indicate the presence of woolly adelgids.*

May

*May is the best time to be a gardener in Pennsylvania.*

Fragrant lilacs scent the air, crabapple flowers glorify cobalt-blue skies, and fresh summer annuals add colorful new life to the front yard.

Even the weather is generally well-behaved. March winds and April showers give way to frequently pleasant, sunny May days that kick plant growth into high gear. The threat of overnight freezes ends this month—already in the Philadelphia region and by Memorial Day even in the cold pockets of northwestern Pennsylvania.

That clears the way for the widespread planting of annual flowers—the petunias, the zinnias, and the begonias that color our landscapes until frost returns in fall.

There's no need to wait for those to thrive though. Our biggest concentration of tree, shrub, and perennial flowering also happens in succession throughout May, ranging from native Virginia bluebells to the gazillions of Asian-bred azaleas and rhododendrons that decorate so many house walls.

The spring bulb show joins in with its last main hurrah, in particular the tulips but also late daffodils, Spanish bluebells, and the year's peak month for ornamental onions (*Allium*). It all adds up to a delightful and diverse setting at a time that's usually not too hot or too cold and not too wet or too dry.

But don't sit on that bench under the tree gawking for too long. There's plenty for the gardener to do to maximize the current display and set the stage for the rest of the growing season. Those early-blooming shrubs will need to be pruned. The fading bulb foliage will need to be cut. And your new plantings will need to go in the ground before it gets too hot in June and beyond.

Yeah, it's a busy time for gardeners—one of our busiest. But you won't hear much complaining.

## PLAN

### ALL

This is like Christmas season for garden centers. Everybody swarms to buy plants this month, seemingly on the second Saturday of May. Get out on a weekday, if you can, to avoid peak crowds, lines, and spats over who gets that last dark-leafed elderberry.

You'll be less confused if you get to the garden center already knowing what you want to buy. All of those blooming plants practically cry out, "Buy me! Buy me!" It's easy to end up with two of this and three of that. And that's when you end up wandering around the yard trying to figure out where to plant everything.

You don't necessarily need a detailed landscape drawing for your shopping (although that helps), but at least know basics such as how much space you have to work with, the kind of light you've got, and any particular site challenges (wet soil, tree roots nearby, lurking animals, and so forth).

Watch for sales and coupon deals. They're plentiful this time of year, and they could save you a lot of money.

### ANNUALS & TROPICALS

May is by far the top-selling month for annual flowers. Yes, make your list before you head out to buy, but be ready to shift gears if you can't find your top pick, or if you see something new that grabs your eye.

When should you pull the trigger and plant those warm-season annuals? Frost will kill or severely damage most of them. The "real" last frost dates vary widely from year to year and from place to place. In Pennsylvania, the *average* last spring frost dates range from mid-April in the warmer Philadelphia area to almost mid-May in the coldest regions. However, the all-time *latest* killing frost dates range from late April in the Philadelphia area to end of May in the coldest regions.

How do those dates translate into your buying decision? If you're a gambler and use the average last-frost dates, you'll get an early start half the time, but get frosted the others. If you play it safe, wait until the all-time record frost date passes. A sensible middle ground is to watch the expected overnight lows in the ten-day forecast once you get close to the all-time latest frost date. If the forecast calls for nothing close to freezing, you're probably okay to take the jump.

To match flower color to your house trim, paint small strips of wood or plastic with the same paint you used for the doors, walls, railings, and/or shutters. Then take those to the garden center to hold up next to the flowers. An alternative is to get paint-sample strips from the home center, and match those to your trim.

Don't overlook annuals just because the transplants for sale aren't blooming yet. Growers manage to have almost everything in flower by early May so they're enticing for prime shopping time. However, some beauties just take longer to get going, such as blue salvia, browallia, and gloriosa daisy. They might not look like much now, but they'll flourish in a few weeks.

### BULBS

Get your tender bulbs out of storage. Discard any that have shriveled or rotted. Do you need to replace or expand any? How about new types? You'll be able to buy summer bulbs such as dahlias, callas, gladioli, and tuberous begonias now at the garden centers or from mail-order vendors.

Continue to watch for spots where the yard could use more spring-blooming bulbs. The crocuses, hyacinths, and most of the daffodils are done, but May is when you could be getting color from tulips, alliums, fritillaria, camassia, and Spanish bluebells.

### LAWNS

Your lawn should be at its best this month. Grass has had weeks to green and fill in, sunlight is increasing, and soil moisture is usually good. The threat of brutal heat and drought is weeks away. If all isn't well in grassland, think about why (and plan to correct it).

- Are you cutting too short?

- Is the soil nutrition lacking?

- Is the lawn thin, allowing crabgrass and weeds to elbow in?

- Have you had outbreaks of grubs killing off whole patches?

- Are tree roots expanding, signaling it's time to switch to another, more shade-tolerant groundcover?

## PERENNIALS & GROUNDCOVERS

Garden and home-improvement centers have their best selection of perennials and groundcovers this time of year, often in a selection of sizes. Plants in 4- or 6-inch pots are least expensive but will require more patience. Larger plants in quart or 1-, 2-, or 3-gallon pots cost more but have immediate impact.

Look for healthy plants at purchase. Signs of setbacks are:

- Wilted foliage from lack of water.

- Yellow or limp foliage from insufficient light or fertilizer.

- Holes or a stippling of the leaves from insects.

- Blotches or gray coating on the leaves or stems from possible fungal disease.

- Thin, lanky stems from lack of light during initial growth.

- Excessive flowers on an undersized plant from overfertilization.

- Roots emerging from pot drainage holes, which can signal circling roots or a plant that's been in the pot too long.

- Weeds in the container from lack of attention by the seller.

Not all of these are deal-killers. Some are temporary or cosmetic issues, ones that plants will grow through once in the ground. However, the closer you can get to perfection at buying time, the better your odds of success.

One guide to superior perennials is the annual Perennial Plant of the Year award bestowed by the Perennial Plant Association. See the full list since 1990 at www.perennialplant.org. The Pennsylvania Horticultural Society also added top underused perennials to its Gold Medal

■ *When you buy perennials or chrysanthemums (perennials that are sometimes sold as seasonal annuals), buy plants that haven't bloomed yet. That way, you get to enjoy the flowers for longer.*

## FIVE THINGS TO CHECK WHEN SHOPPING FOR HEALTHY SHRUBS

1. Good leaf color; there's no yellowing or dull color that might indicate poor soil nutrition or insect trouble.

2. There's no spotting of the leaves or a grayish coating; those are symptoms of disease.

3. The shrub has a good full shape without broken or missing branches.

4. No wilting, which indicates the plant hasn't been watered often enough or has outgrown the pot.

5. The shrub's roots aren't tightly circling or matted when you gently slip the plant out of the pot.

Award program (see http://phsonline.org/learning/gold-medal-plants), and Devon-based Jenkins Arboretum awards Green Ribbon honors each year to top under-used native perennials (see www.jenkinsarboretum.org/greenribbon.html).

Maximize your first-year enjoyment by picking perennials that have a lot of buds just about to open as opposed to plants already in full bloom.

## ROSES

Garden centers are well stocked with container-grown roses this month, and some are in flower already. Nothing beats seeing the real flowers to gauge exact colors.

Shrub, antique, and groundcover roses are the most disease-resistant types, but breeders have made strides in producing hybrid teas, grandifloras, and floribundas that are more disease-resistant than some earlier varieties.

## SHRUBS

May is peak time for azaleas and rhododendrons, which have the good marketing sense to bloom when everybody is plant shopping. Other May-flowering shrubs to consider include beautybush, cherry laurel, chokeberry, coralberry, deutzia, lilac,

shrub dogwood, tree peony, sweetshrub, viburnum, and weigela.

## TREES

What size tree should you buy? Some gardeners use a "bigger-the-better" approach, but small to mid-sized trees—4 to 6 feet tall at purchase—offer several advantages. They're less expensive, easier to transport, easier to handle when planting, and quicker to establish once in the ground. Small trees often catch up size-wise to larger ones in a few years because their rootballs are more in balance with their canopy.

When tree shopping, look for well-spaced, firmly attached branches, a trunk without wounds, and the same five traits as healthy shrubs. (See "Five Things to Check When Shopping for Healthy Shrubs," left.)

If your yard is weak in May-blooming trees, consider Carolina silverbell, fringe tree, Japanese snowbell, Kousa dogwood, hawthorn, horse chestnut, and some magnolias.

## VINES

Honeysuckle, ornamental kiwi vine, and spring-blooming clematis are three vines that add vertical color in May.

Think about adding more annual vines this season. These allow you to change the look from year to year. Examples are purple hyacinth bean, scarlet runner bean, black-eyed Susan vine, moonflower, and mandevilla. May is the best month to plant all of those.

## PLANT

### ALL

"Transplant shock" refers to the wilting that can happen to plants soon after they're moved to a new location. It can happen both to existing landscape plants that are dug and moved, and to newly bought potted plants going into the ground from a sheltered greenhouse. Minimize transplant shock by planting on a cloudy day, or at least out of the hot, midday sun (early morning and evening are good). Always soak a plant's roots well immediately after it's planted or transplanted.

## ANNUALS & TROPICALS

Once you're convinced frost is done, get busy planting those petunias, geraniums, angelonias, and other warm-season annuals. One foot apart is good spacing for most. A few, including geraniums, lantana, and most petunias, spread quicker and more vigorously and can go 15 to 24 inches apart. (See "Here's How to Plant Annuals," right.)

If you're using transplants that you started from seed (less expensive than buying transplants), be sure to "harden them off" first. This means gradually getting them used to increasingly more light and outdoor exposure over a seven- to ten-day period before planting.

The end of frost means it's time to direct-seed annuals into the ground. Ones that start well this way include calendula, cleome (spider flower),

■ *This flowerpot uses the classic pairing of a "thriller, filler and spiller." See page 92.*

### HERE'S HOW

### TO PLANT ANNUALS

1. Loosen the planting bed to 10 or 12 inches deep and work in 1 to 2 inches of compost, mushroom soil, rotted leaves, or similar organic matter. Also mix in a light scattering of granular organic flower fertilizer or a pelleted, gradual-release flower fertilizer.

2. Open a planting hole, deep enough so that the plant will end up at the same depth it was in its pot or cell-pack.

3. Squeeze the sides of the pot, invert, and gently slip the plant out into your hand. Set it in the hole.

4. Gently firm the soil so the rootball is covered. Water well.

5. Mulch isn't necessary, but if you use any, keep it to less than 1 inch deep and away from the stems.

## HERE'S HOW

### TO PLANT AND CARE FOR PLANTS IN CONTAINERS

1. Think *big*. Smaller pots dry out faster than larger ones. Also, terra cotta dries out faster than plastic, foam, concrete, and metal.

2. Fill the pot about two-thirds full with lightweight potting mix, or so the soil line will end up an inch or two *below* the pot lip once the plants are planted. An option is to work in a *small* amount of hydrogel crystals to absorb water (which will be released over time later).

3. Set your plants, spaced almost to touching, and cover the rootballs with additional potting mix.

4. Lightly scratch a scattering of granular, gradual-release flower fertilizer into the surface, and soak the pot well until water runs out the bottom.

5. Start your season-long care. Figure on daily soakings (except in cool, cloudy, and rainy weather), and add a half-strength flower fertilizer to the water once a week throughout the growing season.

6. Snip back stems of plants that are overtaking neighbors or growing too long. Deadhead spent flowers.

cosmos, marigold, nasturtium, nigella (love-in-a-mist), sunflower, and zinnia. Loosen the soil, scatter the seed, and cover with the soil to the depth listed on each variety's seed packet. Keep the bed watered until the seedlings are up. Snip off excess seedlings with scissors.

May is the time to put together containers of summer annuals. The classic design is an upright "thriller" as the centerpiece, several bushier bloomers as the "fillers," and one or more "spillers" to trail around the edges. You don't have to stick with that, though. A pot filled with a single type of showy flower, 'Dragon Wing®' begonias, for example, can be simple but elegant. Or if you like a more action-packed cottage-garden look, go with a collection of "onesies."

Once frost is done and nights stay above 50 degrees Fahrenheit, take houseplants outside for their "summer vacation." Gradually acclimate them to the outside over seven to ten days; don't just set them outside in full sun all day right off the bat.

### BULBS

Tender bulbs can go in the ground once all danger of frost is gone. Clean off any soil, and discard any shriveled or rotted bulbs. Divide dahlia tubers, making sure each separate tuber has an "eye," or growing tip. Separate begonias and gladiolas, and plant those separately too.

Gradually acclimate tender bulbs you've started inside before transplanting into the ground. Ditto for that amaryllis you've been growing inside all winter. Amaryllis can be planted in the ground, or left to grow in a pot outside over summer.

Don't have any tender bulbs? You'll find dahlias, gladiola, callas, cannas, tuberous begonias, and more on sale now in bulb form at the garden center. These can be planted throughout May, once all danger of frost is past.

One other plant you'll find in bulb form this time of year is the lily. Most lilies are winter-hardy and will come back year after year. Buying them as bulbs is less expensive than buying them in plant form. They can be planted this month.

Spring-flowering bulbs that are done blooming can be dug, divided, and transplanted. Gently

■ *Cut a piece of sod to snugly fit the patch area. It's better to cut it slightly larger and then trim it to fit as necessary. Use a large, sharp knife to cut the sod.*

## HERE'S HOW

### TO PLANT AND CARE FOR HANGING BASKETS

1. Lean toward larger baskets, which won't dry out as fast as smaller ones. Line the inside of the frame with sphagnum moss or with a ready-made moss or fiber liner. Reduce evaporation loss by lining the inside (but *not* the bottom) of your basket with a sheet of thick plastic.

2. Fill the basket with lightweight potting mix about two-thirds full. An option is to work in a small amount of hydrogel crystals to absorb water.

3. Set your plants, spaced almost to touching, and cover the rootballs with additional potting mix. The mix should end up an inch or two *below* the lip.

4. Lightly scratch a scattering of granular, gradual-release flower fertilizer into the surface.

5. Install the hanger hooks and chain. Make sure the hangers are sturdy enough to hold the weight of the basket, potting mix, and water. Hang the basket.

6. Once in place, soak the basket until water drains out the bottom.

7. Start your season-long care regimen. Check regularly for water (daily watering is the norm in hot, dry weather), and add a half-strength flower fertilizer to the water once a week throughout the growing season.

8. Snip back stems of plants that are overtaking its neighbors or growing too long. Deadhead spent flowers.

dig up masses, and shake away excess soil. Tease apart individual bulbs. Discard any bulbs that are damaged or diseased. Replant some of the bulbs in the original spot, and plant the rest where you'd like to spread the colony. Cut the foliage once it's turning yellow.

## LAWNS

May is still a month to plant grass seed but the sooner the better. Grass can be planted all summer, but it's harder to germinate grass and keep it damp when it's boiling hot and bone dry.

An alternative to seeding bare lawn spots in the impending heat is to use sod. Sod is sections of already-growing grass—complete with roots and soil—that are sold like strips of carpet in garden centers. Sodding is more expensive than seeding, but sod sections can be laid right on top of loosened soil, tamped down, and watered to produce an instant lawn. (See September's "Here's How to Start a New Lawn from Sod," page 163.)

## PERENNIALS & GROUNDCOVERS

May is still an excellent time to plant perennials and groundcovers. Just be vigilant with the water since we're heading into the hot season. (See April's "Here's How to Plant Perennials," page 74.)

Perennials aren't just for in the ground. Coralbells, hosta, brunnera, Japanese forest grass, and others with colorful foliage are excellent additions to flower pots. Mix them with color-coordinated annuals or create entire pots using long-blooming and/or colorfully leafed perennials.

## ROSES

Cool nights and comfortably warm days make this an excellent planting month for container-grown roses. The process is similar to planting any other shrub, except that in the coldest regions of the state, plant so that the bud union (where the top part of most roses have been grafted to the rootstock) is set 2 to 4 inches below ground. (See March's "Here's How to Plant a Shrub," page 55.)

Get your potted miniature roses that you've been growing inside into the ground immediately this month if you didn't do it in April.

## SHRUBS

The vast majority of flowering and evergreen shrubs are sold as container-grown plants these days. May is one of the year's best months to plant them. (See March's "Here's How to Plant a Shrub," page 55.)

Azaleas and rhododendrons require special attention since plants in this family (*Ericaceae*) don't prefer the conditions many homeowners give them; that is, compacted, clayish, alkaline soil in

### HERE'S HOW

#### TO PLANT AZALEAS AND RHODODENDRONS

1. Dig a hole three to four times as wide as the rootball but only as deep.

2. Mix in enough coarse sand and compost or peat moss so that you'll have equal parts of existing soil, sand, and compost or peat moss for your backfill mixture. Set this aside.

3. If your soil isn't acidic enough (a pH of about 5.5 is ideal), work sulfur into the planting mix. A soil pH test will give you a reading and tell you how much sulfur is needed.

4. Remove the plant from the pot and fray out the roots. It's okay to remove most or all of the soil in the process, and to make a few vertical cuts if necessary to resolve tight matting or circling roots.

5. Set the plant in the hole so that the top of the rootball is about 2 inches above the surrounding grade. Fill in with the amended soil mix until the roots are covered.

6. Add 1 or 2 inches of pine needles, bark mulch, or rotted leaves to the soil surface, kept back away from the trunk by a few inches.

7. Soak the roots well and keep the soil consistently damp throughout the entire first three growing seasons.

hot, dry locations. Other related shrubs appreciate the same specialized planting, including pieris, mountain laurel, and heather. (See "Here's How to Plant Azaleas and Rhododendrons," left.)

## TREES

May is a good month to plant both container-grown and balled-and-burlapped trees. (See March's "Here's How to Plant a Tree," page 56.)

Most nurseries and garden centers will plant trees that you purchase from them (at an extra fee) if you can't or would rather not plant your new tree.

Earlier advice to remove branches at planting to "balance the roots with the aboveground growth" has been found counterproductive. Remove *only* broken or torn branches at the time of planting. More wood means more leaves to grab the sun's energy and feed energy to the growing roots. Wait a year to start corrective pruning and training.

## VINES

Most annual vines are best grown by direct-seeding them into the ground. Once danger of frost is done, loosen the soil, scatter the seed, and cover them with soil according to instructions on the seed packet. These include purple hyacinth bean, scarlet runner bean, black-eyed Susan vine, morning glory, moonflower, cypress vine, cardinal climber, cup-and-saucer vine, and climbing nasturtium.

It's also warm enough to plant annual vines normally grown from transplants, including mandevilla, dipladenia, bougainvillea, jasmine, sweet potato vine, and passion vine. Loosen the soil and plant these as you would any other annual flower. (See "Here's How to Plant Annuals," page 91.)

Passion vines sometimes survive winter in the warmer parts of the state, especially ones growing near heated walls. Watch for new shoots and cut off last year's dead growth to allow the new growth to take over. If nothing's emerging by mid-June, it's time to plant a new one.

May is also fine to plant container-grown woody and perennial vines, such as climbing hydrangea,

■ *Keep mulch a few inches away from the base of trees to avoid rotting the bark.*

Japanese hydrangea vine, clematis, honeysuckle, and trumpet vines. Plant all at or just above-grade, except for clematis, which prefer to grow at, or an inch or two *below*, grade.

## CARE

### ALL

May is mulch month. The soil has warmed enough now that you don't have to worry about trapping cold or root-rotting excess moisture. May is ideal mulch timing for two reasons: mulch excels at stopping weeds, many of which germinate in May, and mulch conserves soil moisture, which is needed as summer heat, dryness, and peak sunlight arrive.

Don't overmulch. Use no more than 3 to 4 total inches around trees and shrubs. Two inches is plenty around perennials, and 1 inch is enough around annuals. In all cases, keep mulch away from trunks and stems so as not to encourage rot.

If you already have the above mulch totals, don't add more. Resist the urge to automatically top the beds with more and more mulch, just because you like the look of fresh mulch. If you have enough

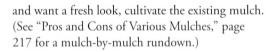
■ *Stakes and cages are two ways to support plants.*

and want a fresh look, cultivate the existing mulch. (See "Pros and Cons of Various Mulches," page 217 for a mulch-by-mulch rundown.)

When working compost into new beds, you'll end up with slightly raised beds that are ideal for almost all plants. To keep mulch from sliding down the sides and onto the lawn or sidewalk, taper the bed edges down to 2 or 3 inches *below* grade. That'll create a "lip" to catch sliding mulch.

## ANNUALS & TROPICALS
Nurse newly planted annuals through a hot spell by erecting temporary shade over them for a few days. An inch of organic mulch (chopped leaves are ideal) over the bare soil will discourage weeds and keep the soil moist and cooler.

Watch for new sprouts from last year's self-sowing annuals, such as cleome, nigella, and larkspur. These can thickly carpet a bed if you don't thin them early with scissors. Or dig and transplant "volunteer" seedlings.

## BULBS
Some summer bulbs such as lilies, gladioli, crocosmia, and dahlias can get tall enough to flop once they flower. Erect supports or install plant

rings soon after the shoots are up. That'll corral them more neatly than trying to bring floppers back under control later. Be careful you don't ram stakes into the buried bulbs.

As the foliage of daffodils, tulips, and other bloomed-out spring bulbs yellows and starts to collapse, cut it off and compost it.

## LAWNS
Let your grass clippings remain where they fall. They decay quickly and return nutrition and organic material to the soil. They don't cause thatch, that spongy layer composed mostly of dead roots at the soil surface. Mulching mowers cut blades multiple times before dropping them, but even ordinary mowers disperse clips without matting if you're mowing often enough.

Now that the grass is growing at peak rate, raise the blade on your mower to 2½ or 3 inches. Taller grass retains soil moisture, chokes out sunlight to weeds, and provides more chlorophyll for stronger grass-root growth.

Continue mowing often enough that you're never removing more than one-third of the grass blade at a time.

New lawn weeds are popping up to join ones returning from last year's roots and ones that sprouted in early spring. Now's a good time to control all of them. Spot-spray scattered outbreaks with a liquid broadleaf weed-killer, or broadcast a granular broadleaf weed-killer if they're all over the lawn. Handpick or dig out larger lawn weeds such as dandelions, hawkweed, plantain, and thistle.

If you're using a crabgrass product that both stops crabgrass from sprouting and kills it in its early stages, such as ones containing dithiopyr (Dimension), May is an ideal time to apply it. A good cue from nature is when dandelions are blooming.

## PERENNIALS & GROUNDCOVERS

May is still okay to dig and divide perennials that already have bloomed or that bloom in fall, although it's not as desirable as the cool of earlier spring. We're heading into hot, dry weather soon. That's more stressful on a newly moved plant. Be extra vigilant with summertime watering of May-divided perennials. (See April's Here's How to Divide Perennials, page 77.)

Taller perennials benefit from staking or similar supports to keep them from flopping later. Get your support in place now so the plants grow within them. It's easier than trying to corral flopping plants later.

For supporting tall perennials, use plant rings or similar store-brought metal staking gizmos available at garden centers. Or build your own by hammering bamboo stakes around the clusters in need of support and trying jute tightly around the staking. The stakes should be slightly shorter than the plant's maximum height.

Neaten perennials that have finished blooming by "deadheading" them—snipping off their spent flowers and/or flower stalks. Use shears to speed the job of deadheading masses of perennials with clustered flowers, such as candytuft, dianthus, and creeping phlox.

Keep late-blooming perennials from flopping by shearing them back this month. Mums are the best example, but sedum, aster, goldenrod, beebalm, boltonia, and even coneflower and black-eyed Susan can be trimmed by one-third to one-half. The plants will look ragged for a few weeks and bloom slightly later, but they'll bloom fuller and be markedly more compact.

## ROSES

Fresh mulch under roses not only discourages weeds and retains soil moisture, it prevents last year's fallen disease spores from splashing up on the stems. Keep it to no more than 3 inches total. Top off what you have, or remove and replace the mulch if you're tackling disease problems.

■ Climbing roses are often grown as vines but they are not true vines. These plants have long canes, or stems, that must be tied and trained into place to encourage them to grow upward. Use twine or twist ties if stems are light; insulated wire or rubber strips if they are woody.

Fasten the canes of climbing roses to their supports as they grow. These don't cling or twine on their own. Loop soft ties around the cane, then around the trellis to fasten. Do not tie skinny ties too tightly. That can cut into the wood.

Remove fallen leaves around the roses and discard them; they might harbor insect eggs and disease spores.

Finish your beginning-of-the-season cutbacks very quickly this month if you didn't get to it in April. Also watch for new stems growing from below the graft. Their foliage usually looks noticeably different from that of the main plant. These are unwanted shoots coming from the rootstock and should be pruned off.

## SHRUBS

Is it dead? That's a common question after a particularly cold winter that's caused a lot of branch dieback and brown leaves and needles. New buds should be poking out of most shrubs by the end of May to early June, so that's the surest way to tell what's alive and what's not. Be patient and watch for new growth.

Once you're sure branches are dead, prune them off. Occasionally, cold winters kill sensitive shrubs such as bigleaf hydrangeas, butterfly bush, and crape myrtle completely back to the ground. If that happens, cut off the dead top growth to make way for new growth emerging from the base.

### TWO TESTS TO ASSESS LIVE OR DEAD WOOD

1. Bend a branch in question, and see if it's flexible or brittle. Bending is good; snapping is bad.

2. Scrape a sliver of bark off a stem or two with a fingernail or blade. If there's green or pale moist tissue beneath, it's probably still alive. If it's brown and dry underneath, that wood is dead.

Prune spring-blooming shrubs right after they're done flowering, such as quince, azalea, daphne, fothergilla, deutzia, and weigela.

Snip off faded blossoms from large-flowered rhododendrons as they finish blooming. Go down to the next lower truss to control size. Rhododendrons are best not sheared.

## TREES

Most trees will have leafed by now. If you're seeing bare branches or leafless tips, that wood is likely dead and will have to come off. Perform the two live-wood tests (see sidebar) or wait a few more weeks to be sure.

May is a good time to prune spring-flowering trees once they're done flowering, although it's a little harder to see the branching now than over winter. Examples include dogwood, redbud, flowering cherry, flowering pear, and early magnolias. (See February's "Here's How to Prune a Tree," page 43.)

Some trees "bleed" sap profusely when you prune them this time of year. Maples, yellowwood, snowbell, birch, and elm have this tendency. This sap loss isn't harmful, but it can make the job needlessly messy. Avoid this leaking by pruning during the winter dormant season.

Do not pile soil on top of tree roots. Gardeners sometimes do that to cover exposed roots or to help keep grass growing in the losing competition with bigger tree roots. You can get away with maybe 3 or 4 inches, but covering tree beds more than that starts to deprive the roots of oxygen.

## VINES

Make sure trellises are installed several inches out from walls to allow air circulation. This will protect wall surfaces from mildew and marks from the vine. Building them so they're also detachable is convenient for painting or repairing the wall surface.

Prune off any winter-killed wood from woody vines. Most everything should be leafed out by the end of May. (See sidebar on page 98 for two tests you can do to determine if wood is dead or alive.)

Pyracantha being trained as a vine can be sheared, or it can be pruned a branch at a time. These tolerate pruning and shaping well, but keep in mind the more you prune, the more fruits you'll give up. A good balance is to thin out about one-third of the side shoots back to the main trunk right after the plant finishes blooming. Then shorten remaining branches, cutting *above* clusters of flowers. Sections that flowered will produce fruits in fall.

## WATER

### ALL

Even if it's rained recently, soak plants immediately after planting. This settles the soil around the roots and makes sure there's plenty of moisture to encourage root penetration. Don't count on that sure-fire soaking rain that's being forecast.

### ANNUALS & TROPICALS

Annuals are shallow-rooted and benefit from frequent watering, especially in the first four to six weeks after being planted. Water them every other day when it doesn't rain—or whenever the top few inches of soil is dry when you insert your index finger into the soil.

For annuals you're starting by seed directly in the ground, sprinkle the surface daily until the seeds are up. Then give them slightly deeper waterings every two or three days for the next four to six weeks.

Annuals and tropicals in containers typically need water daily, especially ones in a sunny location. Soak them until water comes out the bottom drainage holes.

### BULBS

Avoid watering summer bulb beds so much that the soil becomes soggy and rots the bulbs. However, keep the soil consistently damp until the shoots of newly planted summer bulbs are up. You'll likely need to water two or three times a week until that happens. Then cut back to a weekly soaking when it's hot and dry. These need less water than new annuals.

Bulbs growing in pots need more water more often than in-ground ones. Check the pot daily and soak until water runs out the drainage holes if the pot is noticeably lighter in weight and the soil is dry when you insert your finger.

### LAWNS

Keep the soil under newly seeded or sodded areas consistently damp. Otherwise, established lawns seldom need much—if any—irrigation in May. The exception is an unusually early drought.

### PERENNIALS & GROUNDCOVERS

New perennials are generally larger and deeper-rooted than annuals and so need a little less water in the first few weeks in the ground. Two soakings a week are usually plenty for the first four to six weeks after planting.

Most established perennials need little to no water in May, unless the month is unusually hot and dry, in which case a weekly soaking is helpful.

New groundcovers benefit from watering once or twice a week for the first four to six weeks after planting, but established ones seldom need any supplemental water in May.

### ROSES

Roses survive well with little water, but they perform and flower better in consistently damp soil. Your goal can be your guide here. If you're growing shrub roses and/or trying to minimize maintenance, skip watering them, or soak occasionally only in a drought. If you're trying to maximize performance, soak the ground around your roses two to three times a week whenever it's not raining.

Whenever watering roses, water the ground and not over the bushes. Damp leaves are more prone to blackspot and other disease problems.

## SHRUBS & TREES

When there's no rain, soak new shrubs and trees two to three times a week for their first two months, close to the rootball where the roots are. Then soak once or twice a week for the rest of their first season.

A rough guide for the water needs of a new tree is 1 to 2 gallons for every inch of trunk diameter at shoulder height. For new shrubs, apply 3 to 5 gallons of water per watering. As roots spread, widen your watering area and increase amounts to 1 gallon of water for every square foot of soil surface.

Trees and shrubs that have been in the ground for at least three or four years usually won't need water in May and most times only in extended hot, dry summer spells.

Trees and shrubs growing in containers need water more often, usually daily. Water until it drains out the bottom.

## VINES

Treat direct-seeded annual vines (black-eyed Susan vine, purple hyacinth bean, moonflower, and so forth) as you would any other annual flower—sprinkle daily until the seeds are up, then water deeply every two or three days for the next four to six weeks.

New vine plants should be watered two to three times a week for the first four to six weeks after planting. Lean toward deeper watering twice a week for perennials, and lighter waterings three times a week for smaller annual vines.

Established woody vines seldom need any water in May, unless it's been abnormally hot and dry. Then, a once-a-week deep soaking is fine.

## FERTILIZE

### ALL

Now that your plants are actively growing, watch their leaf colors. Yellowing, paleness, or light tissue between dark veins are signs of possible nutrient deficiencies. Before you guess and take the wrong action or buy the wrong product, test your soil if you haven't done that lately. Penn State offers

do-it-yourself kits, available at County Extension offices, many garden centers, and online at http://agsci.psu.edu/aasl/soil-testing/soil-fertility-testing.

## ANNUALS & TROPICALS

If you added compost and/or granular slow-acting fertilizer to the soil when preparing your beds, you don't need more fertilizer now. If you prefer water-soluble flower fertilizer, apply your first dose as you water your new plants after planting. Then follow the timing on your product's label, which is typically once a month.

Annuals in pots and baskets need more fertilizer more often since the frequent watering carries many nutrients out when the water drains. In addition to the slow-acting fertilizer at planting, use a water-soluble flower fertilizer at half-strength each week. Some gardeners use a quarter-strength dose each time they water.

## BULBS

Although summer bulbs, corms, tubers, and rhizomes store energy for the plant to use, high performers such as dahlias and begonias produce flowers all summer and welcome some extra nutrition. Use a product formulated for bulbs or one that's higher in potassium and phosphorus than nitrogen (a ratio of 5-10-10 is good). One option is to scatter a dose of slow-acting, granular bulb fertilizer over the soil within a month of planting. Another is to apply a water-soluble bulb fertilizer in that same time frame and another dose in June or early July. Don't overdo it by pumping on too much nitrogen.

## LAWNS

If you're using an organic program and fertilizing twice a year, May is the month to apply the season's first application. (Late September through October is the ideal time for the other.)

If you're using a three-times-a-year program, whether organic or with a chemical lawn fertilizer that's high in slow-release nitrogen, May is also a good time for the season's first application. (Products that are high in slow-release nitrogen are coated in order to release the greening effects of nitrogen more slowly and over a longer period of time. Fertilizer bags list the percentage of nitrogen that's slow-release.)

*May is a good month to fertilize the lawn, especially right before a soaking rain.*

If you're using a commercial "four-step" lawn-fertilizer program, you should've put down Step 1 in late March to early April. Wait until late May through late June to put down Step 2.

Good timing to apply lawn fertilizer is right before a soaking rain. The water starts to dissolve the fertilizer and carry it down into the root zone.

## PERENNIALS & GROUNDCOVERS

If you worked compost and/or slow-acting granular fertilizer into your soil at planting, there's no need to add more fertilizer now to new perennials.

Established perennials also don't need additional fertilizer now, especially if you did a scattering of a slow-acting granular fertilizer over the beds last month. Just watch for signs of poor growth or nutrient deficiencies, and act on those accordingly. Otherwise, you're off the fertilizer hook here.

Established groundcovers and ornamental grasses also hardly ever need supplemental fertilizer. The exception is if poor growth and a soil test indicate a deficiency.

## ROSES

As with watering, fertilizing roses can be linked to your expectations. Most roses (shrub and antique types in particular) perform adequately with no fertilizer, or with an annual springtime scattering of a granular, slow-acting fertilizer formulated for roses. But for peak performance, roses benefit from an additional scattering of rose fertilizer this month, as well as another in June, another in July, and another in early August.

## HOMEMADE ORGANIC ROSE FERTILIZER

Here's a recipe for making homemade rose fertilizer out of organic ingredients. It's one that many amateur rosarians use:

8 parts alfalfa meal

2 parts cottonseed meal

2 parts rock phosphate (not super phosphate)

2 parts bone meal

1 part blood meal

1 part Epsom salts (magnesium sulfate)

Combine all of the above and scratch the mix around each rose bush. Use 1 cup for each foot of bush height (i.e. 3 cups around a bush that's 3 feet tall). Water well after applying.

## SHRUBS, TREES & VINES

Routinely fertilizing established trees, shrubs, and woody vines is not necessary. Skip fertilizer unless poor growth or a soil test indicates a nutrient deficiency; then address it specifically. Adding more fertilizer where it isn't needed wastes time and money, may pollute waterways, and can be counterproductive to plant health.

## PROBLEM-SOLVE

### ALL

*Lots* of bugs become active now. Monitor your plants regularly and learn the difference between ones that do no, little, or only cosmetic damage vs. the relative few that are more serious plant-health threats.

### THREE MAIN TYPES OF INSECTS THAT DAMAGE PLANTS

1.  **Chewing insects.** These eat plant tissue such as leaves, flowers, buds, roots, and twigs. Damage is often seen as holes or missing tissue around the leaf edges or between the leaf veins. Key plant-chewers are beetles and caterpillars.

2.  **Sucking insects.** These insects insert their beak (proboscis) into leaves, twigs, flowers, or fruits to feed on the plant's juices. Damage shows up in discolored tissue, drooping leaves, and tiny spots in the leaves ("stippling"). Suckers include aphids, mealybugs, thrips, and leafhoppers.

3.  **Boring insects.** These are the most destructive and hardest to detect because they feed inside stems or beneath bark. Damage includes dead branch tips, wilting, and even death of the whole plant. This family includes the dreaded emerald ash borer as well as the oldie-but-baddie dogwood borer and assorted bark beetles.

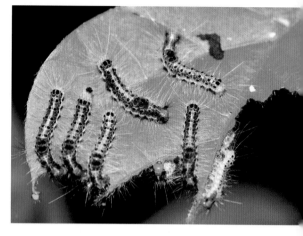

■ *Caterpillars are a chewing insect.*

■ *Aphids are a type of sucking insect. Control them with natural predators such a ladybugs.*

One common May pest in Pennsylvania is the aphid. Aphids are small green or black pear-shaped insects that suck chlorophyll out of leaves and can be seen on a wide variety of plants from sedum to roses. They can be blasted off with a stiff spray of water, killed with insecticidal soap or chemical insecticides, or left for the lady beetles to clean up (that is, eat).

A second common bug is the tent caterpillar. Moths lay eggs in a variety of trees and some shrubs, resulting in masses of caterpillars that feed inside of web-like bags (their "tents"). The bags are usually seen in branch crotches (at the base of where two branches meet). Insecticides control them, but just as effective is whacking open the bags to let birds have a feast.

## ANNUALS & TROPICALS
Deer, rabbits, voles, chipmunks, and groundhogs are fond of many of the tender new annuals you've just planted. Your plants will become less attractive as they grow, but in the short term, think about using repellents or installing a protective fence.

Slugs occasionally chew on young annuals and tropicals, especially those planted in shadier spots. (See April, "Problem-Solve, Perennials," page 84 for control ideas.)

## BULBS
Deer and rabbits are still on the lookout for the last of your tulips, so keep the repellent handy.

Rabbits are especially fond of lilies, and they sometimes nibble the young shoots as they're emerging. If you're seeing this, spray the new plants with a rabbit repellent, or scatter granular rabbit repellent over the bed.

Watch for early mildew or leaf spot problems with your young tuberous begonias. The best defense is a good offense. Make sure they have good air circulation, don't water over top of the foliage, pick off infected leaves, and clean up fallen diseased leaves.

## LAWNS
You may see tearing-type holes in the lawn. The culprit is usually skunks (sometimes birds) in search of grubs, which are nearing the surface and about to pupate into adult beetles next month. It's annoyingly helpful. Scatter new seed and water to patch the damage. Grubs are very hard to kill at this stage and will turn into adults soon anyway, so there's no sense trying to kill them.

You might also notice volcano-like mounds popping up here and there. Those are the work of moles, which are different from the mouse-like voles that surreptitiously feed on roots and low-to-the-ground stems. Moles are primarily meat-eaters.

Earthworms and grubs are favorite snacks. Solutions include trapping, baiting active burrows, and spraying the area with castor-oil repellents.

Ants often swarm in the lawn and construct small mounds. These are more of a minor nuisance, not nearly as troublesome as the fire ants of the South. Our ants feed on pest insect eggs, and can actually help a lawn. Ignore them.

The arrival of warm, humid air can lead to several lawn diseases, the first of which is "dollar spot," named for the half-dollar-sized yellowish blotches that turn straw brown. In severe cases, the blotches merge into bigger dead patches. Lawns that are low in nitrogen are more prone to dollar spot, so fertilizing can help. Fungicides are options in bad outbreaks.

## PERENNIALS & GROUNDCOVERS
You'll likely see ants swarming over your peony buds this month. They're not hurting the plants; they're interested in a drink of the sugars the buds are secreting. And no, ants aren't needed to make peony buds open.

Don't be surprised if some of your perennials start to disappear late this month and next. Some bloom in spring and go dormant until the following year. Three common examples are bleeding heart, Virginia bluebells, and Oriental poppies. Just cut off the foliage as it yellows and collapses. They'll be back.

## ROSES
Blackspot is the disease bane of roses, especially hybrid teas. Start watching this month for black rings and then yellowing in the lower leaves. Limit its spread by spraying the foliage with organic or chemical fungicides at the first sign of infection. Infected leaves can be picked off to slow the early spread.

Wilting is somewhat common in newly planted roses, especially if a hot, dry, sunny spell follows planting. Be sure new roses get enough water. Consider erecting a temporary shade structure over the plants until the roots begin to take hold.

Sawfly larvae are brownish black caterpillars that chew the needles on pine, spruce, and other needled evergreens. Early infestations can be squished or handpicked. Insecticides control bad outbreaks.

Dog urine may be the culprit if foliage yellows on lower branches of shrubs at corners or along edges of the yard. Erect a small wire fence, or plant prickly groundcover plants around the targeted shrubs to deter the dogs.

■ *Prune rose branches affected with blackspot and throw them away.*

Raspberry cane borer causes unopened buds to droop. Look carefully for a tiny, discolored entrance hole just below the affected bud or at the tops of pruning cuts. Prune off the rose cane below the hole. Prevent entry into pruning cuts by sealing cuts with a dab of white glue.

Thrips are an early-season bug threat. These are tiny, winged, sucking insects that cause discoloration of the flower petals. A variety of insecticides control them if they're getting out of control.

The roseslug is another early-summer rose pest. It's a type of sawfly whose larval stage looks like a half-inch-long caterpillar. Roseslugs chew on rose leaves. The damage won't kill your plants and will stop in a few weeks as the insect graduates into adulthood. Sprays will kill them if you're impatient.

## SHRUBS

De-icing salt problems may show up now as scorched lower leaves or twig dieback on shrubs near the street or sidewalk. If you suspect this problem, drench the soil with copious water to leach out remaining salts.

■ *A string trimmer is an effective tool for trimming grass in areas around your yard where a lawn mower cannot reach.*

Lilacs not blooming? Issues to consider are a lack of sunlight and pruning at the wrong time (fall, winter, or early spring during which the formed flower buds are being cut off). Old lilacs often bloom poorly and benefit from rejuvenation pruning. Late this month or in June, cut off one-third of the biggest, oldest shoots right to the ground. Then shorten the remaining shoots by one-third. Keep doing the same thing each year, and you'll eventually end up with all younger wood that flowers best. Infections of powdery mildew in summer also weaken—but seldom kill—lilacs.

## TREES

Anthracnose is a common fungal disease of American dogwood. If you see brown splotches with purplish "halos" forming on your dogwood leaves this month, that's probably it. Anthracnose can kill twigs and branches and generally weaken the tree over time. Prune off dead wood, get rid of any fallen diseased leaves, and in bad enough cases, treat with a fungicide as soon as the leaf buds open in spring.

Protect tree trunks from getting whacked by string trimmers and lawn mowers this season by carving out mulched beds around them instead of allowing grass to grow right up to the trunks.

Bacterial leaf scorch is an increasing early-season threat to red and pin oaks. It's caused by a bacterium spread by insects. The disease clogs the channels that carry nutrients from the tree's roots to its leaves. Watch for browning and withering leaves, then dying limbs. There's no good cure for this one.

## VINES

Vining euonymus isn't as prone to scale insects as some of the variegated-leaf bushy types, but check anyway for what look like white flecks on the stems and leaves. These are the shells giving protection to sucking insects underneath. Plants often grow through minor outbreaks, but severe and repeated infestations can kill euonymus. Horticultural oil or an insecticide might be warranted in that case.

## HERE'S HOW
### TO TRANSPLANT A TREE OR SHRUB

1. The sooner and younger you can move plants that are in the wrong place, the better. The two best times for transplanting are end of March through May and from Labor Day through October. The best weather is a cloudy day or when rain is in the forecast.

2. Water the to-be-moved plant well a day or two before the move.

3. Dig and prepare the hole in the new site. Then dig as much of the plant's rootball as you can handle. Dig down, in and around the perimeter, circling until the plant is loose.

4. Wrap the rootball in burlap or use a tarp to carry the rootball to the new hole. Try to prevent soil from falling off and tearing roots along with it.

5. Replant immediately at the same depth. Water well, mulch the soil, and generally treat the moved plant as you would a new plant.

June

*June is a bridge month. It's a time when spring hands off to summer, and May's flurry of gardening activities settle into a more maintain-and-monitor pace.*

Daytime temperature highs typically run in the 80s. Nights are warm enough that freezes go off the radar. And rain usually happens often enough to keep lawns and flowers chugging along. On the other hand, the season's first upper-90-degree heat waves often show up, accompanied by the beginnings of midsummer drought or humidity. Most years, June brings a little of all of these.

Depending on how the weather leans, plant disease can become a June issue. Problems such as blackspot on roses, rust on crabapple leaves, and mildew on hydrangeas can pop up along with the humidity readings. Bugs arrive in full force too—the pesky, up-your-nose blackflies for those who live near streams, and the leaf-chomping, lawn-killing Japanese beetles that are pretty much everywhere by late June into July.

Most of our woody landscape plants finish blooming in June, especially with the month's prolific peaking of roses and hydrangeas. Perennial flowers pick up the slack, with daylilies, coreopsis, astilbe, and hardy geraniums being some of the more common. May-planted annuals also bulk up enough by June to impress.

Keep an eye out for four-legged garden pests, in particular rabbits, groundhogs, chipmunks, voles, and deer. These vegetarians appreciate the buffet you've set out for them. It's all so nice, tender, and tasty this time of year. Weed germination tapers off slightly in June, but enough types continue to sprout in summer that you'll still need to be on alert. Patrol your beds regularly, and keep yanking so no weeds go to seed.

Now if only you could train those groundhogs to switch to an all-weed diet …

## PLAN

### ALL

Are you keeping track of the plants you're adding? Some people insert labels next to their plants, while others map their plantings in a garden journal. Either way, it's easy to forget which plant is which unless you have a record somewhere.

If your outdoor plant labels keep blowing away or breaking, think about converting to something more durable. The thin plastic models that come with plants are not very long-lasting. Metal, ceramic, or sturdier plastic ones are available at garden and home-improvement centers. Cut-up old vinyl window blinds to make a free homemade alternative. Use a china marker or wax pencil to write names on the labels. It helps to insert them in the same place at every plant so you always know where to look.

If you've planned well for wildlife, you should be seeing a variety of birds, pollinators, and butterflies starting to show up in the yard. If that's not happening, evaluate what's missing.

### ANNUALS & TROPICALS

It's not too late to finish planting annuals in the ground or to put together another flowerpot or three for the deck. Plant sizes generally increase at the garden center, from May's 4-packs and 6-packs to larger, individual plants in 4- and 6-inch pots.

## HERE'S HOW

### TO ATTRACT BIRDS AND BUTTERFLIES TO YOUR LANDSCAPE

1. Avoid spraying insecticides whenever possible. Those caterpillars you're killing might turn into beautiful butterflies, while birds could be eating your pesticide-laced bugs.

2. Plant a diverse variety of plants, especially natives and especially ones that bloom at various times throughout the season.

3. For butterflies, include both host plants on which to lay eggs and nectar plants to provide food as adults. Good host plants include fennel, dill, parsley, marigold, snapdragon, turtlehead, milkweed, clover, and many native trees. Nectar favorites are ones with clustered flowers and bright colors, especially purple, red, yellow, orange, and hot pink. Good nectar plants include cosmos, pentas, salvia, catmint, coreopsis, goldenrod, Joe-pye weed, mountain mint, and beebalm.

4. Set out a mix of different feeders in protected areas in late winter and early spring to lure hungry birds to your yard.

5. Include shrubs and trees in the landscape that provide fruits in fall and winter, such as winterberry holly, crabapple, and native honeysuckle.

6. Don't forget shelter and nesting plants, such as a few taller trees, some dense evergreens, and grasses for nest-building.

7. Add a water source, such as a water garden, birdbaths, and a mud puddle or two that butterflies use for extracting salt and dietary minerals.

8. Add a few rocks for butterflies to sun themselves.

9. Set out a mash of overripe fruit as a sweet attractant.

■ *Providing water with a birdbath is certain to attract birds, such as these cedar waxwings.*

Don't overlook the houseplant section for seasonal color. Almost all tropicals are happy growing both in pots and beds during our hot, humid summers. It reminds them of home. Dracaena, cordyline, and palms make especially nice pot centerpieces. Aluminum plant, wandering Jew, and Moses-in-a-boat make colorful summer groundcovers in the shade. Most tropicals can then do double-duty as indoor plants if you pot them before fall frost.

Think about adding annuals that you can *use* in addition to just looking at. Salvia is superb for attracting hummingbirds. Old-fashioned heliotrope adds a scent of vanilla to the deck. Celosia and strawflower dry well and are useful in craft projects. Gloriosa daisy makes a striking cut flower.

Annuals really start to show their stuff this month as warm weather settles in. Take time to record which plants do best and sidestep bug, animal, and disease problems.

## BULBS

This year's spring bulbs are barely finished, and already you're getting catalogs and pitches to pre-order new ones for fall planting. Advantages to ordering this early: the bulbs you need are fresh in your mind; you'll have first choice of varieties in limited supply, and suppliers often offer a discount for early orders. Pre-ordered bulbs are shipped at the appropriate planting time in fall.

## LAWNS

May's growth spurt slows as summer heat arrives. This is a good time to decide whether you're going to allow the lawn to go brown in a dry spell this year or try to keep it green and growing by irrigating. A healthy lawn can stay brown for four to six weeks in summer and quickly green up when rain returns. Summer dormancy is a survival skill of cool-season grasses. Keeping it green all summer despite a drought is more of a cosmetic decision by the lawn-owner. It's possible but requires a lot of water.

## PERENNIALS & GROUNDCOVERS

After all of that lawn mowing in May, this is a good time to think about whether you have too much space tied up in turfgrass. Trees

■ *Anything can become a "groundcover" when planted* en masse.

underplanted with shady groundcovers will gradually convert sunny open areas into shade, while mixed beds of shrubs, perennials, and groundcovers offer a colorful and more pollinator-attractive sunny yard than an ocean of grass.

Keep track of when your different perennials are starting and ending bloom to help with selecting new varieties to plug those bloomless gaps.

Groundcover plants need not be just trailing and low-growing. Almost any plant can become a "groundcover" when planted *en masse.* Ones that grow a little taller actually shade out weeds better than the ground-huggers. Some attributes of an effective groundcover: it grows and spreads fairly rapidly but without getting out of control; it's easily removed if it oversteps its bounds; it does not need frequent grooming, watering, and feeding; and it holds up over many years.

Be patient with young perennials. They're a little slower to establish themselves than annuals. It's often not until their second or even third year in the garden that they really show their stuff.

## ROSES

June is peak month for rose bloom, so it's a good time to visit public gardens with rose displays to see potential habitants of your yard in "real life" before buying. Morris Arboretum, Hershey Gardens, Wyck (Philadelphia), Renziehausen Park Rose Garden (McKeesport), Malcolm Gross Memorial Rose Garden (Allentown), Longwood Gardens, and Penn State University's H.O. Smith Botanic Garden are among sites to see plenty of roses.

## EVALUATING SHRUB PERFORMANCE

Now that your spring shrub performance is still fresh in your mind, assess the troops by asking these questions:

1. Are you happy with the color, the bloom length, and other performance issues?

2. Any shrubs running into health issues that are either unacceptably ugly or threatening the plant's survival?

3. Are the maintenance levels acceptable, or are plants some taking up more than their fair share of your workload?

4. How are the sizes? Anything crowding out neighbors, blocking windows, or generally overpowering the assigned space?

5. Are you satisfied with how your shrubs are fitting into the overall look and design?

6. Are the shrubs still getting adequate light, or has tree growth allowed shade to creep in and limit flowering?

7. Has something new come along that you believe will look and grow better than your struggling oldster?

8. Do you even know what all you have?

Answers to these questions will help you decide what changes to make with your current shrub lineup. As you look at each plant, you've got three options:

1. **Remove.** Sick, old, or overgrown plants may have reached their useful life span or are taking more care than you're willing to give them.

2. **Renovate.** Healthy shrubs that are overgrown might be able to look almost new again with pruning, especially by removing dead wood and tangled or gangly growth that hasn't been touched in years.

3. **Transplant**. Some shrubs may be perfectly fine, but they're just not in the right spot. Most shrubs move better than you might think. Younger is better, but moving any laggard to, say, more light or roomier quarters can make a world of difference. (See May's "Here's How to Transplant a Tree or Shrub," page 105.)

## SHRUBS

Fewer shrubs flower from here on out, but June certainly isn't colorless. Among flowering shrubs that bloom in June are abelia, elderberry, hydrangea, Japanese spirea, mock orange, nandina, ninebark, potentilla, smooth hydrangea, St. Johnswort, and Virginia sweetspire.

## TREES

June is a good month to do the same kind of assessment with trees that you did for shrubs (see "Evaluating Shrub Performance," above). As temperatures continue to rise the next couple of months, the lack of shade—and the need for more trees—will be most apparent.

Smaller trees grow well outdoors in decorative planters year-round, if the container is large enough and you keep it watered. Growing a tree in a pot might come in handy in cases where you need shade on a patio, when you plan to move soon and want to take the tree with you for permanent planting, or when you're just not sure yet where you'd like to plant it.

A few trees bloom in June, including Japanese tree lilac, goldenrain, smoketree, and sweetbay magnolia.

## VINES

Vines aren't just for climbing. Without a support, vines will ramble across the ground and/or spill over wall edges, making them good options for adding color to stonework or even as groundcovers.

Some of the bigger vines such as trumpet vine and wisteria show their girth during the two fast-growth months of May and June. Make sure your supporting structure is sturdy enough to handle big vines and that any bolts, eye hooks, and other fasteners are secure.

Japanese hydrangea vine and climbing hydrangea are two woody vines hitting peak bloom in June. Many clematis also flower well through June, and some honeysuckles remain in color too.

## PLANT

### ALL

Container-grown perennials, groundcovers, shrubs, evergreens, trees, and vines can be planted throughout June, but it's a little more stressful than earlier spring. Plant on a cloudy day or in the evening, if possible, to minimize the wilting effects of bright, hot sun on a new planting, and keep your new plants well-watered throughout summer.

### ANNUALS & TROPICALS

Pansies, violas, and other cool-season annuals might start to shut down flowering as heat shows up. Some people milk extra life out of these by transplanting them to shadier spots this month. Or just buy new heat-loving summer annuals to replant the cool-weather stuff that's petering out.

Even in the coldest corners of the state, June is safe to buy new tropicals and move houseplants out for the summer. It's fine to keep these in their pots for use on a deck or patio outside. But most of them do fine planted in the ground, too. Just remember to pot them back up before fall frost if you want to keep them another year. Note: If your houseplants are in pots without holes, either transfer them to pots *with* holes or keep them under outside cover. A heavy rain will quickly saturate the soil in a pot lacking a drainage hole.

Seedlings coming up from last year's self-sowers are large enough to transplant where you'd like them.

### BULBS

It's last call for planting those tender summer bulbs that you started inside in pots.

Time is running out to dig and divide crowded clusters of spring bulbs while the withering foliage is still attached and you can see where to dig. You can dry and store these dormant bulbs until fall, but why bother? Plant them where you want them now, and be done with it.

Plant another round of gladiola corms so you'll have replacements after the first batch fades. These can be planted throughout June.

### LAWNS

June gets harder to plant new grass from seed because it's now hotter and drier. Cover new seed with a light layer of straw, and sprinkle the planting daily. Even twice a day isn't too much. The surface dries quickly this time of year. Water frequently and lightly—not so much that water runs off.

■ *Cover newly planted seed lightly with straw and water daily.*

Sod is much more expensive for patching or installing new lawns, but it usually yields better results in summer because it comes with roots already established. Sod has to be kept well-watered all summer.

## PERENNIALS, GROUNDCOVERS, ROSES, SHRUBS & TREES

It's still okay to plant any of these, but the sooner the better. Remember, lean toward planting on cloudy days, and keep them well-watered, especially over the first four to six weeks but all through summer.

Early morning and evening plantings are options if you can't avoid planting during a hot, sunny spell. Erecting a temporary shade structure for the first few weeks is another anti-wilt aid.

## VINES

You might see shoots coming up from the around the base of some woody vines. These can be dug or severed, and so long as they've got roots attached, they can be transplanted to create new plants. Keep these transplanted "babies" well-watered and ideally out of direct sun at first (one of those shade structures mentioned above can aid these too).

It's not too late to plant annual and tropical vines, including mandevilla, bougainvillea, sweet potato vine, jasmine, and passion vine.

## CARE

## ALL

Summer is more about watering, weeding, deadheading spent flowers, moderate pruning, and watching out for bugs and diseases than digging, planting, and transplanting. But garden care also includes "gardener care"—the important job of admiring everything you've created up to this point. Carve out plenty of time to smell the roses—literally.

If you're down to bare soil over your garden beds (or close to it), it's not too late to lay new mulch. It's a little harder now working around more mature plants, but mulch will slow the summer sun from heating and drying the soil surface and discourage the sprouting of purslane,

prostrate knotweed, pigweed, and other summer-germinating weeds.

## ANNUALS & TROPICALS

New weeds keep popping up thanks largely to the regular watering you're doing to get your annuals off to a good start. Pick weeds regularly, and when they're young. Their sprouting will taper off as the annuals fill in and start to shade space between plants. In the short term, don't let weeds overgrow your annuals and steal sunlight, nutrition, and water.

Some annuals drop or hide their spent blossoms, while others hold on to them. Pinch off faded blooms of any flowers that need it. This "deadheading" neatens the plant, encourages continuing bloom, and sometimes lessens the odds of mildew disease.

Some annuals flower best in cool weather and shut down when it gets hot. They don't die; they just stop flowering. Rather than pull summer slackers like pansies, viola, dianthus, nemesia, osteospermum, and snapdragon, cut them back to a low set of leaves, keep them watered throughout

■ *Lay down more mulch if you can see bare soil.*

■ *Place several stakes in and around a large plant clump to serve as a framework and as individual supports. If one branch is particularly large and floppy, put one of the stakes next to it, about an inch away from the plant stem.*

summer, and they'll likely start blooming again when the weather cools.

A few annuals, such as zinnias, cosmos, and larkspur, may grow tall enough soon to need help from flopping. Get stakes in place, and start tying up long growers as soon as they need it.

Go ahead and start snipping a few flowers to use in bouquets. You might have a few less flowers to look at now outside, but the clipping encourages bushier branching and more flowers later.

## BULBS
Continue staking plants that need support. Some dahlias grow very tall by midseason, and their brittle stems break easily. Stake gladiola stems individually to prevent their large blossoms from flopping in heavy rains.

Pick dahlias and gladiola flowers for indoor display and to stimulate the plants to produce new blossoms.

Remove off any shabby leaves and faded flowers of begonias; ditto for spent alliums.

## LAWNS
Continue mowing often enough that you never remove more than one-third of the grass blade at a time and cutting on a high setting (2½ to 3 inches—no scalping). Let the clips lie.

If you've had a crabgrass problem in the past, and it's been a cool, damp spring, a second application of crabgrass preventer might be warranted. Crabgrass can continue to germinate in early summer, but preventers applied in early spring typically run out of steam by now. Most crabgrass preventers work effectively for eight to ten weeks.

Continue to pull or spot-spray weeds.

Alter your mowing patterns to minimize wear on the turf. Mow in horizontal rows one week, in vertical rows the next, and diagonally the next.

## PERENNIALS & GROUNDCOVERS
Deadhead the spent flowers of perennials as they finish blooming, including cutting off the entire flower stalks of plants that bloom on separate flowering stems. A prime example is the daylily, which hits peak bloom this month. Once all of the flowers on a daylily stem open and brown, cut the stalk off at the base.

Get supports in place for tall perennials, if you haven't already done that.

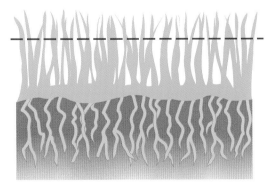

■ *By mowing at the proper height and controlling thatch, water will soak in more efficiently and better quench roots' thirst. You'll use less water and get better results.*

Trim mums in half a second time (May was the first) to encourage denser branching, more flowers, and less flopping in the fall.

Some groundcovers, such as vinca, ivy, and ajuga, may be growing beyond where you want. Cut back the stems and/or dig out runners trying to creep into the lawn.

Don't let English ivy grow up your trees, at least not very far. The stems don't suck the life out of trees, but if the vines grow up and out tree branches, the ivy leaves can block sunlight getting to the tree leaves. Also keep ivy off the house, chimneys, windows, gutters, and such unless you never plan to remove it. Rootlets will be left behind on surfaces if you rip off ivy later.

## ROSES

Cut some roses to use in bouquets, and cut the rest off after they brown. Hand-prune hybrid teas, grandifloras, and floribundas stem-by-stem back to just above where you see a cluster of five leaves. You can cut back even lower to keep your plants more compact. (See July's "Here's How To Cut Flowers for a Vase," page 126, for tips on cutting roses for indoor display.)

Shrub rose types and continuous bloomers don't require pruning and deadheading, but doing so does improve their appearance and keeps the bushes compact. They can even be sheared right after their first main flush of flowering.

■ *Cut roses back to a five-leaflet stem.*

Check climbers and ramblers to make sure they're securely fastened to their supports. Rapid early-season growth sometimes loosens the ties. Newly planted climbers may need additional guidance as their canes continue to grow.

Pick up and discard fallen, diseased leaves from around your roses. This removes disease spores that can reinfect the plants and goes a long way toward reducing disease without spraying.

When working with roses (and sphagnum moss), be aware of a fungal disease called *sporotrichosis* that can affect people. Rose thorns can carry this fungus, which enters the skin through small cuts and punctures. The first symptom of infection is usually a small painless bump (red, pink, or purple) resembling an insect bite on the finger, hand, or arm. See your doctor if you suspect you've got it. For more information, see the Centers for Disease Control and Prevention's website at www.cdc.gov/fungal/diseases/sporotrichosis.

## SHRUBS

Spruce, fir, and pine have finished most of their spring growth by now, so this is a good month to clip off most of this season's growth to maintain size. The new growth is noticeable because it's lighter or different in color than older needles. Avoid cutting spruce, fir, and pine shrubs back so far that you're into this older growth and definitely not back into where the branches are needleless. They won't push new growth from that location.

Add a layer of chopped leaves or bark mulch to the soil surface of any shrubs growing in pots. These dry out quicker than shrubs planted in the ground. Mulch helps slow moisture loss.

It's fine to move potted tender shrubs such as gardenia, fig, croton, and citrus outside now. Just give them seven to ten days of gradually more exposure to help them adapt to the brighter light. These make good options to set over top of garden space opened by bleeding heart, Virginia bluebells, and other perennials that go dormant in early summer.

Continue to prune spring-blooming shrubs as soon as they finish flowering, such as rhododendron, lilac, weigela, pieris, daphne, heath, and mountain laurel.

■ *Cut off suckers at the base of trees as soon as you see them.*

June is a good month to trim evergreen hedges, including yew, boxwood, holly, and arborvitae. Spring is best for heavier cutbacks; summer is better for lighter, neatening trims. Knock off all hedge pruning by the end of August.

## TREES

Some tree varieties regularly send up straight branches from around the base. These skinny, upright "suckers" serve no useful purpose. Cut them off at the base as soon as and as often as you see them. They're particularly common around honeylocust, crabapple, cherry, and pear.

Also watch for branches that don't resemble those on the rest of the tree. On grafted trees, the rootstock sometimes sends up branches that intertwine with those of the more desirable tree variety grafted onto it. Look for branches growing from below the graft union (the swollen knob on the trunk) and that have flowers of different color or type (single rather than double, for example). Cut off the rootstock interlopers at the trunk.

As with shrub-sized spruce, fir, and pine, now is the time to prune tree-sized versions of those species. The idea is to control size by letting new growth occur, then trimming most of it back off. Also as with shrub-sized spruce, fir, and pine, avoid cutting back into branches to a spot that no longer has needles.

Avoid compacting the soil under the canopy of trees, such as by running over it with heavy equipment during a construction project or parking cars on it. That can damage roots as well as impede drainage. Since tree roots typically spread out about twice the distance of the canopy, it's good to keep soil-squishing objects off the ground for that distance.

## VINES

When is an ivy not really an ivy? When it's *poison ivy*. This native vining plant is clambering full speed up trees now, but it'll also romp across the ground if its arms can't find anything to grab onto. A young plant may even look like a baby shrub before it starts its vining habit. Poison ivy has three-lobed leaves that grow in clusters of three, fall berries, and glossy, burnt-red fall color. Remember the saying, "Leaves of three, let it be."

Watch that the spring growth of clinging vines such as climbing hydrangea and Japanese hydrangea vine hasn't crept onto surfaces where you don't want them. If these vines adhere and are pulled off later, they'll leave behind hard-to-remove rootlets.

After wisteria finishes blooming, it generates leafy stems with gusto. This is the time to cut back all side branches to about 6 inches, which not only

■ *Poison ivy growing up a tree.*

controls the size of the plant but encourages the next round of flower buds. If there's also a tangle of excess branches, remove up to one-third of those back to the main stem.

## WATER

### ALL

Since rain can shut off this month, be always ready with the hose, watering can, and/or sprinklers. Plant water demands also go up due to a combination of high growth and rising heat and light.

Continue to pay particular attention to anything new you've planted this spring. The young roots haven't yet spread enough to "mine" much water, so they'll need more help from you and your hose. Focus close to the plant since that's where all of the roots are for now, but apply enough water so that the soil all around and just below the roots is consistently damp. That encourages the roots to grow out and down in search of moisture.

Two guiding principles for all plant-watering are:

1. To the extent possible, water the soil, not over tops of the plants. Wet leaves are more prone to leaf disease.

2. The two best times to water are early in the morning and early in the evening. Wet leaves dry quickly as the sun rises after a morning watering, while an early-evening watering allows time for any wet leaves to dry before dark. Both of those times avoid midday waterings—the time of maximum evaporation loss.

Humans have a built-in soil-moisture meter. It's called the index finger. Insert your finger in the soil a few inches, and if the soil is damp, that's good. If it's dry, it's time to water. If you prefer something more high-tech, soil-moisture meters are sold at garden centers and in catalogs. And digital devices with software applications are now available that send soil-moisture readings wirelessly to your smartphone or computer.

## ANNUALS & TROPICALS

Annuals are shallow-rooted, meaning they dry out fairly quickly when there's no rain. If you see annuals wilting, the best time to water was yesterday. Shallow but frequent watering is the strategy, usually every other day for the first four to six weeks, then slightly deeper waterings once or twice a week as their roots establish.

Annuals in pots and baskets likely will need water *every day*. At least check them daily. Soak the contents until water comes out the drainage holes.

If you have a lot of pots and baskets, consider rigging up a drip-irrigation system. Small, plastic tubes run water to the area, then side tubing with emitters can be installed to spot-water each pot. Attach a timer at the hose to make the whole thing automatic. It's actually less expensive and easier than it sounds.

A light layer of rotted leaves or bark mulch (1 inch or less) helps retain moisture in annual beds.

### BULBS

Hardy summer bulbs such as lilies and crocosmia (ones that you're not lifting each fall for winter storage) usually don't need water, unless it's unusually hot and dry. These function more like perennials.

Tender summer bulbs that you've just planted or replanted in spring are a different story. Their roots are still developing and appreciate a soaking about twice a week—similar to what you'd give a newly planted perennial.

Avoid watering spring bulb beds. Once tulips, daffodils, hyacinths, and such go dormant for the summer, they don't need or want water. They're taking their summer siesta now and aren't doing any growing.

### LAWNS

Our cool-season grasses can start to brown this month when June turns hot and dry early. This is where your green vs. dormancy decision comes into play. Let the lawn go brown and dormant if you can live without summer-long green grass; start irrigating if you can't.

To keep grass green when nature wants to turn it brown, apply about 1 inch of water per week. You can water the full amount with a once-a-week soaking or break it up into ½-inch waterings twice a week. Set out a rain gauge or empty tuna cans to determine when you've applied enough.

Newly planted grass requires a different strategy. Water seed beds lightly at least once a day until the seed germinates, then keep the soil consistently damp in the top 2 inches by sprinkling it every other day. New grass has shallow roots and needs regular moisture near the surface. It'll die if the soil goes bone dry for a couple of weeks. That's a different need than established grass, which needs moisture down to about 6 inches deep and which has the ability to weather dormancy for six weeks in summer.

## PERENNIALS & GROUNDCOVERS

Established perennials and groundcovers, especially drought-tough species such as salvia, gaillardia, and goldenrod, seldom need supplemental water. However, even those perform best when given about 1 inch of water per week, whether it comes from rain or from your hose.

Newly planted perennials are still establishing their root systems, so be more vigilant to make sure these get a good soaking once or twice a week. That guideline of 1 inch of water per week applies here too.

## ROSES

For peak performance, give your roses a deep soaking two to three times a week (over the ground, not the leaves, to limit blackspot disease). Most will perform well with a single, once-a-week, 1-inch soaking, and most will at least survive with as little as an occasional soaking during long, hot, dry spells.

## SHRUBS & TREES

Shrubs and trees are deeper rooted and benefit more from deep soakings once or twice a week than from the shallow, frequent watering preference of new annuals and new lawns. Be particularly vigilant about keeping the soil damp around shrubs and trees planted within the past two or three years. Water regularly enough that the soil is consistently damp all around the rootball and to just below it. You'll probably need more than a 1-inch sprinkling to wet to the bottom of a shrub's or tree's rootball.

How do you know you're applying enough water around shrubs and trees? Insert a stick or probe next to the rootball to determine how deeply your water is penetrating after it's had an hour or so to soak in. A store-bought soil-moisture meter will tell you the same thing. This feedback tells you how long you'll need to water based on how fast your water is coming out and how well your soil drains.

Whether you're holding a hose, using a sprinkler, or adjusting the hose flow to a trickle, water *evenly*. You want to wet the whole rootball, not just one side.

Trees and shrubs growing in containers likely will need daily soakings throughout the summer. These dry out much faster than in-ground plants.

---

### LAWN-WATERING PRINCIPLES

1. Avoid shallow, daily waterings to established lawns. This wets the grass blades frequently and encourages lawn disease. Worse, if you're going the shallow-but-frequent route, you're wetting only the soil surface, which is counterproductive for encouraging deep rooting.

2. Set your sprinklers or irrigation system so that you're watering as evenly as possible. Avoid missed spots and areas that are getting double coverage.

3. Keep the water confined to the lawn. Sidewalks, driveways, and streets don't need watering.

4. Don't apply water so fast that it's running off. Tinker until you get it right because saturation points vary depending on your water pressure, the equipment you're using, and how fast your soil drains.

■ *A soil moisture meter works equally as well indoors to test houseplants as it does outdoors.*

Most established shrubs and trees usually need no water, except for an occasional deep soaking during a drought or unusually hot, dry spell.

If you didn't already do it at planting and/or mulching time, make a ridge around the mulched edge of your young trees and shrubs to help keep water in the root zone instead of allowing it to run off around the perimeter.

## VINES

Newly planted annual vines should get the same watering regimen as other annuals—light watering every other day for the first four to six weeks and then slightly deeper waterings once or twice a week when rain doesn't happen.

Woody vines get the same treatment as shrubs and trees—deep soakings once or twice a week for recent plantings and usually nothing for established ones (except for occasional deep soakings during a drought or unusually hot, dry spell).

Vines in pots and baskets need soaking daily until water drains out the bottom.

## FERTILIZE

### ALL

Only a few types of plants benefit from booster doses of fertilizer over summer. If you've topped the soil with compost or organic mulch and/or scratched in granular, gradual-release fertilizer in spring, you're fine now in much of the garden.

### ANNUALS & TROPICALS

Annuals are heavy feeders and usually benefit from water-soluble flower fertilizer, applied during watering according to the package directions (typically once a month). If your soil is compost-rich, or if you worked in gradual-release fertilizer at planting, that's probably all you'll need.

Annuals in pots and baskets need more regular feeding. These perform best by adding a water-soluble flower fertilizer at half-strength once a week.

### BULBS

No additional fertilizer is needed if you've already worked a gradual-release fertilizer into the soil around your summer bulbs. If you're going the liquid-fertilizer route and applied a dose in May, apply a second dose this month or in early July. A nutrition analysis of 5-10-10 is good.

Don't fertilize spring bulb beds. Those bulbs are dormant and don't need fertilizer over the summer.

### LAWNS

If you're using an organic program and fertilizing twice a year, the first application is generally in May. There's no need for more now. If you did not do that, it's still okay to apply it early this month.

If you're using a three-times-a-year program, your first application would have been in May. Early June is still okay if you didn't get to it then. Otherwise, your next application is late summer.

If you're using a commercial "four-step" lawn-fertilizer program, you would've put down Step 1 in late March to early April. June is good timing for Step 2.

One rule that trumps the previous advice: *Never* fertilize lawns that are stressed by drought or heat. If we've hit an early-season hot, dry spell, and the lawn is already brown or browning, don't add fertilizer—especially high-nitrogen chemical ones. The salts in these can compound the moisture-sapping effects of dry soil. Wait until the grass is green, and rain has returned to apply either a full or half-dose fertilizer. Or skip this treatment in prolonged dry spells, and pick up again with your late-summer application.

## PERENNIALS & GROUNDCOVERS

The granular, slow-acting fertilizer you added to the soil when preparing the garden bed or at planting will continue to feed perennials and groundcovers for weeks. There's no need to add more now.

Perennials in pots benefit from more regular nutrition, since frequent watering leaches nutrients out the bottom with the drainage. Add water-soluble flower fertilizer to the water, similar to the way you're fertilizing annuals (half-strength once a week).

## ROSES

Scratch in another dose of granular rose fertilizer around your rose bushes this month if you're shooting for peak performance. If you're not, that springtime scattering of a granular, slow-acting fertilizer should still be delivering decent growth and bloom. (See May, "Fertilize, Roses," page 101, for a homemade fertilizer recipe.)

## SHRUBS, TREES & VINES

Skip fertilizer unless poor growth or a soil test indicates a nutrient deficiency, then address it specifically. Routinely fertilizing established trees, shrubs, and woody vines is not necessary.

Especially do not fertilize shrubs, trees, and vines when they're stressed by heat, drought, or bug problems. The salts in chemical fertilizers can compound the effects of dry soil, while bugs are often *more* attracted to fertilizer-rich plants.

Newly planted blooming annual vines benefit from a water-soluble flower fertilizer either once this month at full strength or at half-strength two weeks apart.

## PROBLEM-SOLVE

### ALL

In warmer years and in the warmest parts of Pennsylvania, the dreaded Japanese beetle makes it annual appearance late this month. This bug feeds on lawn roots in its larval grub stage and then pupates into shiny, hard-shelled, fingernail-sized, green-and-copper-colored adults in early summer. Japanese beetle adults feed on about *300 species* of plants. (See July, "Problem-Solve," pages 136–137, for ways to control them during peak feeding season.)

For now, a more immediate issue is heading off future grub trouble in the lawn. If you've had regular grub damage or don't want to deal with that prospect this fall, June is the best month to apply a grub preventer. These granular products (usually containing either *imidacloprid* or *halofenozide*) are spread on the lawn so that when this year's adults lay eggs, the young grubs are killed when they start feeding on the treated roots. Ideally, spread your grub preventer right before a rain. Otherwise, water it in well after applying.

Blackflies—often called "gnats"—can get exceedingly annoying this month, especially for people living near creeks and streams. These tiny, black, winged insects don't do landscape damage, but they can swarm in such numbers into eyes and up noses that they make gardening (or any outdoor activity) unbearable. They can also cause small skin welts from biting. State-funded, aerial spraying of waterways is the best solution, but if that hasn't happened, use spray-on repellents before heading out into the yard.

Continue to watch for slugs, especially in the moist, shady parts of your yard. They chew leaves (usually at night), and leave behind shiny trails of dried slime. (See April, "Problem-Solve, Perennials," page 84 for slug-control ideas.)

## HERE'S HOW

### TO SCOUT FOR PESTS AND PROBLEMS

1. Start by knowing what's normal and what's not for your plant. For example, some species naturally slough off bark or drop inner needles each fall.

2. Regularly inspect your plants. You'll notice changes or potential problems sooner. Corrective actions are usually most effective at the beginning of a problem.

3. If something's amiss, look closely both for direct clues (such as dot-sized black fungal spores on the undersides of plant leaves or tiny bugs crawling on stems) and for symptoms (how plants have reacted to a problem).

4. Evaluate whether what you're seeing is causing life-threatening or unacceptable damage to the plant or whether it's something that's temporary and cosmetic. Most leaf damage, for example, is non-life-threatening, but sap leaking from a trunk could be serious.

5. County Extension offices, garden centers, and a host of university and botanical garden websites are good sources for identifying specific problems and their solutions. (See Resources, pages 222–223.)

6. A few common plant problems and their possible causes:

   **Plant is yellowing all over:** Poor soil fertility; extreme heat; light is too intense or lacking; plant is potbound.

   **Young leaves are yellow:** Not enough light; iron or manganese deficiency in the soil; excessive fertilizer.

   **Old leaves are yellow:** Nitrogen, magnesium, or potassium deficiency in the soil; overwatering; natural aging of leaves; plant is potbound; roots are rotting.

   **Random leaves or needles yellowing or browning:** Mite damage; herbicide spray drift; root or stem injury; stem galls.

   **Dead or yellow spots on leaves:** Fungal, bacterial, or viral infection; excessive fluoride in the soil; pesticide damage.

   **Holes in leaves:** Caterpillar, slug, or other bug damage; fungal leaf spot disease; hail or wind damage.

   **Leaves brown around the edges:** Wind damage; excessive salt in the soil; lack of water; excessive fertilizer; pesticide damage; air pollution.

   **Leaves falling off:** Excessive fertilizer; lack of water; reaction to move or transplanting; cold damage; pesticide damage; lack of light; rotting roots; natural life cycle of plant.

   **Leaves wilted:** Under- or overwatering; excessive fertilizer; roots or stems rotting; rodent damage to roots; pesticide damage; frost damage; excessive heat.

   **Weak growth and/or gradual dieback of branches:** Lack of water; root injury or girdling roots; compacted soil; plant was planted too deeply; excessive mulch; poor soil nutrition; lack of light.

## ANNUALS, TROPICALS & BULBS

Since pest insects arrive in the garden before beneficial ones, you may see more pest problems early in the season. A good example is aphids, which often cluster at the new tips of stems and suck the juices out of young plants. Often, lady beetles and other predators swoop in to clean up the infestation (by eating the aphids). Otherwise, a stiff spray of water or a spray of insecticidal soap or light horticultural oil will control them.

Animal problems can still crop up. Some plants are growing enough by now to become less attractive to the bunnies and chipmunks, but you still never know when you'll find some of your petunias buzzed off at the base one fine morning. Keep the repellents handy.

## LAWNS

Besides the possible late-month arrival of Japanese beetles, you might notice a much bigger bug flying out of and over the lawn. These are June beetles, and they're about the size of a thumbnail and shiny green in color. Their wings are so big that they buzz, causing some people to think these are some kind of bee. June bugs don't sting, and they don't do nearly the plant damage of Japanese beetles (in part because of lesser numbers). But their larval grub stage does do lawn damage. The same chemical grub preventer that you apply this month for Japanese beetles will control June beetle grubs. Swat the adults with a tennis racket in the meantime if it makes you feel better. It's good exercise.

When temperatures reach into the upper 80s and the humidity rises, a lawn disease called "brown patch" can start to thin lawns or cause brown,

■ *June beetle*

■ *Leaf miner damage on a tomato*

blotchy patches that can extend as much as 2 to 3 feet across. The disease is caused by a fungus, and it's encouraged by overfertilizing and by too-frequent watering. In other words, it's a case where you're killing with kindness. Solutions include cooler, drier weather and cutting back any excess fertilizing, although fungicides are an option.

Some people like moss, but others find it annoying when they're trying to grow a carpet of grass. Moss grows best in shade, dampness, and acidic soil, although it can do well reasonably well without any of these. A good place to start if you're trying to "de-moss" a lawn is to create less favorable conditions, such as by limbing up and thinning out nearby trees to improve air circulation, aerating the soil in fall to improve drainage, and applying lime to make the soil more alkaline.

## PERENNIALS & GROUNDCOVERS

Watch for leafminer activity. Leafminers are bugs that feed between the upper and lower surface of leaves, leaving behind tunnels through the foliage; columbine is a favorite. Clip off infested leaves, and you'll remove the bugs along with the leaves. Give the plants a good watering, and they'll push out new foliage shortly.

You might notice elongated brown spots on your iris leaves this month. It's most likely a fungal leaf spot disease, and it's more prevalent after cool, damp springs. Cut off infected foliage, and add a fresh topping of mulch around the plants to discourage spores from splashing up. Also consider dividing your irises (now is a good time) if you haven't done that in the last three years. Too-thick patches are more prone to disease because air can't dry out the leaves as quickly.

You might also notice chewing damage around the edges of some of your perennial leaves. Caterpillars are often the culprit, but keep in mind that most of those soon will turn into the butterflies and moths you've been trying to bring into the landscape. Tolerate this temporary leaf damage. It won't kill your plants.

## ROSES

Mites often attack roses that are stressed by heat and drought. Look for fine webbing on twigs and leaves. Disrupt light infestations with a stiff spray of the hose to leaf undersides every day or two for a week. Stubborn infestations of these tiny sucking insects can be controlled by insecticidal soap or neem oil.

The rose midge is another pest that becomes active as the weather warms. The damaging stage is a larval maggot that feeds at the tip of new shoots, causing buds to wilt and die. Multiple generations can occur throughout summer. Cutting off the stem tips along with the bugs may help. Or consider spraying the maggots while they're feeding or applying an insecticide to the soil to interrupt the next generation after the maggots drop to pupate.

June is when you might notice C-shaped sections of rose leaves missing from around the edges, almost as if someone has carefully cut them out with scissors. This is usually the work of leaf-cutter bees. This damage is temporary and cosmetic. Ignore it.

Continue to watch for—and treat, if necessary— blackspot disease. This is one that causes black spots, leaf yellowing, and then leaf dropping, typically from the bottom up. Thrips and roseslugs are other bugs that are often still active in June. (See May, "Problem-Solve, Roses," page 104 for these.)

## SHRUBS

Shrub leaves looking pale and turning yellow between dark green veins? It's a condition called "chlorosis," and acid-preferring species such as rhododendron, mountain laurel, and blueberries are particularly prone to it. The problem is a lack of iron in the plant tissue. Often, there's sufficient iron in the soil; the plants just aren't taking it up because the soil isn't acidic enough to dissolve the amounts the plant needs. A soil pH test will confirm this. Adding sulfur to lower the pH (make the soil more acidic) is usually the solution, although adding iron or an iron-and-sulfur product should correct it too.

The leaves of bigleaf hydrangeas, shrub dogwoods, and a few other flowering shrubs may start to develop spots or a whitish cast to the leaves, especially if it's been damp lately. These are fungal leaf-spot and mildew diseases. Damage is seldom bad enough to warrant spraying. First try picking off ratty, infected leaves, then clean up any infected leaves that fall to reduce spores on the ground that can reinfect future growth. Plants usually grow through these setbacks when drier weather arrives.

Bagworms start to do damage this month on a variety of evergreens. These are caterpillars that

■ *Watch for bagworm sacs on evergreens this month.*

feed inside of cone-like sacs that they construct out of the needles of the plant they're inhabiting. Bagworms are harder to detect now because they're small, and the needles blend in with the rest of the plant. They become much more noticeable later in summer when the sacs enlarge and turn brown. But by then, the caterpillars are harder to kill. Check now for little sacs, and either handpick them or spray with B.t., a caterpillar-targeted organic spray.

Scale insects may turn up on evergreen euonymus, holly, and other shrubs. Some types are evident as powdery white spots, others are waxy white bumps that dot leaf and stem surfaces. If there are enough that plants are losing color or dropping leaves, treat with a spray or two of light horticultural oil as directed on the product label.

If you notice wilted or dead shoots on your rhododendrons, two things could be going on. One possibility is phytophthora root rot, a common soilborne fungal disease that kills roots and shoots. Poor drainage is a leading cause, and fungicides may be needed to keep the disease from progressing. The other possibility is rhododendron borer, a bug whose larvae tunnels into stems and feeds on the wood, often killing tissue above the feeding area. Check the branches for entry slits, and either prune off the bug-containing wood or consider an insecticide labeled for borer control.

## TREES
Watch for signs of rust disease on crabapples and hawthorns. The telltale sign is rusty orange spots on the leaves. Leaves drop prematurely, and twigs and branches can die if the infestation is bad enough. Fungicides may be needed. The best solution is to choose disease-resistant varieties in the first place, and avoid planting junipers near crabapple and hawthorn because rust jumps back and forth between these two host families.

Watch for gypsy moths, which are caterpillars that can cause significant chewing damage to many tree species, especially oaks. Trees can grow through limited and occasional attacks, but repeated heavy infestations can kill them. Spraying and setting out

■ *Gypsy moths can cause significant damage to trees.*

baited traps are options. Egg masses also can be scraped off of trees, and burlap wraps near the base of trees will trap females as they search for a place to lay eggs.

Anthracnose and similar wilt diseases can cause an early leaf drop that may happen regularly, although it isn't "normal." A prime example is sycamore and their plane tree cousins, which can drop almost their entire first set of leaves early most summers due to anthracnose. Trees often just cope with it by growing a second flush of foliage.

Trees also run into many of the same issues as shrubs, including chlorosis, leaf spot, mildew, bagworms, and scale. (See "Problem-Solve, Shrubs," page 122, for more on those.)

## VINES
As pyracantha flowers fade, you should see small green berries forming that will turn orange later in the season. What sometimes happens, though, is that these young berries turn black and fall off. That's usually pyracantha scab, a fungal disease that's also characterized by leaves and stems that have velvety, sooty spots. Rake up fallen infected leaves and fruits to head off future infections. In bad or ongoing infections, you might need to intervene with fungicide sprays, ideally every seven to ten days starting when the buds first open in spring to two weeks after the flower petals drop.

July

*There's no mistaking it. Summer is here now.*

July is Pennsylvania's hottest month, a time when the mercury can hit 100 degrees Fahrenheit, and the conditions can start feeling like Dallas, Texas. Sometimes the rain shuts off, and gardeners end up spending more time with their hoses than their significant others. Other times, the broiling humidity is enough to make gardeners sweat just *thinking* about weeding the flowerbed.

But in a merciful July, warm days and well-placed summer thunderstorms can add up to a beautiful month in the landscape. Enjoy the summer-blooming perennials, the colorful flowerpots and hanging baskets (which should be hitting peak lushness by now), and especially that water feature you added with its cooling cascade or waterfall.

If you've been keeping up with the to-do list in May and June, July should be a month to kick back a bit and enjoy what you've created. Garden time this month is mainly about monitoring for pests and diseases, patrolling for weeds, keeping new and water-wimpy plants damp, and generally puttering. July gardening can be done mostly in first gear instead of spring's more harried third gear.

While you're out there puttering, assess how well you've done with plant planning. July can be a dead time in gardens if the gardener did all of the plant shopping in May and therefore loaded up on spring bloomers. That can lead to a no-color, game-over look from July on.

The solution is to scope out July-interest plants that grab your eye. Go back to the garden center now. Visit a public garden or two. Notice plantings that neighbors have that are looking good this month. Then make it a point to add some of them to your yard—even if they're out of bloom at planting time.

## PLAN

### ALL

If you don't have a pond or water feature in the yard, would you like one? Most people say it's the sound of moving water they like best, but water adds a cooling "feel" in summer and provides a drink for wildlife.

Garden centers get fresh shipments for fall planting and may be able to add your request for that plant you couldn't find in spring to their fall order. There's usually no charge.

### ANNUALS & TROPICALS

Harvest annual flowers this month both for fresh use in a vase and for drying for craft projects. For cutting, flowers are at their best just as they're opening early in the morning or at dusk. Flowers for drying are best cut around midday and chosen at peak bloom. Most flowers air-dry, but some dry best in silica gel and/or borax and sand. Keep cutting into fall as flowers keep coming.

### BULBS

Now that the spring bulb season is done, note what worked, what didn't, and why. That information will help you plan for next season in advance of this year's fall bulb planting.

### LAWNS

If you're planning a vacation, will someone cut the grass while you're gone? Unusually long grass can be a sign to burglars that no one is home. Grass won't get out of control in a week or so, but if you're gone two weeks or more, it might need a trim.

Double-check the automatic lawn-sprinkler system before you leave on that vacation. This is when these systems pay for their keep, but if a malfunction or leak develops, you won't be there to catch it.

### PERENNIALS & GROUNDCOVERS

Turfgrass under trees suffers when July's heat and dryness combine with the shade and hefty roots of trees. Growing grass under those conditions is an uphill battle. A better solution is to switch to groundcovers that tolerate dry shade and root competition. Liriope, barrenwort, pachysandra, and hosta are four of the best, and barren strawberry, sweet woodruff, leadwort, and foamflower are four others that compete well.

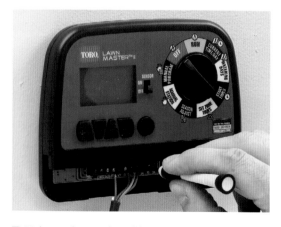

■ *Make sure the control panel for your automatic sprinkler is in top condition before you go on vacation.*

## HERE'S HOW

### TO CUT FLOWERS FOR A VASE

1. For longest vase life, cut flowers in early morning or at dusk when the air is cool. Take a container of tepid water into the garden with you.

2. Select flowers in the late bud stage and just about to open instead of ones that are fully open.

3. Use sharp pruners or scissors to make a clean cut. Cut the stem longer than you need for the intended vase.

4. Immediately immerse the cut stem in the container of water. Continue harvesting until you've got what you need.

5. Once inside, mix floral preservative in tepid water and fill your display vase about three-quarters full. Make a fresh cut immediately before placing each of the cut flowers in the vase.

6. Change the water with new preservative at least every two or three days. Make fresh cuts to the stems before putting them in the replaced water.

Bloomless gaps in the perennial garden can happen now as the spring bloomers finish but the later ones aren't yet peaking. Three ways to plug this gap are to add July bloomers such as butterfly weed, coreopsis, black-eyed Susan, and liatris; add more perennials with colorful foliage; and spot more season-long annuals to bridge the gap between perennial bloom times.

## ROSES

Evaluate how your roses are faring against bugs, disease, and heat. These observations will help with future choices as well as which varieties might be "culled" due to repeated, unacceptable trouble.

A new national rose-trialing program called American Garden Rose Selections will help gardeners hone in on the best new high-performing, disease-resistant varieties. It'll start announcing winners in upcoming years and include regional picks as well as special honors such as roses with superior fragrance. Awards are listed online at www.americangardenroseselections.com. The AGRS replaces the defunct All-America Rose Selections program, which had done similar testing since 1938.

## SHRUBS

The first round of shrubs that bloom on "new wood" (branches that have grown this season) kick into flower in July. Ones that give color now include abelia, butterfly bush, compact crape myrtles, rose-of-Sharon, smooth hydrangea, panicle hydrangea, St. Johnswort, and summersweet.

That Fourth of July cookout hammered home the realization that you need more privacy around the patio, eh? Other than a fence, one way to achieve that is by a shrub hedge. Flowering ones give you privacy during the growing season (when you need it the most), while evergreen ones give you privacy year round. In most cases, plants that mature at 6 feet are tall enough to do the job.

Good flowering choices for hedges include viburnum, elderberry, winterberry holly, shrub dogwood, lilac, ninebark, and the panicle, oakleaf, and smooth hydrangeas. If you have the space and like its loose habit, forsythia is another option.

Good evergreen hedge choices include: blue holly, upright yew, upright Japanese plum yew, cherry and schip laurels (warmer regions of the state), upright boxwoods ('Dee Runk' is a good narrow one), Hinoki cypress, and the green- or gold-thread falsecypresses. Prickly shrubs such as barberry, pyracantha, and quince make people-crossing barriers in addition to privacy screens.

*A well-designed trellis supports climbing plants during the growing season, and it also contributes to the appearance of the yard during the off-season when the plants die back.*

## TREES

Most trees are done blooming now, but a few put on a July show. These include crape myrtle, goldenrain, and stewartia.

Healthy, well-selected trees not only add beauty to a home landscape, they increase its monetary value. Top specimens can be worth thousands of dollars. Take time to inventory and photograph your trees every few years. Store the information in a safe place so it'll be available to insurance adjustors, if necessary.

## VINES

If you need more deck or patio privacy but don't have much space, a vine-covered trellis is a good solution. It's a more colorful and "gardeny" way to add privacy than erecting a fence. Build a lattice support or use multiple trellises—bumped side by side—to screen whatever length along the patio that you need.

Choose vine supports based on what kind of vine you plan to use. Small trellises and lattice supports are fine for small-to-medium vines such as clematis, honeysuckle, and all of the annual vines. But you'll need more muscular support (think 4-by-4 posts and bolted lumber) for larger vines such as wisteria, climbing hydrangea, Japanese hydrangea vine, and kiwi vine.

## PLANT

### ANNUALS & TROPICALS

Last call to get a few last summer annuals in the ground or in pots. You'll likely find them on sale as demand for annuals plummet and unsold ones threaten to become compost.

It's possible to grow annuals in the dry shade under trees. The secret is planting in sunken pots. Annuals have little chance of thriving next to big masses of trees, but if you can sink wide, shallow pots without damaging larger tree roots, you'll give annuals a protected home. The pots will shield the tree roots from encroaching into the annuals' territory. Cover the pot edges with mulch to disguise them. You'll need to regularly water these sunken-pot annuals, but at least not as often as aboveground pots. Be sure the pot bottoms have drainage holes.

It's not too late to plant sunflower seeds. They grow quickly and still have time to produce their striking golden or burgundy flowers by early fall. Water daily until the seeds are up.

### LAWNS

Patching a few bare spots with seed or sod is possible despite July's heat, so long as you keep the water coming. If you're looking at a new lawn or thinking about revamping a poor one, wait until after Labor Day if you can. Otherwise, be ready to sprinkle on an almost-daily basis to get through summer.

### PERENNIALS, GROUNDCOVERS, ROSES, SHRUBS, TREES & VINES

It's not the ideal month to plant because of the heat and typically dry conditions, but container-grown perennials, groundcovers, shrubs, evergreens, trees, and vines can be planted throughout summer. Plant on a cloudy day or in the evening to minimize transplant shock, and stay on top of watering!

## CARE

### ALL

If you're taking an extended vacation, consider recruiting someone to come in to keep a lid on weeds and aggressive growers. It's disheartening to leave a garden and return to a jungle.

How's the mulch holding up? If it's thin and you're getting a lot of weeds, now is a good time to add a fresh topping. A total of 3 to 4 inches is plenty around trees and shrubs, and 2 inches is fine around perennials.

Weedy viners such as wild grape, poison ivy, Oriental bittersweet, Japanese honeysuckle, and mile-a-minute vine don't mind the heat at all. They seem to grow up trees right before our eyes. Don't let these vining invaders spread over your tree foliage, blocking the leaves' access to the sun. Disconnect woody vining weeds at their base, and the top growth will die. Then you can pull the foliage down, or it will eventually fall and/or decay.

To keep your container gardens looking good, regularly remove faded flowers.

Dig out the weed's root if you can. Otherwise, paint the stems and lower foliage with a root-killing herbicide such as glyphosate.

### ANNUALS & TROPICALS

Revive wilted annuals by soaking them well and adding an inch of chopped leaves or dried grass clippings (which have not been treated with weed-killer) around their base to keep the soil cool and to better retain moisture.

Stake tall plants that are flopping (sunflower, larkspur, cosmos, and so forth), patrol for weeds, and pinch spent flowers to keep the flower display chugging along neatly.

Yes, annuals can be clipped if they're getting long or leggy. This is especially true in pots where bold growers such as lantana, petunias, and coleus may need July "haircuts" to keep them from dominating. Hand-pruners do the job nicely. Often, these cuts stimulate bushier growth and a new spurt in flowering.

It doesn't take long for Japanese honeysuckle vine to take over.

To limit unwanted seeding of reseeding annuals such as cleome, larkspur, and nigella, snip off the flower heads before seedheads mature.

## BULBS

Deadhead spent flowers as dahlias, cannas, lilies, gladioli, and other summer-blooming bulbs finish their show.

Stake tall dahlias, lilies, gladioli, and others that are flopping if you didn't do that last month when it was easier. Be careful not to poke your buried bulbs and tubers with the stakes.

## LAWNS

Continue mowing if the grass is still green and growing; skip it if it's not. This is when it pays to let the grass stand taller, say, 3 to 4 inches instead of 1 or 2. Long blades shade the soil, keeping it cooler and damper. That means your grass will stay greener longer as the weather gets hotter and drier.

Stay off the grass as much as possible if it's browning from dryness. Early signs of drought stress are wilting blades and noticeable footprints left behind when you walk on the lawn. Grass gets brittle as it dries, and walking on it then can crush the crowns (the point where the blades emerge).

Dig or spot-spray weeds with a liquid broadleaf herbicide for lawns. Summer is a good time to eliminate weeds, clearing the way to fill the openings with grass seed right after Labor Day. Especially eradicate weeds before they go to seed.

Forget aerating now. You won't get very good cores or plugs anyway. The aerating machine probably will bounce across the hard, dry surface. Plus, new holes mean more openings to lose moisture.

## PERENNIALS & GROUNDCOVERS

Continue to deadhead flowers, cut off ratty or diseased foliage, and regularly patrol the perennial and groundcover beds for weeds.

Stake tall perennials if you didn't already do that last month. Some may be flopping by now, but all it takes is one, brief summer storm to blow those 3- or 4-footers over.

The first week of July is the end of the line for one last cutback to keep mums compact.

## ROSES

Continue pruning as repeat bloomers open and then brown. It's fine to clip lower on each stem than just the tips where the flowers were. This more aggressive pruning keeps the bushes more compact.

Pick off diseased leaves and remove fallen ones to discourage the continued spread of blackspot and other fungal diseases.

Remove weed competition from around the roses, and add a fresh inch of mulch if it's getting thinner than 2 inches. Keep mulch from touching the rose canes.

## SHRUBS

You should be finished pruning spring-blooming shrubs by now (azalea, weigela, and lilac, for example). Leave them alone to form next year's flower buds. Bigleaf hydrangeas can still be pruned, ideally early in the month.

Spent flower heads can be pruned off of summer-flowering shrubs as they brown, such as ninebark and the oakleaf, panicle, and smooth hydrangeas. They really *should* be regularly pruned off of butterfly bushes because many butterfly bush varieties seed into the wild (which equals invasive) if their flowers are left to mature into viable seed.

July is a good month for the season's last, light, neatening trims to yew, arborvitae, boxwood, holly, laurel, and other evergreens being used as hedges and privacy screens.

Patrol regularly for weeds.

## TREES

Limit tree pruning to removing broken or diseased branches, clipping off useless "suckers" growing up from around the base, and removing the stray branch that's whacking you on the head as you mow. The dormant winter season and spring through early summer are better times for more widespread shaping, thinning, and size-reduction cuts.

Watch for cracked-off-but-hanging limbs after summer storms blow through. These may get caught in the tree for awhile and then drop on unsuspecting passersby below. Prune off ones you can safely reach, and hire a pro to remove ones you can't.

## VINES

Keep tying and training twining vines that need guidance.

Shorten the ends of large woody vines such as trumpet vines, kiwi vines, climbing hydrangea, and Japanese hydrangea that are outgrowing their supports or growing beyond where you want.

Prune wisteria if you didn't do it last month. Thin out excess branches altogether, and cut back side shoots you're keeping to 6 inches.

Prune back and thin out large-flowered clematis varieties that bloomed in June. Cut back stems at least halfway to stimulate possible repeat bloom later in the summer.

## WATER

### ALL

Don't try to water your entire garden in one fell swoop, unless it's small. It's easier to break up the job by doing a thorough soaking in one area one day, then giving other areas their due on other days.

When you water, be sure you've applied enough to moisture the roots. It doesn't help to wet just the mulch or the top ½-inch of the soil.

Remember, apply water to the soil, not over top of the plants. And try to water early in the morning or early in the evening when evaporation losses are less but any wet leaves will dry quickly.

## ANNUALS & TROPICALS

In-ground annuals now have bigger, deeper root systems than when first planted (hopefully), so they'll benefit from deeper waterings about twice a week instead of the more frequent, shallow waterings of the first four to six weeks.

Tropicals planted in the ground for summer are usually a bit more durable and able to get by with one weekly soaking.

Annuals and tropicals in pots and baskets will continue to need daily soakings. If you're going away on vacation, arrange for someone to take over this duty. Or rig up an automatic drip-irrigation system if you have a lot of pots. Or group pots together while you're away so one sprinkler hooked up to a timer can water them all at once.

## BULBS

Summer bulbs growing in pots usually need daily soakings, the same as with annual flowers.

Summer bulbs growing in the ground can get by with a single 1-inch soaking once a week or less, similar to perennial flowers.

## LAWNS

Lawns often turn straw-brown this month when it's hot and dry. They're not dead. They're just employing the survival skill of going dormant in unfavorable conditions. By shutting down growth, grass can conserve enough moisture in the crowns (where grass blades emerge) to go six weeks or more in this state.

If a drought drags on, and the lawn is straw-brown for six weeks and counting, give it a watering of about ¼ inch per week. That's enough to replenish

## DRY-SEASON WATERING PRIORITIES

Divide dry-season watering into priorities so that if you can't keep everything watered, at least you'll get to the most important things first.

### HIGH PRIORITY

- Newly planted trees and shrubs that are the most expensive investments and ones at risk if their young root systems aren't kept damp.

- Hanging baskets and container plants that will die in a matter of days without water.

- Any sentimental favorite or expensive specimen plants in the yard that you really don't want to lose.

- Newly planted lawns.

### MEDIUM PRIORITY

- Established but shallow-rooted trees and shrubs, such as azaleas, rhododendrons, dogwoods, hollies, and blueberries, especially if they're wilting or showing signs of drought stress.

- Newly planted perennials (more at risk than established ones).

- Annual flowers and vegetables.

### LOWER PRIORITY

- Established perennials and established trees, shrubs, evergreens, and roses, especially ones that are adapted to cope with dry soil.

- Groundcovers unless they're starting to badly wilt and turn brown.

### BOTTOM

- An established lawn. Lawns are "smart" enough to go dormant in droughts. They can go six weeks or more in this straw-brown state with no lasting damage. One good rain and otherwise healthy grass will green up again.

moisture in the crowns without stimulating the grass to resume growing.

Good reasons why you should *not* try to keep grass green when it wants to go brown are:

1. You'll use a lot of precious (and expensive) water.

2. If you don't water deeply enough, grass roots will develop near the soil surface, where the moisture is. That makes the lawn *less* drought-resistant in the long run, more at risk of heat injury, and more likely to develop excess thatch (that spongy layer of mostly dead roots between the growing grass and the soil).

3. Beetle grubs proliferate best when the soil is moist during egg hatch in July and August. They'll thank you for irrigating.

4. Grass that's frequently wetted is more prone to disease.

If you're dead set on a summer-long green lawn, assume applying 1 inch of water per week. It's better to water the full amount once a week or ½-inch waterings twice a week than daily, shallower waterings. Measure how much your irrigation system applies so you'll know.

## HERE'S HOW

### TO TELL IF YOU'RE WATERING ENOUGH

1. Your goal should be to keep the soil consistently damp but not soggy all around and to just below a plant's root system.

2. Frequency and amount varies by plant size and age. Newly planted annual flowers, for example, benefit from shallow waterings every day or two. New trees and shrubs have much bigger roots and benefit more from deeper soakings two or three times a week.

3. A rough guide for the water need of a new tree is 1 to 2 gallons for every inch of trunk diameter at shoulder height. For new shrubs, 3 to 5 gallons of water per watering. As roots spread, widen the watering area and increase amounts to 1 gallon of water for every square foot of soil surface.

4. A good check is to give the water fifteen minutes to soak and then use your finger, a stick, a probe, or a soil-moisture meter to determine if the soil is damp to the edges of the roots. If so, you're done. Do the same thing next time. If not, apply more and make note to water additionally next time.

5. Never apply water so heavily that it runs off instead of soaks in. The moisture needs to go to plant roots, not the sidewalk.

6. Water evenly all around a plant. Don't sit a hose down in one area and never move it.

7. Water often enough that your plants aren't wilting, losing vibrant color, or showing other signs of water stress. If plants wilt, the time to water was yesterday.

8. Pay attention to the weather. Plants use more water in hot, dry, windy conditions than in cool, cloudy weather.

*Run a sprinkler for fifteen minutes, and then measure the amount of water in a small cup. This will tell you how much water your sprinkler puts out in fifteen minutes.*

A lawn planted just this spring isn't deeply rooted enough yet to tolerate brutal heat and dryness the first summer. Help it along with the same watering plan of 1 inch per week, either all at once or broken into ½-inch sessions twice a week.

If you were counting on cool, damp weather when you planted grass seed in July and guessed wrong, water daily until the seed is up. Then do ½-inch waterings two to three times a week until cooler conditions return.

## PERENNIALS & GROUNDCOVERS

Perennials and groundcovers planted earlier this spring benefit from twice-weekly soakings. Do the finger-insertion test to be sure, and water whenever the soil is dry in the root zone. Get to it *quickly* if you see wilting.

Established perennials and groundcovers can get by with a once weekly soaking or less. Some of the most drought-tough ones (sedum, salvia, catmint, and most ornamental grasses, for example), almost never need supplemental water in Pennsylvania yards.

Sometimes it's not lack of water that causes plants to wilt in summer. Some perennials and groundcovers are heat-sensitive and may wilt, brown, or die back even with plenty of water. These can include lily-of-the-valley, lady's mantle, delphinium, lupine, lamium, sweet woodruff, and foamflower. Clip off any dead or diseased foliage, but otherwise let these alone to perk up when the temperatures drop.

## ROSES

For roses planted earlier this spring and for established ones that you're growing for peak performance, soak them two to three times a week (over the ground, not over the leaves, to limit disease).

Established roses will be fine with a single, once-a-week, 1-inch soaking, and most will at least survive with less than that.

Temperatures over 90 degrees Fahrenheit can cause roses to wilt because they're losing moisture through the foliage faster than their roots can supply it. First, be sure you're watering deeply enough often enough. Second, consider a foliar spray of liquid kelp in the morning.

## SHRUBS & TREES

For fairly recent plantings or transplantings (within the past three years), count on deep soakings about once a week if rain isn't happening. Apply enough that you're wetting all around and to the bottom of the rootballs. It'll likely require more water than you think. Check with your finger, a probe, or a soil-moisture meter.

After three to four years, most shrubs and trees can be considered "established." In other words, their root systems have grown enough to mine sufficient moisture from the soil that they don't need supplemental water from you—except in unusually long, hot, dry spells. If you're in doubt, though, a weekly soaking won't hurt. Just avoid watering so much that you create soggy soil.

Bigleaf hydrangeas are some of the first plants to wilt on a hot July day. Heat alone can cause wilting, although heat and dry soil can tag-team to create a hydrangea double-whammy. One way to tell the difference is to check your plants first thing in the morning. Heat-stressed hydrangeas won't be wilted; drought-stressed ones will.

## VINES

Annual vines appreciate the same weekly to twice-weekly soakings that you're giving annual flowers and new perennials.

Newly planted woody vines (clematis, climbing hydrangea, honeysuckle, and so forth) also benefit from a weekly soaking. Established vines need little to no supplemental water—the same as established shrubs and trees.

## FERTILIZE

### ALL

By and large, this is a no-feed month in the landscape. That mulch, compost, and/or annual scattering of granular, gradual-release fertilizer that you applied in spring is enough for most perennials, groundcovers, evergreens, shrubs, trees, and vines.

Adding fertilizer—especially fast-acting synthetic-chemical types—doesn't help plants weather a hot summer. It can be counterproductive in two ways. One is that synthetic fertilizers contain salts that can compound the dry-soil stress that threatens many plants in summer. The second is that even if fertilizers are watered in well, they can stimulate growth at a time when plants are trying to conserve energy to survive the heat and dry soil. A good rule of thumb: never fertilize a plant under stress from drought or extreme heat.

### ANNUALS, TROPICALS, BULBS & PERENNIALS

One exception to the no-fertilizer rule is plants growing in pots. These are being watered so often and using or losing nutrients so fast that a continuous supply of nutrition is needed. To maximize performance, feed a water-soluble flower fertilizer at half-strength once weekly.

### LAWNS

Do not fertilize a dormant lawn. The salts in chemical fertilizers can worsen the effects of dry soil, possibly to the point of killing an already-stressed lawn. More than a few people have had lawns "burned" by fertilizer treatments in summer-dormant conditions.

None of the three main lawn-fertilizer regimens call for July fertilizing anyway. The only exception would be the four-step program, and only then in

*early* July if Step 2 wasn't applied in June, and only if the grass is still green and growing.

### ROSES

Rosarians shooting for peak performance usually scratch in another dose of granular, slow-acting rose fertilizer around their bushes in July, so long as they're also continuing to water regularly.

If you're okay with okay performance, skip the fertilizer—especially if it's hot and dry. The nutrients you've added earlier will carry you through.

### SHRUBS, TREES & VINES

No fertilizer is needed this month. What you added earlier in the season will cover you through the summer.

## PROBLEM-SOLVE

### ALL

Heat stress is an underrated plant menace, certainly not as well known as the obvious freezing damage at the opposite end of the temperature spectrum. Heat causes more insidious trouble, starting at around 86 degrees Fahrenheit:

1. Flower buds may wither.

2. Chlorophyll production goes down, robbing leaves of their healthy green color.

3. Pollen can become non-viable, preventing fruiting plants from producing their fruits and berries.

4. Chemical makeup changes in plant leaves, rendering them more vulnerable to bug attack.

5. Soil temperatures heat to the point where root activity slows and plant growth is stunted, especially on unmulched soil.

6. And most noticeable: moisture loss from plant leaves increases, making plants more susceptible to dry-soil injury.

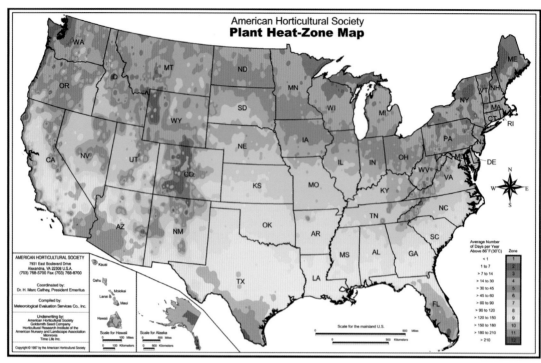

American Horticultural Society
**Plant Heat-Zone Map**

| Average Number of Days per Year Above 86°F (30°C) | Zone |
|---|---|
| < 1 | 1 |
| 1 to 7 | 2 |
| > 7 to 14 | 3 |
| > 14 to 30 | 4 |
| > 30 to 45 | 5 |
| > 45 to 60 | 6 |
| > 60 to 90 | 7 |
| > 90 to 120 | 8 |
| > 120 to 150 | 9 |
| > 150 to 180 | 10 |
| > 180 to 210 | 11 |
| > 210 | 12 |

Reproduced with permission of the American Horticultural Society (www.ahs.org).

You can't air-condition your yard, but you can take heat-busting measures, such as mulching bare soil, watering regularly (which cools the soil besides adding moisture), choosing heat-tough plants for your yard's hot spots, and moving heat-wimpy existing plants to cooler spots come fall.

The American Horticultural Society has created a Plant Heat Zone Map (above) that's similar to the Cold Hardiness Map. Heat-zone ratings are listed on *some* plant labels, but the whole concept has never caught on that well. A copy of the map and more details on heat zones are on the AHS website at www.ahs.org/gardening-resources/gardening-maps/heat-zone-map.

The notorious Japanese beetles shows up between late June and the first two weeks of July. This double-trouble bug chews on the foliage of some 300 plant species as a shiny, brown-and-green adult, and then kills off lawn patches in its larval "grub" form in fall and spring. July is the worst month for aboveground plant damage. That's when adults swarm, feed, mate, and lay eggs, usually in sunny turf near favored plants. The eggs hatch in August into fat, white, C-shaped wormy-looking

critters that feed on grass and plant roots. (See June and September, "Problem-Solve," pages 119 and 172, for tips on dealing with beetle grubs.)

Japanese beetles particularly like roses, grapes, crabapple, cherry, hydrangea, and a range of flowers and vegetables. While their chewing damage is chiefly cosmetic (plants typically

■ *Japanese beetles*

■ *Leaf damaged by spider mites*

recover), massed attacks can leave behind a bloomless, tattered garden. Damage is worse some years than others. If the damage exceeds your tolerance level, Japanese beetle controls include hand picking and either squishing them or dropping them in a can of soapy water; protecting targeted plants with cheesecloth or a lightweight row cover; and spraying with neem oil or one of several insecticides labeled for beetle control.

What about those Japanese beetle traps? They *do* attract beetles, and if they were everywhere, they might make a dent in the population. The problem is if you're the only one using them, you'll *attract* beetles to your yard. A better situation would be if everyone *around* you had them, and you didn't. That's why there's some merit to the advice, "Give beetle traps to your neighbors." If you're going to use traps, at least set them as far away from your attacked plants as possible.

Spider mites are tiny bugs that thrive in this hot, dry month. They suck chlorophyll out of the foliage of many plants, including hemlock, azalea, multiple annual and perennial flowers, and their seeming Pennsylvania landscape favorite, the dwarf Alberta spruce. Look for stippling damage on foliage and fine webbing among the twigs and branches. Repeated stiff bursts of hose water over several days can control them. Or spray with insecticidal soap or a pesticide labeled for mite control.

## ANNUALS & TROPICALS

Impatiens used to be easy to grow. Then a deadly disease called downy mildew swooped into the state, wiping out huge swaths of home plantings

in just a few weeks one July. The disease spreads readily and survives winter in the soil, meaning it's likely here to stay. Look first for a grayish cast to the leaf undersides, then stunted growth, then a fairly fast melting-out death. There's no good control once you've got it. The recommended solution is to switch to mildew-resistant New Guinea impatiens or resistant hybrid SunPatiens® or Bounce® types or to another shade-tolerant species altogether, such as coleus, begonia, or browallia.

Powdery mildew is another damaging but less destructive fungal disease that causes a white coating on some annuals, particularly zinnias. Pick off infected leaves in an early infection, or use a fungicide labeled for powdery mildew for cases spinning out of control.

## BULBS

Gladiolas sometimes get brownish gray patches on their leaves and flowers that turn brown and slimy. It's usually most prevalent in rainy summers. The likely problem is botrytis, a fungal disease. Fungicides can head it off if applied early, but once you have it, the best solution is to yank the bulbs and try fresh ones next year.

## LAWNS

High heat in the triple-digit range can kill some grass species and lead to a thin lawn by summer's end. Perennial ryegrass is among the most

■ *SunPatiens® are a type of impatiens that's resistant to downy mildew; this one is Spreading Variegated White.*

heat-sensitive. Overseed a heat-thinned lawn in September or October.

If you're using grub preventers to head off a repeat of past lawn-grub damage, get this year's application down immediately if it wasn't done it in June. Eggs will hatch into new grubs next month. The insecticide needs to be in place at root level by then.

Sod webworm activity in the grass is signaled by small moths flitting above the turf. These moths are laying eggs that will hatch this month into light-brown caterpillars that chew grass blades, mostly after dark. A second generation feeds in late summer. Brown lawn patches result. Nematodes and insecticides are control options in bad outbreaks.

## PERENNIALS & GROUNDCOVERS

Powdery mildew—that white coating on leaves—can do significant damage to some perennials this month, especially tall garden phlox, beebalm, and some coreopsis and veronica. Fortunately, it usually happens after peak bloom period. Fungicides can be used at the first sign of infection, or just cut off and remove foliage when it looks bad. Plants usually survive to bloom again another year.

An increasing daylily problem is leaf streak, a fungal disease that starts with small brown splotches on leaves that coalesce into longer streaks and finally into widespread leaf browning. Daylilies are tough enough to grow through it. Just cut off and remove diseased foliage—including cutting whole plants back to the ground, if necessary—and plants will grow fresh foliage that usually lasts until frost.

Hollyhocks often suffer from rust, a fungal disease that causes brown-orange spots all over the leaves and then widespread browning. There's not much you can do once the disease gets going, other than pick off and remove diseased leaves, then spray fungicides to protect the rest. Preventive fungicides are often needed to grow rust-free hollyhocks. They usually return each season to flower despite ongoing rust issues.

## ROSES

Japanese beetles and blackspot disease are the two main issues this month for roses. Handpick or spray the beetles, and pick off and clean up diseased leaves and/or spray fungicides every two weeks to control blackspot.

## HERE'S HOW

### TO IDENTIFY ROSE WOES

1. A multitude of bugs and diseases appreciate roses almost as much as people do. Early detection is the best course to head off problems that warrant action. Monitor your plants regularly for the first sign that something's amiss.

2. Get an accurate diagnosis before taking any action. Bugs generally eat holes in leaves or chew leaf edges and tissue. Most diseases cause discolored or spotted or splotchy leaves. Extension offices, garden centers, local rosarians, and online rose websites are all investigative resources.

3. Determine if the problem requires action or is a cosmetic or temporary issue. If action is needed, target it to the specific problem. Not all leaf-chewing requires action, for example. Spraying a fungicide on a bug or viral problem will waste money and effort. Ditto for spraying an insecticide for a fungal disease.

4. Keep roses as healthy as possible by adequate water, adequate nutrition, and proper pruning.

5. The American Rose Society is a valuable resource for all things roses. Members rate rose performance to help you pick the most trouble-free, high-performing types, and connect you with "cyber rosarians" willing to answer questions. The Society's website is www.ars.org.

Rose midge larvae can continue to be a problem this month, too. (See June, "Problem-Solve, Roses," page 122).

## SHRUBS

If the leaves of your azaleas, pieris, rhododendrons, and mountain laurel are looking pale, check for lace bugs, a small flying insect with clear wings that feeds on the leaf undersides. Lace bugs suck plant juices as opposed to chewing, and can run through up to three generations per year, from May through September. Insecticidal soap, horticultural oil, and several chemical insecticides control them, but sprays are most effective early (May or early June) and when sprayed underneath the leaves.

Bagworms become more noticeable this month on needled evergreen shrubs. Pick as many dangling "bags" as possible from shrub branches. Or spray with B.t. (*Bacillus thuringiensis*) or other insecticides labeled for bagworm control.

## TREES

The lace bug family—those little clear-winged insects that suck the chlorophyll from leaf undersides—has members that prefer hawthorn, sycamore, and some species of oak trees in summer. These discolor leaves but usually don't cause enough trouble to warrant treatment.

Japanese beetles *love* fruit-tree species, including their more ornamental cousins the crabapple and flowering cherry. Linden is a favorite too. But surprisingly, beetles also sometimes feed on needled evergreens. The damage might look bad, but large, healthy plants such as trees almost invariably grow through this chewing without treatment.

If tips of your pine and spruce trees are dying, be suspicious of the white pine weevil. The larva of this insect feed just under the bark of branch tips high on trees, especially at the top of the main leader. Most of the damage is done in late spring, but it's typically July until the needles brown enough that people notice. Controls include cutting off infested tips, monitoring in April for

■ *Wilted leaves are usually a sign of clematis wilt, a problem that is caused by a fungus. Remove and destroy affected parts.*

brewing trouble, and spraying outbreaks with insecticides labeled for pine weevils.

## VINES

Clematis wilt is a fungal disease that can quickly brown out whole stems of clematis vines and even whole plants. Big-leafed and big-flowered clematis varieties are especially prone. Planting resistant varieties (*viticella* types, for example) is the best solution, but if existing ones get it, prune out wilted stems, remove dropped and diseased leaves, keep plants watered in dry weather, and consider preventive fungicides if wilt becomes an annual, unacceptable problem. Plants usually send up replacement stems after you cut the dead ones.

August

*One more muggy month to go before things start cooling off, and gardens (as well as gardeners) begin to look fresh and perky again.*

As in July, August's daytime temperatures often park themselves in the 90s with stifling humidity to boot. It's our second warmest month. August also is one of Pennsylvania's drier months, although that can vary depending on whether your yard is in the path of sporadic summer thunderstorms or any hurricane remnants. This month's moisture tends to come in dumpings instead of the gentler multi-day soakings of spring and fall rains. Be ready with the hose during those hot, dry spells, but don't be surprised by the occasional August gully-washer.

August gardening is much like July—more puttering than, say, the pruning and mulching frenzy of spring or the clean-up and cut-down marathon of fall. It's prime time for harvesting the vegetables, but also for admiring the coneflowers, serenely gathering cut-flower bouquets from the yard, and sipping a cool drink on the patio.

The annual flowers should be hitting peak too if you've kept them fertilized, watered, and out of the mouths of rabbits, groundhogs, and deer. Plenty of perennials and shrubs flower in August, so there's no excuse if your yard is devoid of color. If it is, make note to get yourself some coreopsis, gaura, perennial sunflowers, Russian sage, tall phlox, goldenrod, caryopteris, dwarf butterfly bush, panicle hydrangea, and shrub roses.

Enjoy this semi-siesta month. Labor Day will be here before you know it, marking the de facto end of summer, and the beginning of the year's second main window for planting, transplanting, dividing perennials, and similar jobs that the heat of July and August rendered impractical.

## PLAN

### ALL

How's your yard weathering the summer? If things are tired or baked, maybe you need more trees to nurse the plantings (and you) through our oven months. Temperatures can be 10 degrees cooler in summer under a shade tree than in full sun.

Heat-beat August yards might be telling you that you need more mulch, should be watering more often, or need more heat-tolerant plant choices. Have you thought about adding rain barrels at downspouts?

Consider buying a chipper-shredder. These chopping machines will turn that pile of tree and shrub trimmings into mulch, and your fallen leaves into ideal compost fodder or winter garden insulation. Yeah, they're noisy and use gas. But they recycle almost all yard waste, and they pay for themselves in disposal savings and less mulch or soil amendments to buy. Too expensive? Split the cost with neighbors, and share ownership.

### ANNUALS & TROPICALS

The celosia, lantana, vinca, and other heat-loving annuals that you picked back in May are paying dividends now. They're happy with 95-degree

■ *If you have lots of shrubs or trees, or enjoy pruning, a chipper-shredder could be a great investment.*

Fahrenheit days and usually keep going until frost takes them down. But cool-preferring lobelia, osteospermum, nemesia, and pansies probably have stopped blooming, if they're not fried altogether. Give them a chance to bounce back when the weather cools. Otherwise, plan to replace them next month with mums or with a fresh round of fall pansies, violas, and ornamental cabbage or kale.

### BULBS

Spring-flowering bulbs will show up at garden centers late this month. It's too hot to plant them, but you can buy now to get the best selection. You might be able to give them a cooler, drier storage area than the garden center until the more ideal planting time in late September through October.

If you're buying bulbs online or through a catalog, place your order now if you haven't already.

Although now's a tad early to plant bulbs, you can get a new bulb bed ready. Remove any turfgrass, loosen the soil 10 to 12 inches deep, and work in about 2 inches of compost or similar organic matter to create slightly raised beds. Rake smooth, top the soil with about 2 inches of bark mulch, and you're ready to insert bulbs in fall.

■ *One of the simplest, most inexpensive, and most environmentally responsible ways to water a lawn is by tapping a system that collects rainwater and stores it for controlled irrigation.*

■ *You can prepare a bulb bed now by digging the soil and adding any needed amendments.*

Enjoy resurrection lilies, aka "naked ladies," that pop up this time of year. This type of hardy *Lycoris* produces spring leaves that die back in early summer. Then leafless flower stalks that bloom pale pink pop up in late summer. Don't have any of this curious bulb? Add some to your shopping list.

## LAWNS
Assess whether you're running into the same weed, pest, or disease problems in the lawn year after year. Rather than continuing to treat each year, explore underlying causes. Mowing higher, overseeding with more bug- and disease-resistant grass varieties, and other changes in care might be more effective and less expensive in the long run.

That lawn that looked so good in May can look so worn and weed-infested in August after the stresses of a hot, dry summer. Evaluate how much of your "lawn" is still desirable grass vs. weeds or "junk grass." A rule of thumb: If you've got at least 50 percent grass, it's worth rehabbing. If weeds are the majority, it might be easier to kill off everything, improve the soil, and start from scratch. The best two months for both of those are coming up in September and October.

Call now if you're hiring a company to do a major lawn renovation. Get on the calendar for September if you can. If you wait too long, companies may not be able to get to your job until prime grass-planting time has passed.

## PERENNIALS & GROUNDCOVERS
South- and west-facing slopes are some of the toughest spots to keep a lawn looking good, as

August weather often makes apparent. The sun's summer angle bakes these spots, not to mention the difficulty of mowing on a slope in the first place. Think about converting struggling south or west grassy slopes to mass plantings that will perform better with less care, including shrub roses, ornamental grass, spreading juniper, daylily, sedum, and spreading sumac such as 'Gro-Low'.

Some perennials, such as black-eyed Susan, purple coneflower, and gaillardia, self-sow seeds. Decide whether you want that to happen or not. Deadhead spent flowers before the seeds mature if you don't want a plant to self-sow. Let them alone if you do.

This is goldenrod month. You'll see fields and meadows (and maybe your perennial border) aglow with these golden-blooming native perennials. Contrary to popular myth, goldenrod isn't a major cause of allergies. Ragweed is a far more potent sneeze-producer that happens to bloom at the same time as goldenrod. It's just not as noticeable.

Most ornamental grasses produce their plumes and seedheads by late this month. Clip some to go with your flowers in late-summer bouquets.

## ROSES
Many roses bloom continuously throughout summer, even before the more widespread rose "second wind" of September. Not a lot of other woody plants flower in August. Consider adding a few shrub-type roses or other long-blooming types if you need more August color.

■ *Take a look at your lawn; if it's more weeds than grass, like this one, it's time to plan to renovate it.*

## SHRUBS

Some flowering shrubs that offer August bloom are beautyberry, blue mist shrub (*Caryopteris*), butterfly bush, crape myrtle, rose-of-Sharon, panicle hydrangea, and vitex.

## TREES

You'll really appreciate the shade from trees this month. Their cooling effect not only makes the patio more bearable in hot weather, but trees are energy-savers. Trees planted to the south and southwest of homes block the hot afternoon sun, keeping rooms on those sides cooler and reducing air-conditioning need. Plan to add leaf-dropping species to the south and southwest if you don't have any, kept in scale with the size of your yard, of course. When the leaves drop in winter, the sun's rays will warm the house, lessening the load on the heat system.

Evergreens make sense to the north and northwest of a house, where they'll block the prevailing cold winds in winter without blocking the south-originating sunlight.

## VINES

Although they don't have quite the impact of a shade tree, vines planted on or along south- and west-facing walls do have some summer cooling effect on the sun-drenched structures there. Stick with sun- and heat-tolerant vine species in those settings.

Vine-covered trellises are especially useful to block the southern and western setting sun when you're trying to use a deck or patio in the evening. These take up very little horizontal space and can act as a colorful outdoor wall near the patio edge where you may not have a lot of space to work with.

## PLANT

### ALL

August is still hot enough that it's not an ideal month to plant, although most container-grown plants do fine if they're kept sufficiently watered. Conditions get less stressful toward the end of the month in cooler parts of the state, then improve markedly statewide from early September through October as temperatures cool, soil evaporation slows, and it usually rains more often.

### ANNUALS & TROPICALS

If you need to replace dead or damaged annuals to fill out a display or container, go ahead. Just water

## HERE'S HOW

### TO CONSERVE WATER IN THE LANDSCAPE

1. Start at plant-buying time by choosing varieties with low water needs.

2. Improve the soil with compost before planting. Loose, rich soil encourages better rooting to help all plants withstand dry conditions better.

3. Group plants by their water preference. That way you'll have all of the high-need plants together where you can target them. Locate high-water-demand plants near a hose.

4. Add more trees to cool and shade the soil.

5. Maintain adequate mulch over garden beds.

6. Consider a drip-irrigation or soaker-hose system to deliver water directly to the ground.

7. Add rain barrels to collect rain water so it's available when needed.

well. Garden centers usually still have a selection of larger blooming plants to help gardens down the home stretch.

## BULBS

Wait until next month or October to plant spring bulbs. If you're itching to do *something*, dig and divide overcrowded, dormant bulb clusters. The drawback is that you might accidentally slice through buried bulbs. That's why it's easier to do this in late spring when you can still see the foliage.

## LAWNS

Those in cooler parts of the state can get busy overseeding or reseeding lawns toward the end of this month as temperatures cool. For most of the state, after Labor Day is better, unless late August is looking cool and damp.

## PERENNIALS, GROUNDCOVERS, ROSES, SHRUBS, TREES & VINES

If you plant any of these this month, minimize transplant shock by planting on a cloudy day or in the evening. Or erect a temporary shade structure for a few days after planting. Most important, keep the soil consistently damp until the ground freezes.

Another option if you find a bargain that's too good to pass up during a hot, sunny spell—keep the plant in the pot, store it out of the afternoon sun, and water daily until oppressive heat subsides.

Steer clear of plants that are deeply discounted because they're so damaged or stressed that a recovery is doubtful. Dead and dying plants aren't bargains.

## CARE

## ALL

Weeds don't seem to mind heat and drought. Stay on top of them to prevent seeds from maturing. Pull young ones or spot-spray tough ones such as thistle and bindweed that are difficult to control with just elbow grease.

Mulch if you're down to bare or nearly bare soil. That can discourage new weeds while cooling the soil and retaining moisture.

## ANNUALS & TROPICALS

Don't give up too soon and yank annuals that stopped flowering in the heat. Snip off browned-out flowers, and cut back tired stems to green buds or side shoots. Keep them watered, and see if you don't get a new flush of flowers when the weather cools.

If you intend to harvest sunflower seeds for use as birdseed or food, cover the maturing heads with garden fleece or cheesecloth to prevent the squirrels and finches from taking them.

Remove diseased, fallen leaves and any other rotting plant debris from the planting beds. The cleanup lessens the odds of future disease problems.

Continue to stake "floppers," and snip back any overly long stems.

## BULBS

As lily stems yellow and then start to brown and dry, cut them back to the ground. Let the bulbs in the ground. These are hardy and will be back next year.

Continue to deadhead faded blossoms on dahlias, cannas, and other bulb flowers still producing.

Sometimes clusters of small bulbs such as snowdrops or glory-of-the-snow work themselves close to the surface. If you see any exposed ones, dig them, divide them into smaller clusters, and replant 1 to 2 inches deep.

## LAWNS

It's probably time to sharpen the mower blade; every twenty-five hours of cutting is a good guide. One sign of a dull mower blade is brown grass tips. Crisply cut grass blades heal well and stay greener, while ones that are bludgeoned off by dull mower blades are ragged and brown.

Continue to mow high and let the clippings remain as long as the grass is green and growing. Stay off the lawn as much as possible if it's browning or already dormant in dry soil.

Pull or spot-spray lawn weeds so they're out of the way for new grass seed in the coming weeks. Allow

## HERE'S HOW

### TO DEADHEAD FLOWERS

1. "Deadheading" means removing spent flowers. It neatens plants, prevents unwanted seeding, and sometimes encourages repeat bloom.

2. For flowers that produce new blooms from side shoots that grow below a cut stem, such as zinnias, roses, and marigolds, use pruners or garden scissors to snip off the browned-out tips. Cut back to just above live side shoots lower on the stems.

3. For flowers that produce all of their blooms on a single stalk, such as daylilies, coneflowers, and yarrow, cut off the entire spent flowering stalk to the base, leaving the green foliage intact.

4. Deadheading can be done throughout the season, as needed. Time of day does not matter.

six weeks between the time you last use a lawn weed-killer and when you seed.

Crabgrass plants form seeds this month. You may be able to limit the spread of mature seeds by mowing with a bag attachment to catch them. Dispose of them in the trash. Since crabgrass is such a low, sprawling plant, you probably won't get all of the seeds this way. Existing crabgrass plants will die with frost, but you may still need to apply a crabgrass preventer next spring.

## PERENNIALS & GROUNDCOVERS

As summer wanes, the perennial garden may need some primping and clipping to look good again. Cut back leggy stems of catmint, artemisia, goldenrod, and others after they bloom. Clip off spent, diseased, or drought- and heat-injured browned foliage. Deadhead the tall phlox, coneflowers, Russian sage, black-eyed Susan, and anything else sporting brown flowers. And, of course, weed the beds to reduce competition for nutrients and moisture as well as to keep the garden looking tended.

Check the supports of large late-summer perennials. Are they still able to handle the full weight of grown plants, especially when rain and wind add to the burden? Shore up ones that got bigger than you thought with additional stakes or sections of fencing.

## ROSES

Maintain a 2- or 3-inch layer of mulch over your rose beds to hold down weeds and retain moisture.

Many varieties of roses will develop rose "hips," which are berry-like growths that form where flowers fade. By late this month, stop deadheading faded flowers, and allow hips to form. Later in the season, the hips will provide a nutritious meal for birds and other wildlife.

Check climbers to be sure their new growth is securely fastened to their support. High winds that accompany late-summer storms can loosen the long canes and thrash them about, causing wounds to the canes.

Prune off any "suckers" that may have sprung up from the roots or low on the plant. These usually look different than the rest of the bush since they're coming from the rootstock and not the more desirable grafted top growth.

## SHRUBS

Other than snipping spent flower heads off the ends of hydrangeas, butterfly bushes, and other summer-flowering shrubs, limit pruning to removing dead or injured branches. From now through late fall when leaves drop, shrubs are starting to prepare for cold-weather dormancy. Avoid shaping and other heavy cutting that will stimulate new growth at a time when growth should be slowing.

## TREES

Be careful with the weed-trimmer. Nicks in the soft bark of young trees will allow pests and disease pathogens access to tender tissues. This is one good reason why rings of mulch make good sense around trees.

As with flowering shrubs, limit tree-pruning through late fall to removing dead or injured branches. Trees also are starting to prepare for cold-weather dormancy and are slowing growth. Avoid shaping and other heavy cutting that will stimulate new growth.

## VINES

Check that summer storms haven't loosened vines from their supports. Re-tie them, and guide new shoots protruding beyond where you'd like. Or snip off overly long tips.

Watch for wild, invasive vines growing on your property. Many produce fruits and seeds in fall that birds eat and spread to new locations. Oriental bittersweet, Japanese honeysuckle, porcelain berry,

and mile-a-minute weed are common examples. These are best eradicated.

## WATER

### ALL

Getting tired of all of that bucket-carrying, hose-dragging, and sprinkler-moving? Consider investing in a simple irrigation system. In the long run it will save money, water, and time.

For small beds with a lot of plants, rubber soaker hoses that allow water to ooze out along their length is an option. For watering shrubs, or fewer but larger plants along longer runs, consider drip-irrigation systems. These use skinny plastic supply lines that can be tapped into as needed to insert emitters that drip water at the plant roots. Popup sprinklers are a good option for covering large areas such as lawns. All of these can be rigged up to timers to make watering automatic.

Watering bags, tubs, and similar commercially available products are other aids to apply water evenly and gradually. These are installed around young shrubs and trees and are filled once or twice a week. Holes in the bottom let the water seep out slowly, avoiding the threat of runoff from too-fast application. Seeing a big empty bag or tub around your new tree also helps you remember that it might be time to refill it.

Some gardeners make their own homemade watering devices by poking holes in milk jugs, cans, or similar containers, then setting them around recently planted shrubs and trees.

Wilting foliage may mean a plant is hot, rather than sick or thirsty. To confirm this, check wilted plants after the sun and heat of the day have passed. If the foliage has recovered, the problem is heat. If it has not perked up, dryness is a more likely problem. If it does not perk up within a half-hour after a good watering, look for signs of disease or animal chewing around the roots or base.

Don't get faked out by summer downpours. A storm may look like it's dumping more than it really does. Or it may come down so fast that most

■ *To allow rose hips to develop, stop deadheading roses.*

*Use drip-irrigation lines to make watering automatic.*

of it runs off before soaking in. Use a rain gauge or stick your finger a few inches into the soil to assess whether a storm has just wet the mulch or supplied enough moisture where it's really needed, i.e. into your plants' root zones.

## ANNUALS & TROPICALS

In-ground planting roots are often developed enough to do well with moderate soaking once or twice a week.

Figure on daily watering for flowers in pots and baskets. These need even more water now that they're grown and filling the pots with water-needy roots.

Annuals in small hanging pots out in full sun may need water twice a day in August's heat to keep from frying or ceasing to bloom.

## BULBS

Bulbs growing in pots need daily (or more) watering, just like annual flowers. Summer bulbs growing in-ground can get by with a single 1-inch soaking a week or less, similar to perennial flowers.

Spring bulbs that have gone dormant (tulips and daffodils and such) don't need or want moisture in summer.

## HERE'S HOW
### TO WEATHER A SUMMER DROUGHT

1. Add mulch if you're down to bare soil, or close to it. Soak beds well before mulching. A 3- to 4-inch layer is plenty for trees and shrubs, 2 inches is ideal for perennials, and 1 inch is good around annuals.

2. Get rid of weeds. They're moisture competitors for your plants.

3. Monitor soil moisture regularly and look to "indicator plants" that tell you the soil's getting dry. Hydrangea, Japanese maple, redbud, astilbe, ligularia, and impatiens are among the first wilters.

4. Give highest watering priority to new or expensive plants and to plants you really don't want to risk losing. Save water on plants that can fend for themselves.

5. Minimize evaporation losses by watering early in the morning or early in the evening.

6. Make watering more manageable by dividing the yard into zones and watering a zone at a time instead of trying to water the entire yard all at once.

7. Water pots and ornamentals with recycled "gray water" from the house, such as from dehumidifiers, air conditioners, cooking, and dishwashing.

8. Avoid fertilizing and pruning. Both can stimulate growth at a time when plants should be conserving energy.

## LAWNS

Barring a widespread disease or armyworm outbreak, browning lawns this time of year are almost always due to dry soil. It's *dormant*, not dead. Going brown is a survival trick. Once a soaking rain happens, the grass will "green up" in a couple of days and resume growing. If you're okay with that (and the lawn too), skip watering.

The time to think twice about watering a brown lawn is when a drought drags on, and the lawn is straw-brown for six weeks or more. Then, a watering of about ¼ inch per week is enough to replenish moisture to the grass crowns without stimulating the grass to resume growing.

## PERENNIALS & GROUNDCOVERS

Some of the more moisture-sensitive perennials, such as astilbe, primrose, lobelia, and many ferns, benefit from soakings once a week or at the first sign of wilting or browning around the edges. First-year perennials should continue to get weekly or twice-weekly soakings throughout August when there's no rain.

Established perennials, especially drought-tough ones, can survive weeks without water and may need help only in extended hot, dry spells.

Perennials in pots or baskets, either alone or with annuals, dry out quickly and benefit from daily watering.

## ROSES

New roses and ones that you're pushing for peak performance should continue to get soakings two to three times a week. Established roses are fine with a single, once-a-week, 1-inch soaking, and most will at least survive with less than that.

## SHRUBS, TREES & VINES

Focus especially on shrubs, trees and woody vines that you've planted or moved within the past three to four years. Soak them deeply once or twice a week if rain isn't happening, using enough water to dampen the soil all around and to the bottom of the rootballs (most of which is in the top 10 or 12 inches). Check with your finger, a probe, or a soil-moisture meter.

After three to four years, most shrubs, trees, and woody vines are root-established enough that they'll be fine without watering aid except in unusually long, hot, dry spells. When you do water, soak deeply. Wetting the mulch won't help the roots.

When the weather gets hot and dry for weeks, pay particular attention to shrubs growing under trees. Those typically lose the moisture battle to bigger tree roots and may not get much rain in light to moderate storms because the leaves block it. Soak these shrubs every few weeks if it's hot and dry.

Shrubs and small trees growing in planters around the pool or patio can become heat- and water-stressed in the August sun. Keep them watered, cover the soil with an inch of organic mulch, and if you can, move struggling plants to a less sunny spot. Avoid stones or gravel as mulch; they absorb heat.

## ALL

Virtually nothing needs or should get supplemental fertilizer this month. It's counterproductive to fertilize plants that are coping with harsh heat and drought. (See July, "Fertilize, All," page 135.) More fertilizer doesn't help a plant deal with lack of water. Water solves that.

## ANNUALS, TROPICALS & PERENNIALS

An exception to the August no-fertilize rule is flowers growing in pots or baskets. These are using and leaching nutrients so quickly due to daily waterings that they benefit from a water-soluble flower fertilizer at half-strength once a week.

*Plants in containers need daily watering during the heat.*

## LAWNS

Wait until at least September for the next fertilizer application. Definitely do not fertilize any lawn that's brown or flirting with dormancy.

Especially if you're planning to reseed or overseed the lawn next month, test your soil so you'll know what kind of and how much fertilizer to use. Do-it-yourself, mail-in Penn State kits are available at all County Extension offices and most garden centers.

## ROSES

July is typically the end of the line for fertilizing roses. The exception is if you're shooting for peak performance and in the cooler regions of Pennsylvania. Then it's okay to apply one last scattering of a granular, slow-acting fertilizer formulated for roses early in August. From here on out, roses should begin focusing more on storing energy in their roots than pushing new top growth.

## SHRUBS, TREES & VINES

Most don't need fertilizer help anytime, but summer through early fall is the wrong time to apply it. Woody plants start preparing for winter dormancy in the coming weeks and don't benefit from fertilizer that encourages new late-season growth that might not harden sufficiently before winter.

Fertilize woody plants only if poor growth and a soil test indicate there's a nutrient deficiency. Wait to apply it when the plants drop their leaves and go dormant—or until early next spring. Never fertilize a shrub stressed by heat or pest problems.

## PROBLEM-SOLVE

### ALL

Some unusual growths appear in mulch over summer. Most are wood-decaying organisms that are a nuisance but harmless to people, pets, and plants. Tops on the list is artillery fungus, which is notorious for the black, tarry, pinhead-sized flecks the mulch-dwelling fruiting bodies shoot up onto light surfaces. When these spore masses stick and dry, they're almost impossible to remove from siding, fences, white cars, and so forth. This fungus

grows best in shredded hardwood mulch, the most commonly used type. Inspect your mulch-side surfaces over summer for new spores and wipe them off immediately before they dry. Artillery fungus doesn't grow as well in bark mulch or leaf mulch (or inorganic stone mulch).

More noticeable is slime mold, commonly called "dog vomit fungus" because that's what it looks like in its early stage. The blobs start out pale yellow to yellow-orange on the mulch surface and dry into darker blobs that spew a dry gray powder when opened. Bag and toss the blobs if they bug you. There's no spray or treatment to stop them from forming. They'll usually stop forming in very hot, dry weather.

Among the weirdest is a so-called "stinkhorn" fungus that sends up slender, orange, hollow stalks about the size of a pinky with a mushroom-like cap on top. It's harmless and typically blackens, shrivels, and disappears in a matter of days.

Fungal diseases are in their heyday this month because of the warm, humid conditions so many of them favor. Plant-damaging ones cause spots, blotches, or sunken patches on plant foliage, killing the tissues and threatening the stems with dieback. Others clog the "veins" of plant stems, and some rot roots.

Fungicides don't cure diseases but can protect uninfected foliage before or in the early stages of a threatening disease. Different ones work best for different diseases, so it's important to diagnose the specific disease before turning to a spray.

■ *Slime mold in mulch*

■ *Stinkhorn fungus*

While some plant diseases are potentially fatal, plants often grow through leaf diseases—especially ones that occur later in the season. Good sanitation helps. Clip off infected leaves or stems, and put them in the trash to prevent the spread of the disease. Also remove fallen, diseased leaves, which harbor fungal spores that may overwinter to reinfect next year.

## ANNUALS & TROPICALS

Petunias, calibrachoa, nicotiana, and geraniums often suddenly stop blooming this month, leading gardeners to blame hot weather or lack of water. Look closely for small, green caterpillars called budworms that bore into the base of flower buds, causing them to abort. Also look for small holes at the base of flower buds that didn't open. Handpick budworms you can see or spray with spinosyn or an insecticide labeled for budworm control.

Powdery mildew is a common August disfiguring threat to zinnias, annual phlox, and some verbenas. The leaves take on a whitish gray coating and eventually brown and die. Snip off infected leaves, and water the ground, not over the leaves. At planting, space far enough apart for good air circulation. Fungicides can slow outbreaks. A homemade, organic recipe is 1 tablespoon baking soda and ½ tablespoon horticultural oil to 1 gallon water, sprayed every three or four days. The best solution is to plant mildew-resistant varieties.

## BULBS

Powdery mildew also is fairly common on tuberous begonias and sometimes on dahlias. The same treatment options apply as to annuals.

## LAWNS

Beetle grubs hatch this month and start to cause feeding damage in the lawn. The telltale sign is browning patches that pull up like loose carpet. That's because the young grubs have eaten the roots out from underneath. You could also dig up a square foot of turfgrass and examine the root zone for grubs. If you count more than four or five in a square foot, that's enough to cause noticeable damage and warrant treatment.

Grub-preventing insecticides that work well when applied late May through early July don't work as well in late summer and fall. Look instead for products that kill grubs. An organic option is applying predatory nematodes (*Heterorhabditis bacteriophora* and/or *Steinernema carpocapsae*), which are microscopic worms that enter the soil and parasitize the grubs. The year's best timing is late August through mid-September for these.

A slower-acting, longer-term organic lawn-grub option is milky spore, a disease that sickens and kills grubs of Japanese beetles. It can be applied anytime the ground isn't frozen. It's had mixed results, however.

■ *Grubs in the soil*

Rust is a common lawn disease that strikes in late summer. Grass blades develop reddish brown pustules that produce orange-red powder that puffs up as you walk through an infected patch (hence the nickname "the orange shoe disease"). Rust usually resolves on its own without lasting lawn damage, so treatment isn't recommended.

Powdery mildew can affect grass as well as garden plants, causing the same whitish gray coating if you look closely at the blades. It tends to occur mostly on Kentucky bluegrass in shaded areas. Treatment usually isn't needed, but fungicides can control severe outbreaks.

Chinch bugs are small, black, beetlelike bugs that pierce grass blades in hot weather and suck out chlorophyll, causing brown patches in bad infestations. Several generations can hatch per year. If they're bad enough to warrant action, insecticides will kill them.

## PERENNIALS & GROUNDCOVERS

Peony foliage often looks beat up by now due to several late-summer diseases, including botrytis, phytopthora, and powdery mildew. Cut off and dispose of leaves that are looking bad enough to detract from the landscape, including cutting back entire plants to the ground. Badly diseased foliage isn't doing the plants any good. It's late enough that peonies have taken in enough sunlight to recharge themselves to return next spring.

Some black-eyed Susan varieties, including the popular 'Goldsturm' variety, come down with fungal leaf spot disease that some years is bad enough to warrant cutting down and removing all the foliage. Plants usually grow a new set of leaves until frost kills those. In minor or early outbreaks, pick off spotted leaves as soon as you see them.

Perennial or groundcover leaves that are browning around their edges or turning a bleached, pale color could be suffering from lack of water, but it also could be sun scorch. These symptoms happen to young or shade-preferring plants that are getting more sun and heat than their genetics allow. A leading example is variegated hosta. Ones planted along sunny driveways look fried around the edges this month. The best solution is to move them to a cooler, shadier spot. Excess salt in the soil (from winter ice-melter runoff) can compound this scorching damage.

Mites continue to threaten a variety of plants with their sucking damage as they thrive in the dry heat. Watch for pale, stippled leaves and fine webbing on stems. Wash mites off infected plants with forceful sprays of water from the hose, or in severe, persistent cases, spray with insecticidal soap or a pesticide labeled for mite control.

If you're seeing dead or yellowing patches in groundcovers near sidewalks, that's likely due to visits by local dogs. Their urine, which is high in nitrogen, burns plant foliage. Scent repellents can encourage passing dogs to pick a telephone pole instead. Consider a low fence if that fails.

## ROSES

Mites, aphids, and Japanese beetles are bugs that still may turn up on rose foliage. Insecticidal soap can control both of the first two bugs, while handpicking or spraying neem oil or a beetle-killing insecticide are options for the latter.

Blackspot continues to be the main disease threat, but powdery mildew often shows up this month, especially if it's humid. Most fungicides control both of those diseases if handpicking infected leaves doesn't keep a lid on outbreaks.

More serious are rare but usually fatal viral diseases, such as rose mosaic virus and rose rosette disease (see April, Problem-Solve, Roses, page 84.) These stunt rose growth and lead to symptoms such as disfigured, splotchy leaves, and malformed buds. They don't respond to fungicides either. If you suspect a virus, get an accurate diagnosis. If your hunch is right, you'll likely have to dig and remove the infected rose. There is no cure for viral diseases. Disinfect your shovel and tools after digging to prevent spreading the virus to other roses.

## SHRUBS

Old-fashioned lilacs are prone to powdery mildew, but it's also somewhat common on dark-leafed ninebarks, Exbury azaleas, shrub dogwoods, some hydrangeas, and occasionally on butterfly bushes. It's often mainly cosmetic (especially on lilac), but severe or repeated infections can kill branches. Watch for the symptoms and evaluate whether a fungicide treatment is warranted.

Browning tips on junipers, especially the low and spreading types, may look like heat or drought injury, but it's often the symptom of two common fungal blights. Have a few clippings looked at under a hand lens for the presence of pepperlike spores. Early infections can be slowed by snipping the infected tips and pruning to aid air circulation. Otherwise, ongoing fungicides may be needed to prevent increasing damage, including dead plants.

Junipers, spruce, and many other conifers are targets of mites as well. If you're seeing loss of color (usually the first sign), a good mite test is to place a piece of white paper under suspect branches and bang them. If you see little "dots" scurrying around on the paper, you're likely watching mites in action.

Boxwoods sometimes suffer slow deaths from a condition called "boxwood decline," which involves gradual branch dieback. A newer and more serious threat called "boxwood blight" (caused by the *Cylindrocladium buxicola* fungus) recently arrived in Pennsylvania. It starts with concentric brown spots on the leaves and black streaking on the stems, followed by a fairly quick brownout of the entire plant. This blight is thought to spread mainly from infected nursery stock as opposed to blowing around in the wind or being spread by birds and bugs. Be alert for it, though, and report any cases to the state Department of Agriculture, which is tracking its spread (or hopefully, non-spread).

## TREES
Late summer is when you might notice orange-striped oakworms stripping the leaves of your oaks (and maybe hickories, maples, or birch trees). Because these chewing insects with the orange stripes are late-season feeders, they're not a big threat to the long-term health of a tree. They're more of a nuisance, dropping small gobs of oakworm waste over driveways, patios, and sidewalks. Ignore them, or for intolerable outbreaks, spray with B.t. (*Bacillus thuringiensis*), or hire a tree company to apply an insecticide.

Just because a tree is dropping something doesn't mean it's in trouble. Some species routinely drop twigs, fuzzy balls, seeds, flower bracts, last year's leaves, or excess fruit set. Some slough off strips or patches of bark. Evergreens shed older leaves and needles from the inside to make way for fresh growth. It helps to know what's normal for your species, and then to think about worrying only when something is dropping outside of that realm.

Lightning is attracted to tall, isolated targets such as telephone poles, tall buildings, and, of course, trees. Big, old shade trees are frequent victims. Lightning hits can cause large splits in the trunk and branches as the sap inside super-heats. Cells can rupture inside from the electrical charge as well. If you want to protect a valuable specimen tree, consider hiring a company to install a lightning protection system. Cables run down from the tree top to a buried metal grounding rod.

Fat "bumps" about the size of a half-pea on magnolia branches are a sign of scale insects. Magnolia scale is the biggest of the scale family and is best controlled in August. Inspect your branches, and if needed, treat with horticultural oil or a spray labeled for scale control on magnolia.

■ *Older evergreen needles will drop off naturally after they brown.*

September

*May is hard to beat as Pennsylvania's top month in the garden, but September gives it a run for its money.*

The daytime heat of July and August usually backs off into the upper-60s to low-80s, although a last-gasp, upper-90s heat flash can't be ruled out. Toward the end of the month, the cooler parts of the state start flirting with overnight frost.

Rain happens more often. Usually. Although thunderstorm and hurricane-remnant dumpings occur, so do gentle daylong dousings. It's refreshing to see heat-beat plants perk up following a cool, September soaking rain. Just when you thought the landscape was ready to call it quits.

The outlook of cooling temperatures and more frequent rain adds up to a month that's perfect for patching a thin lawn or starting a new one. It's also a great time to plant most plants or move ones you've realized are in the wrong spot. September planting is less stressful than midsummer planting, and usually allows eight to ten weeks of root growth before winter's approach shuts down the season.

A Cornell University study found that fall-planted plants survive best when they have at least six weeks of root growth before the soil temperature in the root zone drops below 40 degrees Fahrenheit. In Pennsylvania, that translates into an ideal-planting cutoff of late October in the warmer parts of the state and mid-October in the cooler parts. September planting gives a buffer of several additional weeks.

Fall planting offers one other plus—reduced weed competition. Far fewer weeds germinate in fall than spring, so when you dig that soil and start watering your new plants, you won't get more dandelions than dianthus.

We're still a month away from fall-foliage glory, but in the meantime, enjoy the mums, asters, goldenrod, sedum, and the year's second-best bloom time for roses.

## PLAN

### ALL

Has watering been a burden this summer? Consider installing drip irrigation or a similar automatic watering system over selected parts of the yard for next season. You might even install one this month if you're adding new beds and need to keep a lot of new plants moist through fall.

Watch for deals on new plants. Many garden centers hold "Fall is for Planting" sales. As fall rolls on, even deeper discounts show up on both plants and garden supplies as retailers try to clear inventory before winter.

Keep the binoculars handy to enjoy the visits of birds to the plants with seedheads and berries.

### ANNUALS & TROPICALS

Don't wait too long to move tender tropicals and houseplants back inside. Many of them start to suffer when nighttime lows reach into the 40s. Most will die if a surprise early frost hits.

While impressions of your garden are fresh in your mind, make notes in your garden journal. What annuals were most successful? In which areas do you wish you had planted annuals? What problems did you encounter this year with what species? Has anything changed in the yard

## GARDEN DESIGN FOR FOUR-SEASON INTEREST

Most gardeners rate four-season interest high on their wish list. Some strategies for achieving that include:

- **Add more variety.** Plant more plants and different kinds of them. You'll get multiseason change and interest just by luck.

- **Make a conscious effort to plan for all four seasons.** Think what each part of the yard will look like in each season, and seek plants that will add interest to any boring gaps.

- **Move beyond two-week wonders.** Many overused favorites are one-dimensional

■ *Oakleaf hydrangea,* Hydrangea quercifolia, *in fall color.*

plants that peak only for a few weeks of the year (azaleas, rhododendrons, lilacs, peonies, forsythia, and burning bush, for example).

- **Look for hard-workers—plants that do more than one thing in one season.** A example is oakleaf hydrangea, which blooms white in late spring, gets burgundy foliage in fall, then shows off peeling bark in winter.

- **Don't plant-shop only in May.** You'll tend to buy only what's looking good then or on sale. Shop in different seasons. Make it a point to go whenever your yard is looking particularly barren.

- **Visit public gardens.** They're great for getting ideas and seeing what's doing what at any given time. Visit these in different seasons too.

- **Pay attention to what other people have planted.** If you see plants nearby doing something interesting at a time when your yard is snoozing, find out what those plants are, and add them to your list.

## USING SPRING BULBS

Spring bulbs can be used in a variety of landscape settings, not just massed by themselves. Some ideas:

- **Interplant with perennials**. Bulbs will poke up and bloom while the perennials are just waking up. Then the perennials take over to hide bulb foliage as it's yellowing.

- **Poke in among groundcovers.** Taller bulbs such as daffodils, tulips, and hyacinths can be inserted into low plantings of vinca, pachysandra, hardy ginger, and such. Their shoots are strong enough to poke up through the groundcover foliage and bloom over top.

- **Mix and match randomly to create a "bulb meadow."** This is a great way to take advantage of year-end bargains of two packs of this, three packs of that.

- **Plant under trees and tall shrubs.** Many bulbs get sufficient sunlight before the trees and shrubs leaf out to recharge themselves for the following year's bloom.

- **Cluster in key spots around the yard.** How about lining the front walk? Around the mailbox or front light post? Maybe some fragrant hyacinths around the back patio? Or how about some golden daffodils at the base of an arbor or in front of a fence?

- **Plant in foam, plastic, and other winter-hardy pots that can be left outside all winter.** Come spring, the bulbs will emerge and flower in the pot. This is less expensive than buying already-flowering bulb plants in spring.

- **Plant in the lawn.** Short, early bulbs work best for this. They'll poke up and flower before the lawn greens. If possible, hold off mowing until the foliage yellows. Good choices for lawn planting are snowdrops, winter aconite, and *Crocus tommasinianus* crocuses ("tommies").

that will affect which annuals you plant where next spring?

## BULBS

We've reached the beginning of prime time for spring-bulb planting, so finalize your plans for what you're adding where. Buy or order quickly, before the choices get picked over or sell out.

Bulb growers grade bulbs by size. Since larger-sized ones usually perform best, they're typically more expensive than bags of bargain-priced smaller ones. Weigh price vs. their intended use. You may decide to pay more for bulbs you're planning to "force" for inside bloom or use out front, but opt for a bargain bag of dwarf daffodils that you're going to naturalize in the back yard.

Check bulbs for firmness and plumpness. A touch of blue mold on the surface is not a problem; neither is a peeling tunic or dry skin. What *is* a problem is soft or rotting bulbs, or ones that are dry and noticeably lighter in weight.

■ *Clockwise from top left: Tuberous roots, rhizomes, corms, tubers and bulbs can all be planted in the fall for spring or summer blooms.*

A few bulbs actually flower this month. Three to consider are autumn crocus, resurrection lilies (or other *Lycoris* species), and sternbergia.

## LAWNS

Labor Day weekend opens the window for major lawn work. September and October are the year's best two months for seeding or sodding new lawns and for rehabbing sad existing lawns.

Like any plant, grass performs best in good soil with adequate nutrition. Unfortunately, many lawns struggle to grow in the heavily graded, compacted soils common to housing subdivisions. A good way to gradually improve poor soil without digging it up is "topdressing." This involves raking a light layer of sifted compost or similar fine, organic-rich topsoil over the soil surface. A ¼-inch layer is enough to begin helping without smothering the existing lawn. Topdressing can be done early each fall until your lawn is thriving.

## PERENNIALS & GROUNDCOVERS

Trying to reduce maintenance? Think about areas to convert to groundcover, such as bare areas around trees, hard-to-mow slopes, or mulched beds under shrubs. The traditional "big three" are ivy, pachysandra, and vinca (myrtle), but many others are good options. For shade, consider sweet woodruff, barrenwort, lamium, moss, ferns, Pennsylvania sedge, hardy ginger, or variegated Solomon's seal. For part shade, consider liriope, leadwort, foamflower, hellebores, or mazus. For sun, consider creeping sedum, thyme, dianthus, creeping phlox, or hardy geranium.

■ *Fall is an ideal time to topdress a lawn.*

Mums aren't the only perennials that peak in September. Others that add color to the fall landscape are agastache, aster, boltonia, catmint, goldenrod, Japanese anemone, Joe-pye weed, lavender, leadwort, liriope, reblooming daylilies, Russian sage, salvia, sedum, toad lily, and turtlehead.

A good reason to leave at least some seedheads on late-season perennials is to provide food for visiting wildlife in fall and winter. Weigh that against whether you want any self-sowing.

Consider what's most important to you before deciding which new perennials to add. Traits might include low water demand, tolerance for poor soil, low fertilizer need, animal resistance, compact size, long bloom, evergreen foliage, colorful foliage, Pennsylvania native, good for cutting, fragrance, bug and disease resistance, ease of propagation, shade tolerance, attractive to beneficial insects, multiseason interest, and attractive flower color.

## ROSES

September is the year's second showiest month (behind June) for roses. Are you taking advantage of it? Lean toward lower-care shrub, landscape, and antique types if you like the idea of the color but not the pest, disease, and fertilizer efforts.

Although roses perform best in full sun, many do surprisingly well in even half-day sun. Again, lean toward the shrub, landscape, and antique types if you don't have a classic open and sunny rose setting. Most climbing and rambling roses do reasonably well trained up trees, where they get only partial light.

For hybrid teas, grandifloras, and floribundas, ideal conditions include at least six hours of sun per day, excellent soil drainage, a soil pH of about 6.5, and good air circulation.

## SHRUBS

A few flowering shrubs bloom in September. Besides roses, take a look at blue mist shrub (*Caryopteris*), butterfly bush, abelia, and panicle and reblooming hydrangeas.

Berries and fruits are an even showier feature than flowers on the shrub front in September. Choices worth including are bayberry, cotoneaster, nandina, beautyberry, chokeberry, St. Johnswort, winterberry holly, juniper, viburnum, and in a warm southeast corner, skimmia.

## TREES

Several tree species sport eye-grabbing fruits by September. The native American dogwood and the Oriental kousa dogwood are two of the best. Also take a look at crabapple, hawthorn, and the evergreen American holly.

Spring and early fall are the two best tree-planting windows. Take a look around, and decide whether your yard is "under-treed." Benefits include shade, showy flowers, winter interest from bark or evergreen foliage, privacy, shelter for birds, and a way to "ground" the landscape so it doesn't look like your house was dropped from a helicopter onto a grassy field.

Is your tree lineup diverse? A problem that occurs when everyone plants the same few species is the decimation when something comes along to threaten those species. It's happened with chestnuts, American elms, and most recently, ash. A diversity of trees not only spreads out the risk of widespread loss, it helps the ecosystem and its inhabitants that keep nature in balance. Remember, just because you've never heard of a species doesn't mean it's a bad choice. And just because everyone plants flowering pears and flowering dogwoods doesn't mean that's what you should plant too.

Some diversity questions to consider are:

1. Does your yard have conifers (pine, fir, spruce, for example) that provide shelter to birds in storms, and cones to feed them and the squirrels?

2. Does it have flowering trees to attract pollinators and add fragrance over multiple months?

3. Does it have fruit- or nut-bearing trees, such as crabapple, dogwood, and serviceberry that support wildlife?

4. Does it have any (or many) Pennsylvania natives, such as redbud, American fringe tree, blackgum, river birch, red maple, serviceberry, American dogwood, and sweetbay magnolia?

## VINES

Do you need some privacy or sun protection on a second-floor deck or balcony? A vine-covered trellis inserted in a window box on the floor is a colorful solution that takes up very little precious floor space.

Pyracantha fruits are maturing into bright reddish orange clusters (or should be if they didn't rot from summer disease). These are at their showiest in fall and early winter and are durable choices that prune well into any size or shape you like. Just be aware they have large, pointy thorns. You'll need to train them upright; pyracantha doesn't twine or affix itself onto surfaces.

Another fall- and winter-fruiting vine is American bittersweet, which is different from the invasive Oriental bittersweet. This native vine gets red berries in fall that birds love, but that are poisonous to people. American bittersweet can twine its way up about 20 feet.

## PLANT

### ALL

"Fall is for planting" isn't just garden-center hype to get rid of plants the stores don't want to overwinter. Fall really *does* offer some planting advantages, such as:

1. The soil temperatures are warm enough to support good root growth at least through the end of October.

2. Shorter days, less intense sunlight, and cooler temperatures of early fall mean less stress ("transplant shock") for plants being evicted from their cozy pots into the untamed ground.

3. Newly planted plants lose less moisture through their leaves in fall than summer, which lowers water demands.

4. Rain usually increases from summer, further reducing the hose duty that new plantings require.

5. Fall-planted plants will have two growing seasons under their belts instead of one (now and next spring) before facing a grueling hot Pennsylvania summer.

6. The bugs are mostly gone.

7. A lot of plants go on sale from here on out.

8. It's more pleasant for the gardener to be out digging in September than in the furnace called July.

Before digging a new bed (especially when using power equipment), find out where your buried utility lines are. Gas and electrical lines are usually deeper than shovel or tiller depth, but cable and computer lines might be only a few inches down. Call Pennsylvania One Call at 811 or 1-800-242-1776 to have lines located. Or visit online at www.pa1call.org/PA811/Public. It's a free service for Pennsylvania homeowners doing their own work. Note that you may need to call utilities directly if you deal with any not covered by the Pennsylvania One Call network.

## ANNUALS & TROPICALS

Replace tired summer annuals with cool-season color plants. The colorful foliage of ornamental cabbage and ornamental kale are two popular choices, but there's also a fresh supply of pansies and violas—most of which are cold-hardy enough to survive winter and bloom again next spring. Or pick from a plethora of mums. Most of those are winter-hardy enough to qualify as perennials, but some people treat mums like annuals. They'll display them in a pot or bed until the flowers brown, then toss them.

## BULBS

The cooler soil of October is the year's best for spring-bulb planting, but September is also fine—especially in the state's cooler regions. (See October's "Here's How to Plant Spring Flowering Bulbs," page 180.)

As you empty your pots of summer annuals, replant a few winter-durable ones (foam, plastic, concrete) with spring bulbs this month and next. Plant at the same depth as in the ground—2½ to

*Freshen up your fall garden by replacing tired summer annuals with ornamental kale and mums.*

■ *Besides planting new bulbs, existing bulbs can be dug, divided and replanted in fall—if you can find them without slicing into them.*

■ *Sprinkle ground cayenne pepper on the bulbs to keep the squirrels from eating the bulbs. (They don't like the taste of the pepper.) If you have serious problems with creatures digging up bulbs, consider making a makeshift cage out of chicken wire. Plant the bulbs in the cage and bury it.*

3 times as deep as their height. Set the pots where they'll get winter snow and rain. The bulbs will chill, root, and then flower on cue next spring.

Existing bulb plantings can be dug, divided, and replanted this month if you've got a patch that's overcrowded or if you want to "expand the flock." Be careful you don't slice into the buried bulbs while digging.

## LAWNS

September is the best month for planting a new lawn and for overseeding and rehabbing an existing lawn. See "Here's How To Seed a New Lawn," on page 162, if you're starting from scratch, or "Here's How to Overseed a Thin Lawn," on page 164 if you're rehabbing. See "Here's How to Start a New Lawn from Sod," on page 163 if you're sodding instead of seeding.

However you seed, good seed-to-soil contact is very important. If you're dealing with a large area that's too labor-intensive to rake by hand, do your seeding after aerating and/or dethatching the lawn. Both of those procedures disturb the soil. Penn State University's Center for Turfgrass suggests dragging large areas with a large door mat or section of chain-link fence to both prepare beds and to incorporate and tamp scattered seed into the soil surface.

Another seeding alternative for large areas is renting a "slit-seeder" or seeding machine. This power equipment has vertical blades that cut shallow slits in the soil. It then inserts seed from hoppers behind the slits.

To zero in on the best specific varieties of each grass type, check out the ratings resulting from trials at Penn State University. Current results are posted on the National Turfgrass Evaluation Program website at www.ntep.org. Select the State Data button, then hit Pennsylvania on the map.

Adding superior seed varieties each autumn or two gradually improves your lawn quality as the older grasses age and die out.

## HERE'S HOW

### TO SEED A NEW LAWN

1. Prepare the soil by removing all vegetation and loosening soil to a depth of 6 inches. Rent a tiller unless you're seeding a small area that can be dug by hand.

2. Add an inch or two of organic material, such as compost, mushroom soil, or peat moss, and incorporate it thoroughly into the existing loosened soil. If your soil already is good, skip this step. A soil test can help you decide.

3. Rake the soil smooth, and scatter grass seed over the surface at about the density you'd salt a steak. Seed doesn't need to be so dense that it touches, but you'll need more than just a few seeds per square foot.

4. Lightly rake in the seed so that some is a ¼-inch deep and some remains on the surface. Lightly tamp, and cover with a thin layer of straw or a lightweight, spun-bonded polyester garden fabric (also called floating row cover) to discourage birds, retain soil moisture, and help prevent erosion from heavy rain.

5. Water enough to wet the soil about 2 inches deep, then keep the soil surface consistently damp with frequent light waterings until the seed sprouts. Assume daily waterings and maybe even twice a day if it's hot and dry.

6. Remove the fabric once the seed is up, and cut back on the watering to every two or three days. Wait until the grass is 3 inches tall to mow for the first time.

## PERENNIALS & GROUNDCOVERS

September planting and transplanting allows two good months of root growth at a time when plants can focus on roots instead of splitting energy demand with flower production and top growth.

As with trees and shrubs, loosen and fray out tightly matted or circling roots before planting.

It's okay to remove the soil as needed. Try not to damage or remove any more roots than necessary to free them.

Perennials with long taproots such as baptisia, balloon flower, globe thistle, columbine, and butterfly weed are more difficult to transplant than most perennials that have more spreading

## HERE'S HOW

### TO START A NEW LAWN FROM SOD

1. Prepare the soil by removing all vegetation and loosening to a depth of at least 6 inches.

2. Add an inch or two of organic material, such as compost, mushroom soil, or peat moss, and incorporate it thoroughly into the existing loosened soil. If your soil already is good, skip this step. A soil test will help you decide.

3. Rake smooth or drag large areas with a mat. It's okay to lightly dampen the soil the evening before sodding, but avoid working on wet soil.

4. Unroll and lay strips of sod, butting them up against each other and in a staggered pattern, similar to the way bricks are overlapped.

5. Fill in any gaps with cut pieces, and fill small cracks with topsoil. Tamp down the laid pieces or go over larger areas with a roller.

6. Water well so that both the sod and the top 2 inches of soil are damp. Keep the planting damp, with daily watering, if necessary, for the first four to six weeks.

# SEPTEMBER

## HERE'S HOW

### TO OVERSEED A THIN LAWN

1. Mow the grass shorter than usual, to about 1 or 2 inches. Rake up any debris.

2. Loosen or at least scratch the surface of bare areas that will get seed. Or plan on overseeding after you aerate or dethatch the lawn or otherwise disturb the soil surface. Germination is low (if at all) if you just toss seed on top of a compacted surface.

3. Scatter seed over the bare or thin areas, lightly rake, and lightly tamp to achieve good seed-to-soil contact.

4. Water enough to wet the soil about 2 inches deep, then keep the soil surface consistently damp with frequent light waterings until the seed sprouts. Figure on daily waterings (maybe even twice daily) if it's hot and dry.

5. Optional: Cover larger areas with a thin layer of straw to help retain moisture. Products also are available that combine seed with paper mulch.

6. Once the seed is up, cut back on watering to every two or three days. Wait until the grass is 3 inches tall to mow for the first time.

and clumping root systems. Dig deeply to get the entire roots of these, or better yet, plant them and leave them.

Mums overwinter best when they're planted in late summer or early fall. The roots have more time to establish before winter. Those have a higher survival rate than ones planted in mid-October and later.

## ROSES

Some say spring is better to plant roses than fall, but most gardeners have good rose-planting success in September. There's no need to fertilize them until next spring.

## SHRUBS, TREES & VINES

September and October are excellent months to plant and transplant almost all container-grown shrubs, trees, and woody vines for the reasons listed in this chapter under "Plant, All." (See March's "Here's How to Plant a Shrub" and "Here's How to Plant a Tree," pages 55 and 56.)

Be careful you don't damage your new plants on the way home from the nursery. An underrated woe is when people toss leafed-out trees and shrubs in the back of an open pickup and drive home on the highway. To a tree, that's the equivalent of enduring a 65 mph windstorm. Cover plants with plastic or fabric for the ride home if they'll be exposed to moving air. Loosely tie or wrap branches to minimize snap-offs. And secure plants so they're not rolling around in the trunk.

It's cooled off enough now that growers begin digging field-grown plants again, which means that fresh balled-and-burlapped trees and shrubs will be arriving at the garden centers.

## CARE

### ALL
Stay on top of the weeds. Dig, pull, spot-spray—whatever it takes. The appearance of new weeds

will slow from here on out, but many existing ones will try to produce mature seeds before frost kills them. Don't let that happen. If mature weed seeds drop and blow around, your problems get worse, not better.

September mulching is fine if your mulch layer has deteriorated.

Edge landscape beds if they're getting a little ragged.

### ANNUALS & TROPICALS
Those palms, crotons, snake plants, and other tender tropicals that have been "vacationing" outside need to go back inside when the nights

## HERE'S HOW

### TO START NEW PLANTS FROM CUTTINGS

Many annuals, perennials, and even shrubs can be propagated by rooting cut stems. Some of the easiest are coleus, geraniums, perilla, plectranthus, ivy, purple heart, and Persian shield.

1. Cut 4- to 6-inch tips off of the end of healthy stems or branches.

2. Remove the lowest leaves so that at least one, and preferably two, nodes are bare. Nodes are the point from which shoots emerge. They're also where new roots will emerge from cuttings.

3. Dip the cut end into a rooting hormone powder (available at most garden centers).

4. Insert a pencil into a pot filled with lightweight potting mix or seed-start medium to create a small hole. Insert the powdered end of the cutting into the moist rooting medium, covering the nodes.

5. Water well, and cover the pot with clear plastic wrap or a plastic bag to maintain a moist environment.

6. Set pots in light, but not direct sun. Make sure they don't dry out. When small leaves emerge, that's a signal roots are establishing.

7. Remove the plastic, and treat the "start" as you would any other young, potted plant. Keep the potting mix damp, and begin adding a dilute fertilizer to the water every other week.

start to dip below 50 degrees Fahrenheit. (See "Here's How to Overwinter Tropicals," below.)

Now's a good time to take cuttings of any favorite tropicals and annuals before frost kills them. (See "Here's How to Start New Plants from Cuttings," page 165.)

Pull dead and badly bug- and disease-ridden annuals, but give the rest a chance to rebound. As temperatures cool and rain returns, many annuals get a second wind, especially ones that prefer these temperatures such as alyssum, osteospermum, nemesia, and pansies. Help them by clipping brown tips or leggy stems, giving them a dose of liquid flower fertilizer, and soaking the ground if rain hasn't done that.

Cut off maturing seedpods on species that you don't want to self-sow.

## BULBS

Take in last year's potted amaryllis, or dig and pot any you've been growing in the ground. Store these bulbs dry so they're dormant for six to eight weeks; room temperature is fine. (See December's "Here's How to Grow Amaryllis Indoors," page 206.)

By late this month in the state's coolest regions, tender bulbs such as cannas, dahlias, and callas might blacken from the season's first light frost. That's the cue to dig them and store them inside for winter. (See October's "Here's How to Overwinter Tender Bulbs," page 184.)

## LAWNS

A common question is, "Does it matter in which order I do all of those things?" For starters, you may not need to do all of these, or at least not every year. You may not have a thatch problem,

## HERE'S HOW

### TO OVERWINTER TROPICALS

1. Tropicals that you've planted in the ground should be dug and returned to pots with fresh potting mix.

2. Before moving the repotted, dug-up tropicals and ones that stayed in their pots all summer back inside, eliminate bugs trying to hitch a ride inside. Either hose off the plants with a stiff spray of water, or spray them with insecticidal soap or a similar bug killer.

3. Once the plants dry, move them inside to appropriate light settings, ones that prefer bright light near south- or west-facing windows, or under plant lights and ones that can take less light by your east- or north-facing windows, or in other dimmer spots.

4. If your pots have holes in the bottom for drainage, place containers under them to keep water off the carpets and floors.

5. Use no or only limited fertilizer over winter (growth needs are low), and water when the soil goes dry, and the pots become noticeably lighter. Do not overwater to the point of soggy soil, which is the leading killer of indoor plants.

## END OF SUMMER LAWN IMPROVEMENTS

All sorts of lawn-improving steps are best done this month. Most are geared toward overcoming the lousy soil you've likely got underneath, and providing more ideal cultural conditions. Jobs to consider:

**Topdressing.** This involves spreading a light, ¼-inch layer of sifted compost or similar fine, organic-rich topsoil over the soil surface. The idea is to aid soil quality and add nutrients and organic content without smothering the existing turfgrass. It can be done annually.

■ *Topdressing*

**Aerating.** Most effective are machines that remove cores or finger-sized "plugs" from the soil and deposit them on the surface. This opens air space in the soil and aids compaction. Machines work best after a rain softens the ground (they'll largely bounce across a hard, dry lawn) and when eight to ten passes are made.

■ *Power-core aerator*

**Dethatching.** Thatch is the spongy layer of mostly dead roots at the soil surface. A ½-inch layer or less is fine, but thicker thatch begins to impede fertilizer and rain penetration. The solution is to rip it out with a dethatching rake or dethatching machine with rotating vertical blades. It's also best done after a rain. Rake off and compost the removed thatch.

■ *Plugs from aerating a lawn*

**Maximizing growing conditions.** Now that punishing summer weather is retreating, grass will resume growing and focus on root growth, the key to a healthier lawn. Get the soil tested if you haven't done that lately, and put down the fertilizer and/ or lime that's recommended.

**Seeding.** New grass seed germinates well this time of year, and root growth gets off to an ideal start in warm soil, rainier weather, cooler temperatures, and less weed competition. (See "Here's How to Seed a New Lawn," page 162 and "Here's How to Overseed a Thin Lawn," page 164.)

■ *Vertical-bladed mower for dethatching*

for example, or your lawn may be at a good acidity level and not need lime. But if you're tackling the whole regimen, start with the jobs that roughen the soil, such as the dethatching and/or core-aeration. Then scatter the grass seed, some of which will fall into the opened holes and slits. Then apply any fertilizer that's recommended by the soil test. Then topdress with compost, which will lightly cover the seed and fill some of the holes and slits. A good soaking is the perfect curtain call.

Some research suggests that lime and fertilizer together can reduce the effectiveness of the nitrogen in the fertilizer. To alleviate that possible conflict, apply the fertilizer first, and wait until a soaking rain dissolves it into the ground before applying any recommended lime. Lime can be applied anytime throughout fall before the ground freezes.

Continue to mow grass at 3 to 4 inches tall until the last cut or two of the season.

## PERENNIALS & GROUNDCOVERS

Dig and divide perennials that are spreading beyond where you want them. Ones that divide best now are those that already have bloomed for the season. Cut or separate the dug clumps into fist-sized pieces. Put one back, and plant the rest in new sites or give them away. Perennials that are flowering now are best transplanted early next spring. (See April's "Here's How to Divide Perennials," page 77.)

Groundcovers are easy to divide and transplant this time of year. Dig up dense sections, pull or cut apart into smaller pieces, and plant them in additional areas. Replant one of the pieces where you removed the clump.

It's hard to stake tall, flopping perennials "nicely" at this point, but prop them up and/or tie them with stakes and jute as best as you can to prevent stems from bending.

Ornamental grasses especially can start to flop apart by now. Bundling their midsections can improve the appearance, as can cutting off the worst floppy-stem offenders from around the perimeter. Grasses that are hulking messes should

be divided. Put that on the calendar for early next spring. (See February's "Here's How to Cut Ornamental Grasses," page 42.)

Continue to deadhead spent flowers of the late-summer bloomers. Snip off the seedheads of species that you don't want to self-sow, but leave those that you'd like to keep for feeding birds.

## ROSES

Potted miniatures that aren't quite winter-hardy for your area should be moved inside late this month, or if you've planted them; dug, and repotted. Hose off or spray leaves with horticultural oil or insecticidal soap to avoid taking bugs inside. Acclimate them to the inside gradually, a few hours at first and then more each day over a week to ten days. Give them a bright window.

Continue deadheading spent blooms on varieties that don't produce rose hips (berry-like fruits) or in cases where you don't want hips or browned-out flowers.

Continue to gather and discard any fallen diseased foliage.

Besides cutting fresh roses for bouquets, dry petals for potpourri. Pick opened blossoms of fragrant varieties after morning dew has evaporated, but early enough in the day so their essential oils are still strong. For a moist potpourri, pull the petals from the blossoms and spread on a drying rack out of light until they go limp. For a dried potpourri, set the pulled petals on a cookie sheet in a warm oven. Keep the oven door ajar to allow moisture to escape. Stir the petals occasionally so they dry evenly and completely. Or dry the petals in a microwave oven.

## SHRUBS

Tender shrubs that you're growing outside in pots (gardenia, citrus, and jade plant, for example) need to go back inside before frost. Hose off or spray for bugs before the move. Make sure to place a container under the pots if they have drainage holes in the bottom. Gradually acclimate them to the inside over a seven- to ten-day period before setting them in their winter home.

Other than snipping spent flower heads off hydrangeas, butterfly bushes, and other late-flowering shrubs, limit pruning to removing dead or injured branches.

## TREES

Check the ties on staked spring-planted trees to make sure they are still lax but firmly fastened around the expanding tree trunk. Loosen ties that are starting to make indents in the wood, or worse yet, starting to grow into the bark. Remove supports from trees planted last fall. One year is enough.

Other than removing broken or dead branches, avoid pruning now at least until the leaves drop.

## VINES

When nights start cooling below 50 degrees Fahrenheit, tender vines that you plan to overwinter need to go inside before frost. These include mandevilla, dipladenia, bougainvillea, Rex begonia vine, and in cooler areas, passion vine. Dig and pot any that you've been growing in the ground instead of outdoor pots. Clip back the stems to 1 to 2 feet and hose off or spray for any bugs trying to hitch a ride inside. Gradually acclimate them to the inside before setting them in their winter home.

To prevent unwanted self-sowing, cut off maturing berries or seedpods of potential thugs, such as porcelain berry, akebia, wisteria, and trumpet vine.

## WATER

### ALL

Plants' water demands start to go down this month as the weather cools, evaporation losses drop, and average rainfall increases. That doesn't mean you can put away the hose. You'll need to regularly soak new fall plantings, and keep an eye on soil moisture when rain doesn't happen.

Be alert for "sneaky" early-fall dry spells. Things may not *look* as dry as during a July or August heat wave, but it's still possible the soil is dry in the root zones if soaking storms haven't happened. Sometimes those shallow rains are enough to keep the lawn green and the mulch damp without wetting plant roots.

### ANNUALS & TROPICALS

Continue to water annuals in pots and baskets. Check daily. In-ground annuals and tropicals should be fine with a weekly soaking when rain isn't doing the job.

### BULBS

Bulbs growing in pots also likely need daily watering. Dahlias, tuberous begonias, and other summer bulbs growing the ground are usually fine with a weekly soaking when the weather's dry.

Soak bulb beds right after planting new ones to settle the soil, but there's no need to water existing beds where dormant spring bulbs already are nestled.

### LAWNS

Newly seeded lawns and overseeded thin patches should be sprinkled daily (twice daily if it's very hot and dry) to keep the seed moist until it sprouts. Once the grass is up, water two or three times a week so the soil is consistently damp 4 to 6 inches deep. That encourages roots to penetrate.

Keep the soil underneath new sod damp as well. You may need to water two to three times a week if rain isn't keeping the soil moist down 4 to 6 inches into the root zone.

### PERENNIALS & GROUNDCOVERS

Water new perennials, ornamental grasses, and groundcovers about twice a week if rain doesn't occur. Soak enough so the soil is damp to the bottom of the rootballs.

Most established perennials need little to no water in September, unless it's been unusually hot and dry. Insert your finger 2 or 3 inches into the soil of your perennial beds to test for dryness. If it's not moist, soak. Check again next week.

If it's been a dry late summer, some of the more moisture-loving perennials may need regular soakings once or twice a week. Pay particular attention to species such as turtlehead, lobelia, astilbe, Joe-pye weed, ligularia, swamp milkweed, and hardy hibiscus. No wilting allowed!

## ROSES

Soak newly planted roses two to three times a week, applying enough to dampen the soil to the bottom of the roots.

Existing roses that you're pushing for peak performance should continue to get soakings two to three times a week as well, although that need might taper off with cooler weather and more rain. Otherwise, a once-a-week soaking is fine if it's hot and dry.

## SHRUBS, TREES & VINES

Water new plantings two to three times a week, directing most of the water close to the main stem(s) and applying enough that it dampens the soil all around and to the bottom of the rootball. Check with your finger, a probe, or a soil-moisture meter.

Established shrubs, trees, and woody vines are usually fine without supplemental water in a usual September. The exception is during an extended hot, dry spell, in which a deep soaking once a week is helpful.

## FERTILIZE

### ALL

If you're digging a new garden, test your soil to see what fertilizer (if any) is needed and in what amounts. Work it into the soil as you're preparing it, in advance of planting. DIY mail-in Penn State kits are available at all County Extension offices and most garden centers.

With a few exceptions, this is another no-fertilize month throughout most of the landscape. Between nutrients being released by decaying mulch and those slow-acting fertilizers you applied in spring, most plants are good to go.

### ANNUALS & TROPICALS

Exceptions to the "All" advice are annuals and tropicals still growing in pots and baskets, which benefit from a half-strength flower fertilizer once a week.

### BULBS

New bulbs don't need fertilizer (their nutrition is already built in), but existing bulb beds benefit from a fall scattering of an organic or slow-acting fertilizer formulated for bulbs. Apply it this month or next, ideally right before a soaking rain. Otherwise, water it in after scattering.

### LAWNS

If you're fertilizing a lawn only once a year, this is it. Not only does the late-summer nutrition help the lawn recover from the stresses of heat and drought, it helps grass plants manufacture carbohydrates essential to root growth that peaks in the coming weeks.

If you're fertilizing twice a year, May was the first application, the second is either late this month or in October.

If you're following a three-treatment regimen, September is prime time for the second dose. (May to early June was the first, and mid- to late November is the last.)

If you're following a commercial four-step program, September is the time for Step 3. (Step 1 is late March to early June, Step 2 is late May to early June, and Step 4 is mid- to late November.)

The general advice is to use a fertilizer that's higher in nitrogen than the other two main nutrients (phosphorus and potassium). Phosphorus may not be needed at all. However, the most accurate game plan is to have your soil tested so you know exactly what nutrients your particular lawn needs and in what amounts.

### PERENNIALS, GROUNDCOVERS, ROSES, SHRUBS, TREES & VINES

For new fall plantings, the compost or other organic amendments you worked into the soil during bed preparation are usually enough to supply enough nutrition. A soil test tells you if you have any specific nutrient deficiencies that can be corrected by working in a targeted fertilizer before planting. Otherwise, you're just guessing and probably applying fertilizers your plants really don't need.

For established plantings, unless growth is poor and a soil test nails down that a nutrient deficiency is to blame, no fertilizer is needed.

## PROBLEM-SOLVE

### ALL

You'll see much flying around a yard this month, but don't panic. Pest insects normally account for only about 10 percent of the insects in a typical yard. The others are either beneficial or benign. Lesson 1: Lots of insect activity doesn't necessarily equal lots of plant damage. Lesson 2: Relatively few insects cause landscape damage, and much of that is cosmetic or temporary.

If you see unacceptable levels of plant damage and trace it to pest insects, one problem could be a lack of beneficial insects keeping a lid on the pests. Some reasons for that:

- Frequently used general insecticides have killed off many of the resident beneficials. Consider switching to more targeted controls and only when necessary.

■ *Garden spiders are beneficial insects that will help keep down the population of pest bugs.*

- Your yard lacks enough plant diversity to attract and support a healthy population of beneficial insects. Remedy that by planting a wider variety of plants, especially natives and others that attract bug-eating birds and beneficial insects.

- You hit a down cycle in key beneficials. The population of beneficial insects drops when their main food source (pest bugs) is low. As beneficials dwindle, the pest population can expand, and there's a lag until the beneficials catch up again. This cycle explains why some bugs are worse some years than others.

- Deer think you've planted all of those nice, new trees and shrubs with the tender bark just for them. To be on the safe side, erect cages, fences, or other protection around new plantings if you're gardening in deerland.

Rodents will nest soon. To encourage them to nest elsewhere, delay renewing the mulch under shrubs until after the ground freezes. Pull groundcover plantings away from shrub stems. And if rodents are a chronic problem, set up wire cages around shrubs to protect the bases from winter gnawing.

### ANNUALS & TROPICALS

You may see all sorts of problems on annual flowers by now—discolored leaves from mites or lace bugs, wilting stems from aphids, a whitish gray cast on leaves from powdery mildew. It's late in the season to invest in controls, especially since annuals don't have much longer to live with frost around the corner. Just yank the dead plants, and tidy the damaged ones until they go downhill enough to detract from the landscape.

### BULBS

Rodents such as squirrels, voles, and chipmunks *love* some bulbs (mainly tulips) and will dig them up almost as soon as you plant them. One defense is to top the planted bed with chicken wire. Bulb shoots will poke through but rodents can't tunnel down. If your rodents are smart enough to move over, tunnel down beside the wire, and go in sideways, line the bottom of your planting bed with wire, bend the sides up to the surface, plant and backfill with soil, then top with a sheet of wire to essentially create a chicken-wire box.

At least don't advertise the fact that you've planted tulips by leaving dried skins over the soil. That's a scent attractant.

Better yet, if you have a rodent problem, plant species that they (and deer and rabbits) don't bother. Daffodils and alliums are at the top of that list, but others include fritillaria, dogtooth violet, glory-of-the-snow, *Crocus tommasinianus* ("tommies"), snowdrop, snowflake, Siberian and striped squills, winter aconite, and Spanish bluebells.

Cover bulb-planted pots with chicken wire to keep rodents from digging those over winter.

## LAWNS
Grub damage becomes very noticeable now. If lawn patches are browning and pulling up rootless like pieces of carpet, that's the likely problem. You'll probably even see the fat, white, C-shaped, wormy things in the soil underneath pulled-off dead patches.

Grub preventers that are applied in late May through early July won't do much good now. Quick-acting insecticides are more effective. Look for products that say "grub killer," not "grub preventer" if you take action. An "organic" option is buying predatory nematodes that parasitize the grubs. And a longer-term organic option (if your grubs are the larval stage of the Japanese beetle) is milky spore, a disease that's applied in powder form.

Holes in the lawn usually mean that birds or skunks are digging for grubs. You could just let the animals have at it and patch the holes with a little grass seed. Or if you kill the grubs with an insecticide, the digging eventually will stop as the dead grubs decay.

Some years a black dust can be seen on lawns in late summer. That's likely sooty mold, a fungus whose reproductive spores are black and powdery. Sooty mold isn't harmful to people or pets, won't hurt the lawn in the long run, and will go away when the weather turns colder and/or drier. Outbreaks often follow a rain.

Assorted mushrooms and related fleshy fungi appear in many lawns in late summer. Most of these are harmless and can be kicked over or ignored. They're growing on decaying organic matter in the soil. However, a few are poisonous when eaten, so if you've got small children or pets around who might sample these growths, it's best to bag and remove them as you see them (unless you've positively identified that they're non-poisonous). There are no sprays or treatments to prevent fungal growths from popping up.

■ *Mushrooms are harmless to your lawn, but can be poisonous if eaten.*

■ *Hosta is a favorite salad choice of deer.*

## PERENNIALS & GROUNDCOVERS

If rabbits, deer, or other animals are sampling some of those new perennials, spray the area with a scent repellent. Or erect a temporary fence to protect the enticing young, tender foliage until it's had some time to mature.

Borers are the bane of iris. The adult is a moth that lays eggs on iris leaves in late summer to early fall. The eggs hatch into larvae that tunnel down iris leaves in spring and into the underground rhizomes, potentially killing whole plants. Some gardeners short-circuit the cycle by cutting iris foliage before the borers reach the rhizomes. Otherwise, insecticides control this pest. Watch for notches or pinholes in the leaves and "sawdust" (borer poop) at the base of the plant. Infested rhizomes have small "worms" tunneling in them.

## ROSES

Powdery mildew and blackspot are both common rose diseases in September. It's getting late enough now that roses won't suffer much harm if the diseases defoliate plants a little early. Pick off and clean up diseased leaves if you opt to avoid spraying. Otherwise, continue spraying a fungicide.

## SHRUBS

You might notice some trees sending out strange-looking shoots, almost as if it's a different plant growing out of the existing one. These are called "witches' brooms" or "reversions," which are either genetic mutations or growth that's returning to an original form of the plant. This growth is often more vigorous than the desired plant (especially if the desired plant is a dwarf variety), so prune off these oddities as soon as you see them. (Cuttings from mutations, by the way, are often how breeders develop new and unusual variations of plants.)

Bagworms are full-sized now, and their cone-shaped, hanging sacs are brown, making them far more noticeable than earlier in the summer. Chemical controls don't work very well now. Remove and destroy as many of the bags as you can to get rid of eggs inside that will hatch into next year's bagworms.

## TREES

Baglike webs toward the end of tree branches are fall webworms at work. Caterpillars feed on leaves inside the webbing. This late-season chewing damage is almost harmless and can usually be ignored. If webworms bug you, poke open their bags with a stick to give the birds a caterpillar feast.

Bagworms are visible now on evergreen trees as well as shrubs. Arborvitae is a favorite species. Pick off and destroy bags that you can reach. Sprays don't do much good now, but bagworm feeding for the season is nearly done anyway. Prevent continuing damage by spraying B.t. (*Bacillus thuringiensis*) or an insecticide labeled for bagworm control next June, soon after new bagworms hatch and start to feed again.

If you're controlling woolly adelgids on hemlocks with horticultural oil, now through early October is good timing for the year's second application.

## VINES

Woody vines such as wisteria, trumpet vine, and sometimes climbing hydrangea are notorious for failing to bloom. Most of the time, it's the age of the plant. Wisteria can take five to seven years from planting to bloom for the first time. Other explanations include pruning after flower buds have formed but not yet opened and soil that's out of balance nutritionally, often excessive nitrogen.

Training vines to horizontal positions also can stimulate flowering.

# October

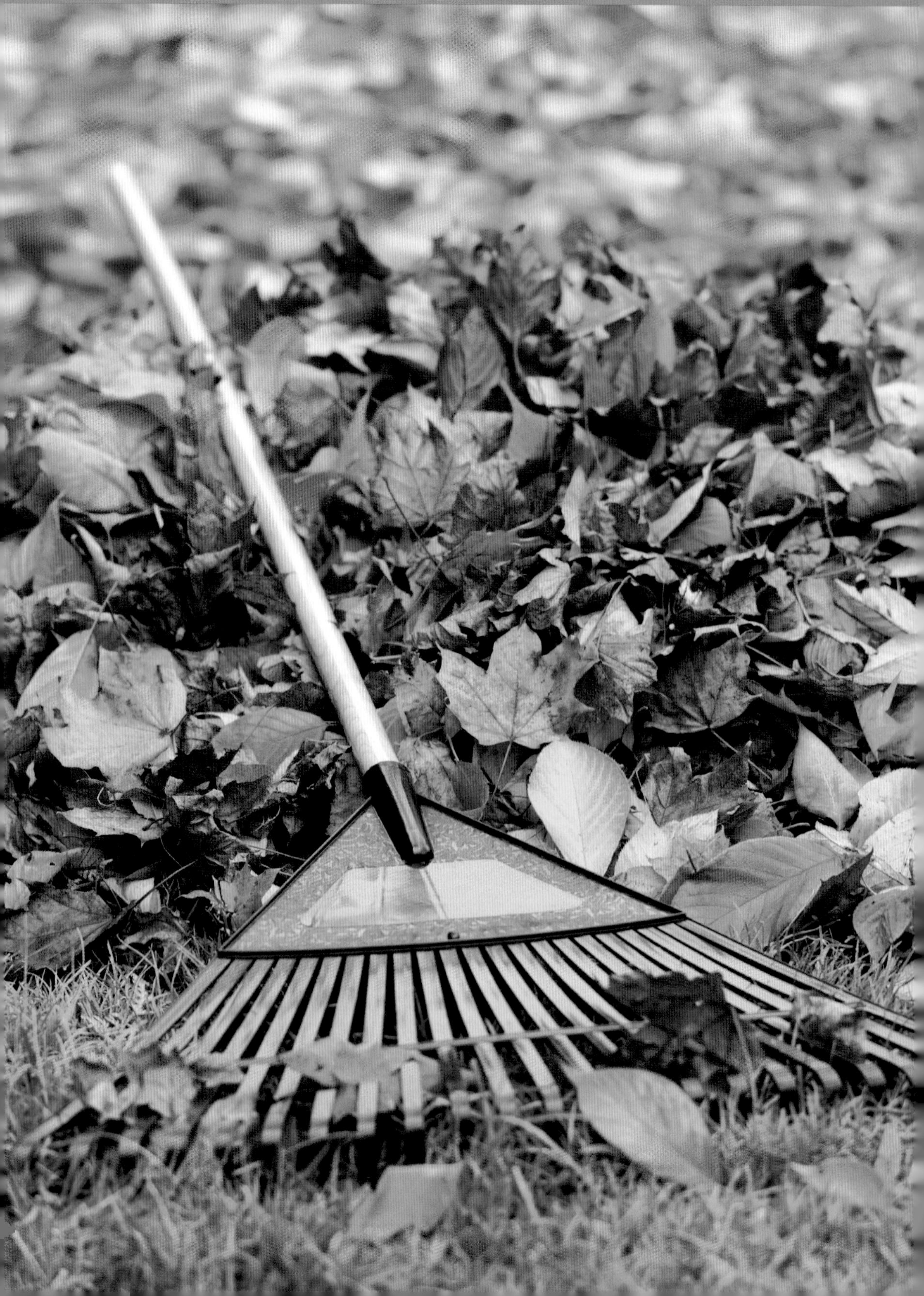

*Although fall officially arrives in late September, October is when it really starts to feel like fall in the Pennsylvania landscape. Daytime highs start dipping into the 50s and 60s, and nights turn noticeably cooler. Frost usually ends the annuals, tropicals, and warm-weather vegetables by early in the month in the cooler, northern part of the state, while even the warmest southeastern corner gets its first killing frost around the third week of October.*

That means a good bit of October's garden work involves preparing for a return of colder weather—moving tropicals back inside, covering annuals to milk them through that first borderline frost, taking cuttings from tender plants before frost zaps them, and so on.

The best part about October in Pennsylvania, though, is the fall foliage. We're in a part of the country that has four distinct seasons, and fall is legendary for its blazing leaf color. Tourists come from afar to see Pennsylvania's forests in their red, orange, and gold fall glory. Maple, sweetgum, blackgum, birch, oak, dogwood, and serviceberry are among the native tree species that are particularly vibrant in autumn.

If you play your cards right, your own yard can be a riot of rich fall color. Many of these same tree species make excellent landscape specimens—even serviceberry, dogwood, and the smaller maples in small yards. What's often overlooked is the many shrubs that turn color. Fothergilla, Virginia sweetspire, summersweet, oakleaf hydrangea, witch hazel, ninebark, viburnum, and blueberries are some of the best choices to make your fall garden go out in a blaze of brilliance instead of a dribble of drabness.

Oh, yeah—don't forget about next spring while you're out ogling the fothergilla. October also is prime time to plant spring-flowering bulbs.

## PLAN

### ALL

Falling leaves, pulled plants, and end-of-season grass clips make a perfect "harvest" for compost. If you don't have a compost bin or three, now's a good time to get busy building. Empty existing bins of finished compost to make way for this year's new "crop" of ingredients. (See "Here's How to Compost," page 177.)

When plant-shopping in October, you'll run into both fresh fall stock as well as spring leftovers. Check the leaves and branches for signs of bug damage or disease. Think twice about those. But if the leaves are just tired and browning, or if the spent flower stems just haven't been snipped, that's not a problem, especially if the price tag says 40 or 50 percent off.

Also assess the roots before buying. Gently slip the plants out of their pots and look for roots that are fleshy and white or creamy, not black and mushy or brown and shriveled. Some circling or matted roots are fine. But if the roots are so badly circled that you can't even get the plant out of the pot, that's more of a drawback. It doesn't mean the plant won't live happily ever after, but it lowers the odds.

Scout for garden-center bargains beyond just plants. You'll likely find discounts on broken or faded bags of potting mix, mulch, fertilizers,

■ *You can compost almost any natural material, but if you're composting at home, don't put any animal products other than eggshells in the compost pile.*

sprays, and more that garden centers would love to unload before winter.

Since all but a few plants have finished blooming by now, you'll have to go by the label photos and descriptions to guide your color considerations. Also pay attention to the size ranges on the label. The #1 landscaping mistake is picking plants that grow too big for the space.

Try your hand at starting a few cuttings from favorite plants, including trees and shrubs, some of which root best from mature tips clipped in early fall. (See September's "Here's How to Start New Plants from Cuttings," page 165.)

### ANNUALS & TROPICALS

Get those tender tropicals back inside if you didn't already do it.

Drape lightweight fabric over still-blooming annuals if an overnight frost is forecast. That might be enough to protect them and keep them going through warm-ups that often follow the first cold snap or two. The *average* first fall frost in the state's coolest regions is September 28, ranging to October 24 in the Philadelphia area. Watch the forecast because each year's dates can happen significantly earlier or later.

How to tell if you had a light frost? Check the impatiens, vinca, or nasturtiums in the morning. Those are three of the most frost-sensitive annuals and will wilt at the first sign of 32 degrees Fahrenheit.

### BULBS

It's possible to have spring bulbs blooming from late January through June in Pennsylvania gardens. The key is choosing a variety of bulb species with differing bloom times. Here's a guide:

**January & February:** Snowdrop, winter aconite, early crocus, *Iris reticulata*

**March:** Spring snowflake, most crocuses, early daffodils, early tulips (*Tulipa kaufmanniana, T. tarda*, and *T. fosteriana* types)

**April:** Glory-of-the-snow, Siberian squill, Grecian windflower, most daffodils, striped squill, hyacinth, midseason tulips, grape hyacinth, spring starflower

## HERE'S HOW

### TO COMPOST

1. Choose an open spot that's ideally out of view and on soil or grass instead of concrete or asphalt.

2. Erect bins that allow piles at least 4 feet tall, wide, and deep. Material options include wood slats, skids, concrete blocks, or wire fencing. Ones that allow airflow are best. Note: bins aren't absolutely necessary; their job is to contain the compost materials and keep them from blowing around.

3. Start adding ingredients. The ideal mix is a blend of high-nitrogen "greens" and high-carbon "browns." A good proportion is three parts browns to one part green. Good browns include shredded paper, fallen leaves, pine needles, sawdust, and wood chips.

Good greens include grass clippings, fresh weeds from the garden (ones that haven't gone to seed), pulled or frost-killed garden plants, and assorted non-meat, non-dairy kitchen waste, such as coffee grounds, banana peels, carrot shavings, salad leftovers, and eggshells.

4. Wet the pile to get it "cooking." Re-wet the pile during unusually hot and dry weather during the growing season.

5. Ways to speed decomposition are to shred or chop materials into small pieces; turn the pile frequently; add worms called "red wigglers;" and add occasional shovelfuls of garden soil or finished compost.

**May:** Spanish bluebells, camassia, crown imperial and most fritillary, late tulips, late daffodils

**June:** Alliums

It helps to map where spring bulbs are going in the yard. Keeping track of them is easy in the spring when the leaves and flowers are up, but after they die back in summer, that's when they tend to get sliced by shovels and planted on top of. Save labels from the bulb packs, and store them with your map.

Bulbs aren't just for full sun. Many species flower well in shady to partly shaded locations, helped by the fact that bulb foliage can take in early-season sunlight before the tree leaves emerge.

Good choices for wooded areas and under trees are snowdrops, Siberian squill, glory-of-the-snow, striped squill, Grecian windflowers, and winter aconite.

## LAWNS

October is still a good month to rehab a crummy lawn or plant a new one. Try to get to it as early in the month as possible to give new grass its best shot of germinating and rooting before the ground freezes.

## PERENNIALS & GROUNDCOVERS

Perennials with colorful foliage give you season-long color beyond the fleeting nature of most perennial flowers. Others have foliage that turns

■ Amsonia hubrichtii *turns golden in fall.*

color in fall. At the top of that list is threadleaf bluestar (*Amsonia hubrichtii*), which has fine foliage that turns bright gold in fall. Another good one is the groundcover leadwort (plumbago), which turns crimson red as its blue flowers fade for the season. And most ornamental grasses take on tan, russet, or burgundy shades in fall in addition to their textural plumes or seedheads.

Deer will eat almost anything rather than starve to death over winter. If you live in deer country and are finishing off fall planting, consider varieties that are low on the deer-favored menu. Good choices include plants that are toxic to mammals (hellebores, cimicifuga, foxglove), plants with fuzzy or silver leaves (lamb's ears, catmint, lavender), and plants with strongly aromatic foliage or stems (anise hyssop, artemisia, and most herbs).

Don't overlook moss as groundcover, especially in wooded areas. Most types prefer shade, acidic soil, coolness, and humidity. To encourage moss, clear the area of weeds, and sprinkle granular sulfur to acidify of the soil (a pH of 5.5 is ideal). Keep the soil damp, and moss may start to appear "magically" from existing spores. Or transplant patches you might find throughout your yard, or buy starter patches of moss that are available online or from some garden centers.

## ROSES

Roses traditionally are planted in their own distinct garden, similar to how vegetables are typically segregated to the vegetable garden. You don't have to limit yourself to that though. If you'd like just a few roses but not necessarily a whole bed of them, tuck a few in a border garden, pair them with color-coordinated perennials, or use them as flowering foundation shrubs along southern or western walls.

## SHRUBS

Trees aren't the only fall-foliage divas. Many shrubs also turn color in fall. Burning bush is the best known. Its leaves turn fire-engine red in fall, but the show is often short, plus it's a species that often seeds invasively into unwanted areas. Some of the best fall-foliage shrubs for landscape use include: fothergilla and panicle hydrangea (gold or gold-red); Virginia sweetspire, crape myrtle, sumac, nandina, and blueberry (blood or bright red); oakleaf hydrangea, viburnum, PJM rhododendron, and ninebark (deep red to burgundy); summersweet, spicebush, winterberry holly, and bottlebrush buckeye (gold); chokeberry (red to red-gold); and spirea 'Ogon' (rusty orange-red).

## TREES

Maples are the best-known of our fall-foliage trees, and that reputation is well-deserved. Almost all of them turn glorious shades of red, gold or red-gold blends in October. Do you have at least one? Match your pick to your yard size—shade tree-sized red maple, sugar maple, or Freeman maple Autumn Blaze® for larger yards, and more compact Japanese maple, trident maple, and paperbark maple for small- to mid-sized yards.

Some other good landscape trees for fall color:

**Over 30 feet:** assorted oaks (gold or red-gold); ginkgo, river birch, and katsura (gold); and blackgum and sweetgum (deep red).

■ *Nandina turns an array of bright fall foliage colors.*

■ *The leaves of the parrotia turn gold to gold red in fall.*

**Under 30 feet:** dogwood (deep red); serviceberry and flowering pear (bright red); stewartia (red gold blend); and witch hazel, parrotia, and American fringe tree (gold).

If you're tempted to cut down a large, attractive tree to make room for new construction or to reduce shade, think twice. Large, mature trees are in demand for large properties, and you may be able to sell it. Call local arborists and nurseries. Professionals have tree spades that allow large trees to be dug and moved. Fall is a good season for moves.

## VINES
A few vines also end the season aglow with brilliantly colored foliage. Two of the showiest are Boston ivy (*Parthenocissus tricuspidata*) and Virginia creeper (*P. quinquefolia*).

## PLANT

### ALL
How late is too late to plant in the fall? Cornell University researched that question by planting sets of the same plants progressively later in the season, then assessing their performance over several years. The conclusion is fall-planted plants survive best when they have at least six weeks of root growth before the soil temperature in the root zone drops below 40 degrees Fahrenheit. In Pennsylvania, that translates into an ideal-planting cutoff of late October in the warmer parts of the state and mid-October in the cooler parts.

This finding doesn't mean you can't plant later. Landscapers will tell you they've planted trees and shrubs in winter and had them survive. The takeaway is that your odds of success start to decrease once you plant past mid- to late October, if Cornell's findings are correct.

Check those plant guarantees before buying. Garden centers often guarantee most plants for a year, but year-end closeouts usually are *not* guaranteed. Guarantees also sometimes don't cover fall-planted species that would rather not face a cold winter right off the bat. These might include crape myrtle, cherry laurel, nandina, Southern magnolia, camellia, variegated or English holly, some roses, mahonia, false holly, cedar, sweetbox, skimmia, and vitex.

October is a good month to prepare new beds, even if you don't plant until next spring. The soil is reasonably dry and workable, and temperatures are more pleasant than trying to dig a bed in July. Prepare the soil, mulch the ground for winter, and walk away. (See April's "Here's How to Turn Lawn into a New Garden Bed," page 69.)

### ANNUALS & TROPICALS
Pot up a few annuals now, such as impatiens, geraniums, coleus, and wax begonias, and a few tender herbs, such as rosemary and basil, for a sunny windowsill. These may not make it all winter, but you can milk a few extra weeks out

■ *To dig a new garden, remove existing grass or vegetation, then loosen the top 10-12 inches of soil.*

of them. Before they go too far downhill, take cuttings of saved tender plants to grow under lights through winter. (See September's "Here's How to Start New Plants from Cuttings," page 165.)

It's not too late to fill beds left vacant by yanked annuals with a fresh planting of cool-season pansies, violas, snapdragons, or ornamental cabbage and kale. Pansies and violas often survive winter to bloom again in spring, but the cabbage and kale die back when seriously cold snaps appear. Remove those when that happens because they'll

rot and start to smell like, well, rotting cabbage. Let the snapdragons alone to see if they resprout in spring before yanking them.

## BULBS

This is the year's best month to plant spring bulbs. The cooling soil triggers bulbs to put down new roots and start the biological clock ticking. Once each variety's genetic chilling time is met, and the weather signals the status of a new season, leaf shoots and then flower shoots will emerge. (See "Here's How to Plant Spring-Flowering Bulbs," below.)

### HERE'S HOW

#### TO PLANT SPRING-FLOWERING BULBS

1. Loosen the soil to 10 to 12 inches deep, and incorporate 1 to 2 inches of compost, chopped leaves, mushroom soil, or similar organic matter. The resulting slightly raised beds are ideal for the excellent drainage that bulbs need. Fertilizer is not needed.

2. Set the bulbs on top of the raked ground where you want to plant them. When the layout and spacing looks good, go back and plant them one by one at a depth that's 2½ to 3 times as deep as the bulb's height. Space small bulbs 3 to 4 inches apart, larger ones 6 to 8 inches apart. The pointy end goes up.

3. Smooth and soak the ground after planting to settle the soil around the bulbs. Top the soil with 1 to 2 inches of bark mulch or chopped leaves. (Note: Include the mulch layer into your planting depth.)

4. If you've had trouble with rodents eating your bulbs, cover the soil surface with a sheet of chicken wire, then mulch over top of it.

**Option for planting bulbs in blocks or rows:** Dig a trench to the correct depth, set the bulbs in the bottom, then cover the whole planting with the excavated soil instead of inserting them one by one.

October's also a good time to pot up and begin the process of "forcing bulbs" so they'll bloom inside over winter. (See "Here's How to Force Bulbs for Inside Blooms," below.) The easiest bulbs to force are daffodils and early bloomers such as crocus, scilla, *Iris reticulata*, grape hyacinths, Dutch hyacinths, and species tulips.

Outdoor bulb plantings look best in clusters or masses as opposed to being lined up single file. You'll also get far more impact by planting in larger amounts, especially when you're using smaller bulbs. A handful of daffodil bulbs doesn't go very far across the whole front of a house.

Plant spring bulbs in a few of your winter-durable pots (foam, plastic, concrete). They can stay out all winter. No special care or protection is needed. Just make sure the pots have drainage holes in the bottom. Set the pots where they'll get winter snow and rain.

It's time to pot and water amaryllis bulbs if you want them to flower in December. Depending on the variety, they'll need six to ten weeks of lead time before blooming. (See December's "Here's How to Grow Amaryllis Indoors," page 206.)

## LAWNS

Grass-seed germination slows as the soil and air temperature drop. Try to get your seeding done by mid-October. If it's warm and stays warm, or if you're in the state's warmer regions, the end of October is still usually okay. Beyond that, seed germination goes downhill, and young grass is increasingly at risk of dying off if a cold spell comes along.

## HERE'S HOW

### TO FORCE BULBS FOR BLOOM INSIDE

Here's the regimen recommended by New Jersey bulb-forcer extraordinaire Art Wolk, winner of numerous Philadelphia Flower Show ribbons and author of *Bulb Forcing*:

1. Fill a mid-sized plastic pot, with drainage holes in the bottom, two-thirds to three-quarters full with moistened, lightweight potting mix.

2. Press bulbs into the mix so tightly that they touch. Add more potting mix to the top, then press down to firm it.

3. Begin chilling bulbs anytime from October through early November to trigger the blooming process. Most bulbs need soil temperatures at or below 48 degrees Fahrenheit for eight to thirteen weeks. The earliest bloomers, such as crocus, scilla, and *Iris reticulata*, need the least amount of chill time. Later blooming varieties, such as Dutch hyacinths and mid- to late-season daffodils and tulips, need the most.

4. One chilling option is burying the potted bulbs in an 18-inch-deep pit outside—covered with 2 feet of leaves to keep the ground from freezing. (Use a stick to mark your site.) Another option is storing the pots in a leaf-insulated cardboard box in an unheated garage or in a window well. A refrigerator (ideally one you're not using to store food) also works well.

5. When the appropriate chill time passes, retrieve the pot, hose it off, and move inside to a cool, bright location (55 to 68 degrees Fahrenheit is ideal). Water when the soil starts to go dry, and turn the pots a quarter of a turn each day so the flowers grow uniformly. Flowers should emerge in one to five weeks.

## PERENNIALS, GROUNDCOVERS, ROSES, SHRUBS, TREES & VINES

All of these can still be planted in October—the sooner the better to give young roots the most time to establish before the ground freezes. Soak the ground well after planting to settle the soil, and cover the ground with mulch to retain moisture and keep the ground warm as long as possible.

All can be transplanted this month, although most roses would rather move in early spring—if at all. Again, the sooner you can get to it this month, the better.

Make a note to check fall-planted plants throughout this first winter. Alternate freezing and thawing of the soil can push poorly rooted plants partially out of the ground (called "heaving"). That exposes the top of the rootball to root-killing, drying winter winds. If that happens, tamp the rootballs back down immediately and water.

## CARE

### ALL

Non-gardeners look at all of the falling leaves as a raking nightmare. Gardeners view them as free mulch! Leaves are useful in lots of ways around the yard:

1. Let them sit underneath trees and shrubs as winter insulation and free nutrients as they break down. If you don't like the look, top them with a light coating of wood or bark mulch in the spring.

2. Chop or shred them as mulch over garden beds. Save a few bags for use next growing season.

3. Mix them with spent garden plants, organic kitchen waste, and season-ending grass clips to make the perfect compost blend.

4. Chop them and incorporate them into the soil while preparing a new bed. They'll be mostly broken down by planting time next spring.

5. Run over light layers on the lawn. The fragments break down quickly and add nutrients and organic matter to the soil.

The seeds of most plants are mature by now, meaning it's a good time to collect seeds to save and start next season. One caveat: some plants (many annual flowers in particular) are hybrid varieties and may not produce the same new plants as this year's, if they produce at all. This seed is free for the taking, and you have nothing to lose (except your time) by giving it a shot. (See "Here's How to Save Your Own Seed," page 183.)

Some of the best candidates for seed-saving are marigold, zinnia, larkspur, cosmos, ageratum, browallia, celosia, cleome, impatiens, nicotiana, petunia, portulaca, salvia, snapdragon, sunflower, gloriosa daisy, and ornamental pepper.

October is a good month to mulch. It's actually easier than summer when full-grown plants are in the way. After frost-killed annuals are yanked and browned-out perennials are cut back, you'll have easier access to open ground.

If you have space, store a pile of extra mulch in case you need it over winter, such as if a heavy rain washes a gully or you decide to plant a live Christmas tree. Mulch may not be available from garden centers and vendors over winter.

Continue to pull weeds from outdoor planting beds to prevent them from going to seed and causing problems next year.

To avoid drainage problems on the property, clean falling leaves from roof gutters. Or install a gutter cover to keep leaves out.

Deal with poison ivy before birds carry its berries away to start even more plants. Pull up small plants with a long plastic bag covering your hand and lower arm. Once the plant is out of the ground, pull the plastic bag off your arm over the plant as you hold it, effectively turning the bag inside out to avoid skin contact with the plant's allergenic oil. Discard in the trash. Spray larger vines with a weed-killer labeled for poison-ivy control. Note: even dead poison-ivy vines have active oil that can cause a skin allergy. And fumes from burning poison ivy can get into your lungs and cause an even *worse* and potentially fatal reaction.

## HERE'S HOW
## TO SAVE YOUR OWN SEED

1. Select seedheads or pods that are browned and mature. Pinch with your fingers to release the seed.

2. Air-dry the seed for at least several days if it hasn't already dried on the plant.

3. Place the seed in marked envelopes so you'll know what's what.

4. Store the saved seeds in a cool, dry place until you're ready to start them. In a jar in a refrigerator is perfect.

## ANNUALS & TROPICALS

Bag and discard bug- or disease-infested frost-killed plants to minimize the risk of infesting next year's plants. Clean but dead plants can go in the compost pile.

Don't till the ground after you yank your dead annuals to "get it ready" for next year. Research shows that tilling increases weed problems, speeds the loss of organic matter, and can harm soil composition—especially when tilling wet soil or pulverizing it. Top the bed with chopped leaves or a light layer of bark mulch, and let it alone.

Some tender plants can survive winter in a sort of "hibernation" state in a freeze-free indoor location, such as an unheated sunroom or basement. Pot the plants (if they're not already in pots), and cut back the foliage to about a foot before stowing. Let them die back or go semi-dormant. There's no need to fertilize. Add just a tad of water every few weeks to keep the roots from drying without pushing new growth. Next May, move the plants into light, begin watering and fertilizing, and in a few weeks you should have a reborn survivor. Good candidates include bougainvillea, mandevilla, some euphorbias, fuchsia, gardenia, tropical hibiscus, princess flower (*Tibouchina*), alternanthera, and many salvias.

Self-sowing annuals leave behind lots of seeds in the soil. If you like that idea, disturb the soil as little as possible. To discourage it, clip off seedheads before they mature and/or remove plants still sporting seedheads. Annuals that frequently self-sow are snapdragon, browallia, calendula, bachelor's button, cleome, larkspur, cosmos, California poppy, impatiens, toadflax, sweet alyssum, money plant, four-o'-clock, bells of Ireland, forget-me-not, corn poppy, nigella, portulaca, and Johnny-jump-up.

Cuttings that you took last month probably have roots by now. Pot them in small containers filled with potting mix. Grow under bright light indoors, and keep damp the mix consistently damp.

## BULBS

Tender bulbs, tubers, and corms, such as dahlia, gladiola, caladium, elephant ear, tuberous begonia, canna, and calla, need to be dug and stored before a hard frost. (See "Here's How to Overwinter Tender Bulbs," page 184.)

The American Dahlia Society also says that dahlia tubers can be overwintered wrapped individually in plastic wrap. The ADS suggests first treating the dug tubers with a fungicide.

A common bulb fake-out is when grape hyacinths send up leaf shoots in fall. This is normal; that's just what this species does. No need to mulch it or cut it. The flowers will happen next spring.

## HERE'S HOW

### TO OVERWINTER TENDER BULBS

1. Just before or immediately after fall's first light frost browns the foliage, cut the plants of tender bulbs to near ground level.

2. Dig the bulbs and let them air-dry for a week or so. Brush off soil, and discard any that are injured or diseased.

3. Store the dried bulbs in a container of ever-so-slightly moistened peat moss, sawdust, or perlite in a cool, dry, rodent-free spot, ideally with temperatures in the 40s. You can store the whole clump now and separate them later, or separate them now.

4. Check the growing media throughout winter, and remoisten if it's dry or if you're seeing signs of bulbs shriveling. If it's too wet and bulbs are rotting, immediately remove them, toss the rotting ones, and store the rest in new, drier medium. The goal is to walk that fine line between too dry and too wet.

Sternbergia foliage emerges with its flowers in October, and will remain all winter, even though the flowers die. It will eventually die back in spring.

## LAWNS

Mow fallen leaves and leave on the lawn, assuming you're cutting often enough that the leaf quantity isn't so great as to clog the mower or leave behind so many leaf fragments that it smothers the grass. Small leaf fragments are beneficial, but you should see mostly grass when you're done.

For large quantities of leaves that you can't shred with the mower, rake or blow them off. Leaf coverings shut off sunlight to the grass. That's not a big issue over winter when grass is dormant, but it *is* detrimental in the shoulder seasons of fall and spring when grass needs light to grow. Matted leaves also trap moisture, increasing the odds of fungal disease. After removing excess leaves, run them through a chipper-shredder (if you've got one) or recycle them elsewhere in the yard instead of paying to have them hauled away (see "Care, All," page 182).

Be careful you don't rip up grass seedlings when you're trying to remove leaves from a newly seeded lawn. Rake gently or opt for a blower.

As grass growth slows and ultimately stops for the season, cut it short for the last time. A 2-inch height dries quicker and heads off snow mold and other cool-season, moisture-related fungal diseases. You could step down in two phases. Lower the height a notch on the next-to-last cut, then lower it to 2 inches for the final cut.

October is an excellent month to add lime to the lawn, but only if a soil test indicates this alkaline mineral is needed. Lime isn't routinely needed. If your lawn's soil already is neutral or alkaline, liming is a waste and maybe even counterproductive.

It's not too late to kill broadleaf weeds in the lawn. Like other plants, they're attempting to store carbohydrates in their roots for winter, which makes herbicide sprays more effective than in slow-growth periods.

## PERENNIALS & GROUNDCOVERS

You don't have to cut every last perennial to the ground as soon as it browns. For one thing, birds appreciate the seeds and nest-building material. For another, many perennials, mums in particular, benefit from the insulation given by dead top growth that collapses around the roots. Go ahead

Cut back perennials when they're fully dormant—in the winter or early spring. Throw your clippings in the compost pile.

and get rid of foliage that's diseased or bug-ridden, but it's okay to save at least some of your perennial foliage for cutting at winter's end.

Don't cut back perennials that are still green. Some perennials stay green all winter and add to the winter landscape, such as hellebores, dianthus, creeping sedum, yucca, and many coralbells. You can always snip off browned-out leaves as they happen later, or cut back or neaten these still-green perennials at winter's end.

Some plants that stay green in winter aren't true perennials at all but are biennials because their life cycle spans two seasons. Examples are foxglove, sweet William, hollyhock, forget-me-not, and poppy. These grow vegetation the first season, then send up flower spikes or stems that drop seed to produce the next generation. Then they die. For first-season biennials, let them alone. If it's their second fall (when they bloomed), they'll die with frost, and you can pull them. Next spring, seedlings of new first-year plants should emerge.

One exception to the leave-the-leaves advice is to rake dense leaf droppings out of the evergreen groundcover beds. Thick layer of leaves can shade and smother plantings of vinca, pachysandra, creeping sedum, foamflowers, and other low-growers that hold their leaves all or most of winter.

Ornamental grasses can be cut when they brown if you like (the plants won't care), but many gardeners enjoy the texture, the sound, and motion of them swaying in the wind, and their winter interest. Let them stand all winter, and cut them back to a stub in early spring before new growth occurs. Or cut them anytime over winter when they get brittle enough that blades start blowing around the yard.

## ROSES

Rose trees, also known as rose standards, aren't hardy in most of Pennsylvania. They involve multiple aboveground grafts, so they are usually more vulnerable to weather extremes. For winter protection, place the entire plant, pot and all, horizontally in a trough, and cover it with mulch. An alternative is to store the potted plant in a cold frame or cool shelter where the temperature never drops much below freezing.

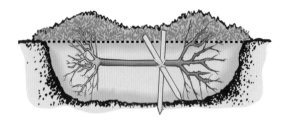

■ *This rose standard has been buried in a trench for winter.*

Many winter-hardy roses will continue blooming through the season's first light frost. Drape a lightweight fabric over your plants if a freeze is forecast to help nurse buds and blooms through the cold snap, possibly buying several more weeks of color.

Continue to gather and discard any fallen diseased foliage.

## SHRUBS

Hold off on the pruning, other than removing dead or injured branches. Early fall is a bad time to prune for two key reasons: You'll stimulate new growth that won't harden off in time before cold weather, opening it to dieback, and your plants (especially evergreens) will look chopped all winter until new growth starts in spring. Shrubs need to prepare now for winter dormancy. Let them do it. If you really can't wait until end of winter, at least wait until the leaves drop, signaling dormancy has begun.

Another issue with fall pruning is that you might cut off flower buds that already have formed on spring-blooming flowering shrubs. If you prune shrubs such as forsythia, lilac, weigela, and azaleas now, you'll cut off next year's flowers.

To prevent pest eggs or disease spores from overwintering and causing problems again next year, clean up fallen leaves and fruits underneath shrubs that ran into bug or disease issues. Put them in the trash, not the compost.

Cut a few berry-laden branches for indoor display in a vase. Beautyberry, viburnum, and winterberry holly are three good choices, coupled with silvery plumes of ornamental grass and other gleanings from the fall landscape.

## TREES

As with shrubs, hold off on the pruning for the reasons listed under Shrubs at left. Trees that "bleed" sap in spring are best pruned during winter, but most others are best pruned at the end of winter or in spring after they've flowered. Limit tree pruning now to removing dead or injured branches.

Wrap or get fencing around tree trunks—especially young ones. That protects not only against rodent gnawing (which picks up once green vegetation dies off), but fall is when deer use trees to rub their antlers.

## VINES

Pull out frost-killed annual vines, such as black-eyed Susan vine, purple hyacinth beans, cardinal climbers, moonflowers, and morning glory. Woody vines, except for spring-blooming clematis, can be cut back anytime after the leaves drop through next spring before new growth resumes.

Don't yank passion vines when frost browns their stems. These are borderline-hardy at best in most of Pennsylvania, but in a warm winter or warm microclimate, they may survive. It's okay to cut back dead stems over winter, but let the roots alone and well mulched until early to mid-June. If you don't see new shoots emerging by then, your passion vine didn't make it.

Purple hyacinth bean seeds are easy to save. Pick pods with plump seeds inside, let them dry, and store in a cool, dry spot until planting out again next spring. On the other hand, morning glory reseeds profusely, so remove plants and their mature seedheads to limit excess seeding. If you weren't deadheading spent flowers throughout the season, you're probably going to have new morning glories anyway for years to come.

## WATER

### ALL

It's still not time to put away the hose yet. Water demand may be headed downward, but those newly planted plants need to be kept consistently damp until the ground freezes. That might not happen until late November to early December.

Be vigilant to keep new evergreens damp because their foliage continues to lose moisture throughout winter. You'll lower your first-winter survival odds if you let their roots head into frozen-soil time already dry.

Be *especially* vigilant with the new broadleaf evergreens, which lose even more moisture than needled evergreens in winter. And be *extra-especially* vigilant to keep the first-fall moisture levels up with new broadleaf evergreens that are marginally hardy in parts of Pennsylvania, such as cherry and "schip" laurels, sweetbox, hardy camellia, osmanthus, some hollies, skimmia, and nandina.

Check moisture regularly in the root zone with your finger because the ground may be drier than the top growth indicates. Soak as needed to keep the soil damp all around and to the bottom of rootballs.

## ANNUALS & TROPICALS
Soak annuals once a week if they're still blooming, and rain is scarce. Continue checking pots and baskets daily. Watering frequency may be a little less, but don't assume you're done just because it's getting cooler.

## BULBS
If rain isn't happening, soak newly planted bulb beds once a week. Their fledgling roots don't need a lot of water, but they appreciate some dampness. Existing bulb beds are usually fine without fall watering.

## LAWNS
Sprinkle newly planted lawns up to two to three times a week to keep the soil damp in the top 4 to 6 inches. You want those young roots to penetrate as quickly and as deeply as possible before the ground freezes.

Existing lawns seldom need water in the fall, so long as they're green and growing. If it's an unusually dry fall and grass is wilting or browning, water once or twice a week to prevent lawn roots from going into freeze season already dry.

## PERENNIALS, GROUNDCOVERS & VINES
Continue watering new perennials, ornamental grasses, and groundcovers about twice a week if

it's dry. Established ones should be fine, unless it's unusually dry, in which case a weekly soaking is helpful.

Also keep an eye on moisture-loving perennials (astilbe, ligularia, lobelia, and so forth), and water those if they're showing signs of wilting or browning.

## ROSES
Continue soaking new roses two to three times a week if it's not raining. Established ones should be fine with a once-a-week soaking.

## SHRUBS & TREES
Continue soaking new trees and shrubs two to three times a week if it's dry. Pay particular attention to keeping new evergreens damp until the ground freezes, especially broadleaf ones.

Established trees and shrubs are usually fine without water in fall, unless it's been unusually dry, in which case a deep, weekly soaking is helpful.

## FERTILIZE

### ALL
Not everyone agrees whether fall is a good time to fertilize most landscape plants. One school says fall fertilizer—especially when applied in late fall—is the best time of year. Another school says that fall fertilizing—especially when it's done toward early fall—is a bad idea because it can stimulate new growth that won't harden in time for winter. The agreement overlap seems to be late fall, so if your plants need the nutrition, apply it toward the end of October in the state's cooler regions and in early to mid-November in the warmer regions.

### ANNUALS & TROPICALS
Keep fertilizing still-blooming annuals and tropicals growing in pots and baskets once a week with a half-strength flower fertilizer. There's no need to fertilize ones growing in the ground.

### BULBS
New bulbs don't need fertilizer (their nutrition is built in), but existing bulb beds benefit from a fall scattering of an organic or slow-acting fertilizer

formulated for bulbs. Apply it this month if you didn't already do it in September. Water it in well.

## LAWNS

Most turfgrass researchers now recommend against so-called "winterizer" fertilizers that are high in phosphorus and potassium, the last two numbers on the fertilizer label. Current thinking is that most soils already have sufficient phosphorus for growing grass, and that, as it is in spring, nitrogen (the first number on the label) is still the most important nutrient.

So far as timing, if you're only fertilizing twice a year, May and again in late September or October are the two recommended times.

If you're following a three- or four-treatment regimen, you have applied an early-fall dose in September, and then will apply the last treatment in mid- to late November. That means nothing goes on this month.

## ROSES

It's past time to fertilize the roses now. Pick it back up again next spring.

## PERENNIALS, GROUNDCOVERS, SHRUBS & TREES

An early-spring application of a granular, slow-acting fertilizer is usually enough for all of these, if even that is needed. More fertilizer in the fall usually is not needed, unless growth is lagging or symptoms of nutrient deficiency are showing up. In that case, first test the soil to nail down exactly

what's needed and in what amount. Good timing for a fall application is late October in cooler regions of the state and early to mid November in warmer regions.

## PROBLEM-SOLVE

### ALL

This month's hue and cry is about bugs getting into the house. As winter approaches, some bugs that overwinter as adults seek warm shelter, and our houses look very inviting. The big three are boxelder bugs, lady beetles, and stink bugs. These hard-shelled bugs are more nuisance than threat, but when their numbers swell, they can become a vexing nuisance.

The best solution to the bug-in-the-house problem is to look for holes and openings that let them in. Look for cracks around windows, openings between walls and pipes, and holes in screens. Seal or caulk openings. Some people try killing congregating bugs on outside walls with a soapy spray or quick-kill insecticide, and others use vacuum cleaners, hand picking, and light traps to deal with populations inside. A drawback of indoor insecticides is that you're left with lots of dead bug bodies in places where you might not be able to remove them (such as inside walls).

### ANNUALS & TROPICALS

There's no sense treating any bug or disease problems on plants that are going to die with the soon-to-arrive frost. For tender plants you're

■ *Boxelder bugs*

■ *Lady beetle*

■ *Stink bug*

potting to take inside, hose them off and/or spray with insecticide to avoid taking any aphids, whiteflies, spider mites, and such inside. Eggs could be under the leaves even if you don't see any active bugs.

## BULBS

Topping bulb beds with chicken wire is one way to discourage tunneling rodents. (See September, "Problem-Solve, Bulbs," page 171 for more on that.) Another option is working about 10 percent sharp gravel, ground slate pieces, or similar jaggy minerals into the soil before planting. This adds enough jagged texture to make it uncomfortable on rodents trying to tunnel in it.

If you're forcing bulbs for indoor bloom, one thing that can go wrong is not giving them enough chill time outside before taking them in. They won't bloom if that's the case. Don't store them too warm inside; 70 degrees Fahrenheit is too warm while leaf and flower shoots are forming. Use plant lights if you don't have a bright window.

## LAWNS

Grubs gradually stop feeding on lawn roots and start digging deeper as they prepare for winter underground. Although the feeding tapers off until they head toward the surface again next spring, the damage they did in August and September is still apparent in October. You'll have a hard time killing them now (and next spring, for that matter), so you're better off reseeding the dead grass, and making note to consider applying a grub preventer next June to disrupt a repeat of this year's damage.

You may notice a stiff, yellowish grass sticking up above the rest of the darker green lawn grass. This isn't technically a grass but is a weedy grass lookalike called nutsedge. Broadleaf weed-killers don't kill it. If you have just a few patches, pull it up. Loosen the soil so you get the little bulblet underground. For widespread trouble, pros have access to two herbicides that control nutsedge without harming turfgrass.

## PERENNIALS & GROUNDCOVERS

Voles start to become threats to plant roots again as aboveground vegetation dies back. Cages around susceptible plants (foamflowers, dianthus, hosta, lilies, and foamybells) can help, or set out cage traps or snap traps baited with peanut butter.

## ROSES

Deer may start to nibble on rose canes and any foliage that remains on shrubs prior to a hard freeze. If you're seeing damage, spray a deer repellent or cage the roses for winter.

## SHRUBS

No or few berries on your hollies? That's a common dilemma, especially with the deciduous winterberry holly, which is grown primarily for its brilliant fall fruits. One explanation is that you have male plants. Only female hollies produce fruits. A second problem could be that you have females but no male nearby to pollinate the flowers. You'll also need the right male to pollinate the right female – specifically, ones that overlap flowering time. Winterberry hollies are fairly picky about this one. Other explanations can include lack of pollinating insects; plants are too young to produce fruits; you cut off the pollinated, forming berries with a summer pruning, or plants have been seriously stressed, such as by extreme heat or a bug or disease problem.

## TREES

Some needled evergreens shed their older needles this time of year. White pines are particularly notorious for dropping copious quantities of these needles, which turn yellow before dropping, making many homeowners think the tree is dying. Assuming the needles are falling only from the inner section of the branches and not the tips, this is normal. There's no need to do anything. These needles make excellent mulch, by the way.

Hurricanes, heavy thunderstorms, and the occasional tornado aren't strangers to Pennsylvania. Even healthy, established specimens can blow over or lose limbs in these rough weather events. One way to reduce damage risk at least a little is by thinning out overly dense branching. That means a more open structure that lets wind blow through better, reducing the "sail effect" of a dense canopy. Wait until after trees lose their leaves to do thinning.

November

*Oh, back to cold. Even the warmest parts of Pennsylvania almost always record a killing frost by early November, officially ending another growing season. Most years, that's already happened sometime in October.*

The arrival of frosty nights turns the tender annuals into brown blobs, causes leaves to drop from the deciduous trees and shrubs, and sends perennials into winter dormancy. By late November or early December, the soil's root zone has dropped to below 40 degrees Fahrenheit, slowing root growth to a crawl, if even that. Above ground, expect to see the season's first few wet snows, or worse yet for plants, branch-snapping freezing rain or an ice storm.

The first visit of winterish weather doesn't mean it's time to run inside and close the blinds. Warm reprieves often follow the first cold burst or two, making for a fair number of pleasant days to get outside and finish some of the cleanup that October's fast demise didn't allow. The landscape is far from bare.

Some tree and shrub species (parrotia, stewartia, fothergilla, and Virginia sweetspire, for example) are late to turn color and long to hold onto their colorful leaves. They still look pretty good into Thanksgiving some years. Fruiting species also are key late-fall pleasures, in particular winterberry holly, viburnum, crabapple, dogwood, bayberry, nandina, juniper, and the spectacular BB-sized metallic purple fruits of beautyberry.

November is a time when colorful-leafed evergreens really come into their own, ranging from woody species such as golden falsecypress and blue juniper to evergreen (or almost evergreen) perennials such as golden creeping sedum, variegated liriope, and lime-green coralbells.

Take advantage of those last few warm days to get a good, long look at what's left of this season's landscape color. Anytime now, things could turn all white.

## PLAN

### ALL

Studies show that family outdoor-life patterns change every seven years or so as children grow, pets come and go, and adults develop new interests. How are you, or will you, be using the yard? Is anything changing that's affecting your landscaping game plan?

As plant work ends, turn to yard jobs that can be done in cool or cold weather. Repair the fence or pergola. Re-do the patio. Dig that new bed. Waterproof or paint the arbors and trellises. Put in a new walkway. Terrace a slope with landscape timbers.

Cut a few berry-laden branches to display inside in a vase. Or scavenge the landscape for fall and winter outdoor decorating materials. (See December's "Here's How to Use Landscape Plants for Holiday Decorating," page 208.)

Organize your plant tags, labels, seed packets, notes, photos, and other memory-joggers to help you keep track of what you've been doing and planting where.

### ANNUALS & TROPICALS

Make note of annuals that did well this year in case you want to grow them again next year. Also note what fizzled so you don't make *that* mistake again.

■ *After frost is a good time to turn to hardscaping projects, such as building a new brick walk.*

### HERE'S HOW

#### TO PROTECT WOODY PLANTS OVER WINTER

1. Wrap the trunks of young trees and shrubs with paper or plastic tree wrap to head off animal chewing damage.

2. Erect a deer fence or start spraying deer-favorite plants with a repellent if these four-legged plant-eating machines are nearby.

3. Protect foundation evergreens and shrubs from snow and ice sliding off the roof by erecting a burlap protector or a plywood lean-to over them.

4. Make sure the soil of newly planted plants is damp as the ground freezes.

5. An option is to spray antidesiccant on broadleaf evergreens in windy areas to discourage cold, winter winds from browning the leaf margins. Reapply twice more over winter on above 40-degree Fahrenheit days to get maximum benefit. (Note: Some research claims these have no to minimal effect.)

Many tropicals are adept at cleaning dust, bacteria, mold spores, and even chemical toxins out of indoor air. NASA tests of nineteen species found that philodendron, spider plant, and golden pothos were the best at removing formaldehyde. Gerbera daisies and potted mums were tops for removing benzene. Other plants that filter one or more indoor-air pollutants: English ivy, peace lily, Chinese evergreen, bamboo or reed palm, snake plant, red-edged dracaena, cornstalk dracaena (corn plant), Janet Craig dracaena, Warneck dracaena, and weeping fig. To clean the air in an average 1,800-square-foot house, NASA suggests fifteen to eighteen plants in 6- to 8-inch pots.

### BULBS

Check the garage, basement, mud room, or tool shed for bulbs you may have bought but forgot to plant. It's still okay to plant them.

Potted bulb kits start showing up in stores this month. Amaryllis and paperwhite narcissus don't need chilling and can go right in a pot with moistened potting mix. Look for hyacinths listed as "pre-chilled" if you plan to grow them in a vase inside.

## LAWNS

Grass tends to be what we plant unless we think of something better. "Something better" might include a bigger patio, wider foundation beds, new gardens, or a swimming pool or water feature. Think about reallocating some of your lawn. On the other hand, maybe you'd like to return some areas to grass if that use makes more sense.

## PERENNIALS & GROUNDCOVERS

Not all perennials and groundcovers die back with frost. Vinca, pachysandra, ivy, and European ginger are four creeping groundcovers that hold their foliage all year long. Dianthus, liriope, coralbells, foamflowers, some ferns, and creeping sedums are perennials that look good through most winters. Hellebores even bloom toward the end of winter. All of these are candidates for a winter garden or just for winter interest throughout the yard.

Consider a plant's salt tolerance when you're planting along roads, driveways, and sidewalks where salt-laden ice-melters can splash or run off into the beds. Salty soil can stunt growth and leave plants more vulnerable to drought injury. Salt-tolerant perennials

■ *Don't limit your groundcover garden to short plants. Any fast-growing plant that takes the place of grass can be considered a groundcover.*

### TO PREPARE YOUR LANDSCAPE FOR WINTER

1. Clean off and take inside anything at risk of winter breakage, including terra-cotta pots, ceramic statuary, gazing globes, ornaments, and fountains.

2. Take in anything not needed now that might weather, rust and/or blow away, such as lawn furniture, metal plant supports, stakes, flags, and so on.

3. Blow excess leaves out of evergreen groundcover beds and off the lawn if there are too many to mow or chop into fragments. Otherwise, let leaves in place to mulch bare soil or insulate trees and shrubs.

4. Double-check to make sure you've brought in all tender plants you want to keep.

5. Either now or at winter's end, remove dead foliage from perennials as frost knocks it back. Compost clean foliage; bag and toss diseased and bug-ridden leaves.

6. Weatherproof, paint, or stain wooden trellises, arbors, pergolas, fences, and decks.

7. As the ground freezes and watering ends for the year, disconnect, drain, and take in hoses. Also drain and shut off sprinkler systems so they don't freeze and break. Disconnect, drain, and invert or store rain barrels.

8. Once you're done with the shovel, pruners, mower, and other outside tools, clean and sharpen them for next season.

9. Keep the birdbath water from freezing. Put baths in the sun, floating a table tennis ball to keep a small area open during a mild freeze. Or invest in a birdbath heater.

and groundcovers include armeria, artemisia, baptisia, beebalm, black-eyed Susan, butterfly weed, campanula, candytuft, columbine, coralbells, coreopsis, daylily, dianthus, most ornamental grasses, gaillardia, globe thistle, hardy geranium, hardy ice plant, hosta, iris, lavender, liriope, New York aster, Russian sage, sea holly, scabiosa, sedum, stokesia, veronica, yarrow, and yucca.

## ROSES

Rose flowers might be history, but their red, yellow, or orange pea-sized fruits—their "hips"—offer fall and winter interest. Some varieties produce more and showier hips than others, primarily rugosa types and other heirloom or antique varieties. Consider adding a few of these if you're missing this fall interest for roses.

## SHRUBS

Evergreen shrubs planted along roads, driveways, and sidewalks are at risk from salt-laden ice-melter splashings or runoff. A telltale sign of salt damage is browning that occurs only on the road or driveway side. But even leaf-dropping shrubs can suffer from excess salt in the soil. Some of the more salt-tolerant shrub species include arrowwood viburnum, bayberry, beautyberry, butterfly bush, forsythia, hydrangea, inkberry holly, juniper, lilac, mugo pine, potentilla, red chokeberry, St. Johnswort, sumac, summersweet, spirea, and snowberry.

Several low shrubs are useful as groundcover plants where you want an evergreen over winter. Spreading juniper and bird's nest spruce are the most commonly used, but the spreading English yew 'Repandens' is a good choice in a shadier spot. Spreading euonymus and some cotoneaster are low broadleaf evergreen options. In Zones 6 and 7, consider sweetbox, spreading Japanese plum yew, and box honeysuckle.

## TREES

Avoid salt-sensitive species near roads, driveways, and sidewalks. Lean toward salt-tolerant ones. Choices include American fringe tree, American holly, Austrian pine, baldcypress, blackgum, Bosnian pine, Colorado blue spruce, cryptomeria, elm, ginkgo, goldenrain, hawthorn, hedge maple, honeylocust, Japanese black pine, Japanese tree lilac, Japanese white pine, Kentucky coffeetree,

larch, sweetbay magnolia, sweetgum, white oak, willow, witch hazel, and zelkova.

If you're planning to buy a live balled-and-burlapped evergreen to use as a Christmas tree this year, dig the hole now. The ground might be frozen later when you're ready to plant. Fill the hole with mulch, and cover with a tarp or board. Store the saved soil in the garage or other spot where it won't freeze.

## PLANT

### ALL

Now that the time window is fast shrinking until frozen-soil time, the success rate of new plantings is somewhat less. Broadleaf evergreens, which lose the most moisture over winter, and species that are borderline hardy to your area are most at risk from late-season plantings. That doesn't mean you can't give a bargain purchase a try. Top the soil with 2 or 3 inches of insulating mulch after planting, and keep your new plant watered until the ground freezes to maximize your odds.

One risk of late-planted plants is that the rootballs are prone to being shoved up and partially out of the ground during alternate freezes and thaws, which can dry out the roots. Check that regularly over winter, and tamp any "heaved" rootballs back into the ground immediately.

Some gardeners nurse fall bargains through winter above ground instead of planting them. They'll set still-potted plants in larger containers that are insulated with leaves, bubble wrap, or foam packing peanuts and topped with a couple of inches of bark mulch. The plants are then stored over winter in a protected spot, such as along a heated wall, in a walled-in courtyard, in a cold frame, or in an unheated garage. Check regularly to make sure the soil stays damp.

### ANNUALS & TROPICALS

As long as the ground remains unfrozen, it's okay to plant pansies and violas.

### BULBS

You can also plant year-end bulb bargains or ones you bought and forgot to plant. The potentially complicating factor now is that the ground can be frozen. Hack through the frozen crust if you must to plant, or watch for an afternoon thaw to get them in. The sooner you plant them now, the better.

Leftover hardy spring bulbs can be planted in winter-durable pots if you can't get them into the ground.

Amaryllis and paperwhite narcissus bulbs will root and bloom without a chill period. Just pot them and water them to start growth. Paperwhites usually bloom within four to six weeks of potting, while amaryllis take more like six to ten weeks. Start some every few weeks to spread out the flowering over winter. Toss paperwhites when they're done, but save amaryllis for future years. (See December's "Here's How to Grow Amaryllis Indoors," page 206.)

Hyacinth bulbs also can be forced for inside bloom over winter. Look for prechilled ones, and set them in a bulb vase that's narrow toward the top. That vase style holds the bulb at the right height and lets the roots dip into the water below.

■ *Hyacinths can be forced to bloom indoors, usually using a "hyacinth glass."*

## LAWNS

Wait until early next spring to renovate a lagging lawn or to overseed a thin one. However, if you're stuck with bare soil, such as in a new home construction, even a sparse stand of young grass with a light layer of straw is better than bare soil, mud, and winter gullies. Another option in this case is securing straw mats that are embedded with seed.

## PERENNIALS, GROUNDCOVERS, SHRUBS, TREES & VINES

Get these in the ground quickly, or if the ground is already frozen, use the insulated-pot option outlined under "Plant, All," page 194.

## ROSES

Are there no rosehips on your roses? It could be you've got varieties that just aren't prone to hip production no matter what you do. But for ones that *are* good hip-producers (especially rugosas and other heirloom types), knock off the pruning at the end of August to allow hips to set.

## CARE

### ALL

Add those fallen leaves, year-end grass clippings, frost-killed garden plants, and other non-diseased, non-bug-ridden yard waste to the compost pile. Now's a good time to start a pile or two. (See October's "Here's How To Compost," page 177.)

If you've been cooking compost all season, empty the bins and use the finished compost to top vegetable gardens, annual beds, or the lawn. Or incorporate it into new beds you're digging to break up the lousy clay. Emptying now clears the space for all of the incoming compost ingredients.

Mulch might start blowing around this month now that wind-sheltering plants have dropped their leaves and debris-catching perennials have been cut back. Hose down exposed mulch if it's dry, or erect a burlap barrier to block prevailing gusts. Some types blow around more than others; cocoa bean shells and bark mini-nuggets carry away more than shredded hardwood or bark mulch.

If the mulch is thin, top it off. Even if the ground has frozen, mulch helps keep it frozen to limit the alternate freezing and thawing that causes young rootballs to "heave" out of the ground.

Continue to mow moderate leaf layers on the lawn. Blow or rake dense leaf covers that threaten to smother lawns or evergreen groundcover plantings. Keep checking the gutters to make sure falling leaves aren't blocking them.

Continue to dig or yank weeds.

## ANNUALS & TROPICALS

Pull dead annuals as frost kills them. Some go down at the first hint of 32 degrees Fahrenheit (yeah, *you*, vinca and zinnia), while others hang in there until a really hard freeze comes along. Don't yank annuals that are still blooming or that have live foliage, such as sweet alyssum, blue salvia, dusty miller, snapdragon, and pansies. These might give you color into December or even survive winter altogether.

## BULBS

Dig, clean, dry, and store tender bulbs such as dahlias, cannas, callas, gladioli, and elephant ears if you haven't already done that. They'll rot in frozen ground.

Fall-blooming hardy bulbs, such as sternbergia and colchicum, have finished blooming by now. Remove collapsed vegetation if you want, or let it decompose over winter.

Cover bulb beds with about 2 inches of bark mulch or chopped leaves if that's not already done. The purpose isn't to protect the bulbs from the cold but to minimize the alternating freezes and thaws that can push new bulbs closer to the surface. If you see bulbs working their way above ground, replant them at the correct depth.

## LAWNS

Gradually reduce the mowing height so the final cut of the season takes the grass down to about 2 inches.

Once you're done mowing for the year, drain any remaining fuel from your lawn mower; change the oil, fuel filter, and spark plug; clean the deck; and sharpen the blades.

■ *Replace the air filter in your lawn mower when you're done mowing for the year.*

November is a good month to add lime, if the lawn needs it. A soil test will tell you.

## PERENNIALS & GROUNDCOVERS

Go ahead and cut frost-killed perennial foliage to (or almost to) the ground if you're a neatnik. If you're leaving some seedheads for the winter birds and nest-building materials for the mammals, postpone cleanup until winter's end. A few perennials—such as mums, borderline-hardy species, and anything planted late in the season—appreciate retaining the collapsed, dead foliage as insulation over winter.

Cut and remove any perennial and groundcover foliage that's diseased or bug-ridden to reduce overwintering bugs or bug eggs and disease spores.

Don't cut perennials or groundcovers that are still green. Some, such as coralbells, hellebores, and dianthus, are evergreen and need just a neatening cut at winter's end, if even that.

## ROSES

There are two schools of thought on late-fall pruning of hybrid teas, floribundas, and grandifloras. Some say let them alone, and prune once at winter's end; others say remove about one-third of the ends to minimize whipping around and breakage over winter, then finish the job next spring. Take your pick. If you're pruning in fall, November or December is fine.

After a hard frost, winterize roses by insulating the base of the plants (about 6 to 10 inches) with soil, bark mulch, chopped leaves, pine needles, wood chips, shredded bark, or prunings from overly long needled evergreens. Remember, this needs to be pulled back at winter's end.

In the state's coldest regions, climbing roses need winter protection. Unfasten the canes from their support, and gather them in a bundle on the ground. Cover with soil, straw, or chopped leaves. Or let the canes up, and mound soil or mulch up 6 to 10 inches around the base as with hybrid teas, grandifloras, and floribundas.

Check the tags that are wired on bushes. Loosen them if any are strangling the growing canes.

## SHRUBS
Set up winter protection for shrubs that need it. That includes broadleaf evergreens in windy sites (especially borderline cold-hardy ones), and shrubs in the line of snow or ice sliding off roofs. Erect burlap screens to block prevailing winds, or snow fencing if drifting snow is a problem. Erect small lean-tos over top of shrubs in danger of being flattened by snow slides.

◼ *Mound extra mulch around rose crowns for winter protection. Remove it in spring.*

Once the leaves are off the shrubs and trees, it's *okay* to prune summer-flowering shrubs and some evergreens. It's *not* ideal timing though. Some gardeners are eager to knock back overgrown plants, or are concerned that big shrubs are more prone to blowing over in winter. The flip side to cutting now is that evergreens might look chopped all winter until new growth resumes, and shrubs that suffer winter damage will need further pruning (maybe more than you would've wanted) at winter's end. Definitely do *not* prune spring-flowering shrubs now, or you'll cut off the flower buds that already have formed. (See April's "Pruning Timing of Shrubs, Trees, & Vines," page 80.)

It's fine to prune off any dead or damaged shrub wood and fine to do some light, selective pruning to harvest cuttings for decorating purposes.

## TREES
Most pruning considerations that apply to shrubs apply to trees. One job that can be done anytime over the dormant season with leaf-dropping trees is thinning out excess branching. Some argue it's best to do it early in winter to lessen the odds of storm damage, while others say it's better to wait and do a single, winter-ending thinning, shaping, and cleanup of any winter damage.

It's fine to prune off dead or damaged limbs and to harvest boughs or berried clusters from hollies or needled evergreens to use in holiday decorating.

## VINES
Fasten the stems of large woody vines such as kiwi, wisteria, and climbing hydrangea securely to their supports. New shoots probably aren't secured. Check ties on this season's growth to be sure they aren't too tight.

## WATER

### ALL
Don't be too quick to put away the hose. Fall can be sneaky-dry. It's important to keep newly planted plants consistently damp until the ground freezes—especially new broadleaf evergreens. You don't want bone-dry roots headed into winter.

## ANNUALS & TROPICALS

Keep the soil damp around potted annuals and tropicals that you've moved inside for winter. But also be aware that water demand drops in winter, leading to potential overwatering, the leading killer of indoor plants. Water these plants when the soil goes dry and the pot's weight becomes noticeably lighter. Once or twice a week may do it. Avoid soggy soil.

## BULBS

In an unusually dry fall, you may need to soak newly planted bulb beds once or twice so the soil isn't going into winter dry. Again, no sogginess!

If you're forcing bulbs outside and have buried pots where rain can reach them, you'll likely not need to water those, except in an unusually dry fall. Forced bulb pots stored out of rain's reach will need moisture help from you. Check weekly and add just enough water to keep the soil damp but never soggy.

Do your first check of tender bulbs (cannas, gladioli, dahlia) stored inside for winter. If you're seeing any early signs of rot, replace the storage medium with dry sawdust, sphagnum moss, or shredded newspaper in ventilated bags, and look for a cooler, drier storage location.

## LAWNS

Established lawns are fine without water now, except possibly in very dry autumns in which the grass is wilting or browning. Continue to water newly planted lawns so the top 4 to 6 inches of soil stays damp. Knock it off once the ground freezes.

## PERENNIALS, GROUNDCOVERS, ROSES, SHRUBS, TREES & VINES

Established plantings should be fine as temperatures cool and normal rainfall happens. Just watch for very dry autumns in which you might need to do a deep soaking or two so roots don't go into winter dry.

Give special attention to anything you've planted this season, especially earlier in the fall. The roots haven't gone out into the soil much yet and might need moisture aid from you and your hose. New plantings benefit from soakings about twice a week when rain isn't doing the deed, right up until the ground freezes. Use your finger as a dampness gauge.

## FERTILIZE

### ALL

Landscape plants are going dormant or at least slowing growth this month, so fertilizing isn't a high priority. The need for fast-acting, water-soluble fertilizers, if you're even using those anywhere other than on potted plants, especially drops now. If anything needs a shot of long-acting fertilizer, apply it before the ground freezes. After that, there's a risk that a cold rain on top of frozen ground will wash fertilizer away.

### ANNUALS & TROPICALS

Annuals and tropicals need little fertilizer inside during the slow-growth winter period. A small amount of slow-acting granular fertilizer scratched into the potting mix will likely suffice. Overfeeding can encourage leggy growth and a buildup of salts. (See "Problem-Solve, Annuals & Tropicals," page 200.) Resume a dilute fertilizer in late winter as growth picks up again.

### BULBS

Scatter a granular bulb fertilizer over existing, unfrozen bulb beds if you didn't do it earlier in the fall. New ones don't need it. Neither do bulbs you're forcing in pots or paperwhites and hyacinths you're growing for indoor winter display.

If you're planning to save amaryllis for future years, fertilize it once a month with a balanced granular fertilizer, starting now and continuing throughout winter.

### LAWNS

If you're fertilizing once a year and missed the ideal late-summer time frame, it's fine to do the application now before the ground freezes. The same is true for twice-a-year feeders. If you missed the fall-application window of late September or October, do it now. May is your other prime application time.

If you're following a three- or four-treatment regimen, mid- to late November is prime time for your final application of the year.

Current advice is to use a fertilizer rich in nitrogen—the same kind that's recommended for earlier applications and not a high-phosphorus,

*Most lawn fertilizers now have no phosphorus, the middle number on the three-digit nutrient formula.*

high-potassium "winterizer." The best game plan, though, is to have your soil tested so you know exactly what nutrients your particular lawn needs and in what amounts.

## PERENNIALS & GROUNDCOVERS

An annual springtime scattering of a long-acting, granular fertilizer is usually enough for these. November is good timing for topping perennial beds with a light layer of compost since the bins can be cleared out for incoming ingredients and plants have been cut back for winter.

## ROSES

Outdoor roses don't need fertilizer now, but if you're using manure, November is a good time to apply it, before the ground freezes.

Indoor miniature roses benefit from either a granular rose fertilizer scattered over the soil surface once a month, or a diluted liquid rose fertilizer every three or four weeks.

## SHRUBS, TREES & VINES

Most woody plants get the nutrition they need from reasonably healthy soil, especially if you're fertilizing the lawn or garden beds nearby. Low-care-leaning gardeners can usually get away with no supplemental fertilizer, opting to watch for signs of poor growth and fertilizing only if a soil test indicates a nutrition deficiency.

Others opt to fertilize young plants (or all landscape plants) with an annual application of a balanced, granular, slow-acting fertilizer. That can be applied either in late fall before the ground freezes or early in the spring before growth resumes.

Soil tests also will tell you if you need to alter the soil's acidity level (pH). Either lime (alkaline) or sulfur (acidic) can be applied this month.

## PROBLEM-SOLVE

### ALL

Deer trouble shifts into high gear as fall arrives. For one thing, the natural food supply dwindles at leaf drop, making your yard full of azaleas, yews, and tender young arborvitae look newly appetizing. For another, increasing development has encroached on deer territory, compressing these stomachs-on-four-legs into hungry pockets near housing subdivisions. Deer often aren't as naturally fearful of humans as they once were.

One line of anti-deer action is using scent or taste repellents. Numerous commercial products are available as well as homemade concoctions using assorted ingredients, such as rotten eggs, hot pepper sauce, bloodmeal, ammonia, urine, human hair, or bars of soap. Repellents need to be reapplied regularly, especially after rain and snow. They're most effective when different ones are rotated so deer don't get used to any particular one.

If repellents fail to discourage deer, try spot-fencing or caging the plants being targeted. Deer (at least the smarter ones) generally won't jump into narrower confined areas from which they might not escape. For widespread, ongoing problems, the best solution is to do what public gardens in deer country do—erect a tall fence around the entire perimeter, 8 to 10 feet tall. Electric fencing is another option.

Bag and dispose of fallen or cut-off foliage of bug- and disease-ridden plants to limit overwintering bug eggs and disease spores. It's fine to leave behind clean foliage or to compost it.

Stink bugs, lady beetles, and boxelder bugs are still trying to get inside your house for winter—or they may be there already. (See October, "Problem-Solve, All," page 188 for options.)

## ANNUALS & TROPICALS

Salt damage is second to overwatering as the cause of indoor-plant death. Symptoms are browning leaf edges and wilting, much like lack of water. Excess salt typically comes from softened tap water and excess chemical fertilizers. Solve this problem by repotting in fresh potting mix, and/or rinsing out salt by copious watering with unsoftened water. Limit future salt buildup by using unsoftened water and fertilizing with organic or slow-release plant foods.

Aphids, mites, whiteflies, and scale are possible indoor-plant bug problems in this less-than-ideal growing environment. Minimize plant stress with adequate light, humidity, and soil moisture. Inspect for bug eggs, and wipe them off with an alcohol-dampened soft rag. Or knock back infestations with bug-killers labeled for indoor pest control.

## BULBS

Place a sheet of chicken wire over bulb beds and top with mulch if you're seeing holes in the ground or other signs of rodent exploration.

Bulbs being grown indoors will lean and bloom toward the window side where the light is. Rotate pots a quarter of a turn daily (or as often as you can remember) for more even growth.

## LAWNS

Dog urine is an ongoing lawn issue for pet owners. The urine load burns grass and creates brown patches, usually surrounded by dark green perimeters where the nitrogen is enough to help instead of burn. Altering a dog's diet doesn't solve this. Either soak the urine spots with water immediately, or train your dog to "go potty" in a

selected area, such as mulched spot or stone bed—maybe adorned with a faux fire hydrant.

Nimblewill is a grass imposter that blends in with turfgrass during the growing season. But when frost arrives, this dense, wiry, upright, grassy weed turns brown and becomes very apparent. It's a problem on three fronts: It's perennial (comes back year after year); it overruns desirable grass; and it's difficult to control without harming the "good" grass. Early infestations can be pulled or sprayed with a selective herbicide. Crabgrass preventers head off new infestations. But for large, existing nimblewill patches, you're probably looking at killing off everything, and reseeding.

Crabgrass browns with frost, making its wiry, groundhugging habit readily noticeable. The seed has matured and dropped, so rather than trying to remove spent crabgrass now, consider applying a crabgrass preventer at the end of winter.

Herbicide sprays don't work very well in cold weather. You can still dig out weeds in the lawn, but you'll get better results from sprays next spring.

■ *To fix dog spots, first flush the soil by watering the area twice a day for three or four days. Then, dig out the top 2 inches of soil and replace it with new garden soil. Next, sprinkle grass seed on top and water the grass seed twice daily until it sprouts.*

*Nimblewill*

## PERENNIALS & GROUNDCOVERS

Cage still-green perennials and groundcovers to guard against rabbit, rodent, and deer damage. These stand out now after so much else has dropped leaves or gone dormant. Or start applying repellents and set out traps.

## ROSES

If miniature roses growing indoors are getting leggy or losing vigor, set them under fluorescent lights for fourteen to sixteen hours a day. Plant lights with a sunlight-like spectrum are even better.

Check indoor miniature roses for pale, stippling leaves, a sign of spider mites. A weekly shower or wash-off under the kitchen faucet might head off outbreaks. Otherwise, consider an insecticide labeled for indoor use against mites.

## SHRUBS

Besides deer, rodents such as mice, voles, and chipmunks often chew on the roots and base of shrubs. Rabbits also may "girdle" stems—chew the bark in a band the whole way around, usually killing the plant. Tender, young transplants are particular targets. Wrap or cage trunks, up as high as 3 to 4 feet to account for snow accumulation that can elevate varmints' reach. Or get traps and repellents in place if you're going that route.

## TREES

Install plastic wraps and/or cages around trees, especially young ones. They face the same animal threats as shrubs.

Not all "evergreens" are evergreen. Larch, dawn redwood, and baldcypress are examples of needled trees (technically "conifers") that turn color in fall and then drop their needles for winter before growing a new set the following spring. Lesson: Don't be alarmed if your larch, dawn redwood, or baldcypress is now, well, bald. It's normal.

## TROUBLESHOOTING CHECKLIST FOR TREES

Now that trees have dropped their leaves, use this checklist from the International Society for Arboriculture to look for signs of trouble:

- Are there large, dead branches in the tree or "hangers" that might drop?

- Does the tree have cavities or rotten wood along the trunk or in major branches?

- Are mushrooms present at the base of the tree?

- Are there cracks or splits in the trunk or where branches are attached?

- Has the trunk started leaning?

- Has the tree or its root zone been injured by nearby work, such as repairing sidewalks, digging trenches, or soil compaction from construction vehicles?

- Did the leaves this year drop or turn color early or grow smaller than usual?

- Has the tree been chopped, topped, or otherwise poorly pruned?

This list doesn't note all signs of impending doom, but they're worth investigating further. An arborist or experienced tree expert can help evaluate for early signs of trouble. Pay particular attention to big trees that have targets nearby if they should fail (people, cars, your house).

December

*The calendar declares it's officially winter late this month, but Pennsylvania weather is usually on the cold, windy, and, sometimes, white side from Thanksgiving on. December can surprise with a few light-jacket days, but more often than not, nights are consistently below freezing, and snow can come at any time.*

Consider it a bonus anytime you can get outside this month to finish fall's jobs. If you're *really* on the ball and luck out with a few nice December days, you might even get a jump on next season with some dormant-season pruning or bed-edging.

For the most part, conditions are more comfortable inside. There you can feed your gardening habit by cleaning the lawn mower, getting the seed-starting station ready, and starting the annual winter ritual of planning how to make next season's garden the best yet.

Sure, you'll have to trade your petunias for poinsettias and your amsonia for amaryllis, but hey, they're all colorful and involve soil. If indoor potted plants aren't quite cutting it for you, December is an excellent month to visit a public conservatory. Pennsylvania is fortunate to have two of the world's best—the Phipps Conservatory in Pittsburgh and nearly 4 acres of gardens under glass at Longwood Gardens in Kennett Square, Chester County. Both of these venues add special displays for December. Longwood has *spectacular* outdoor light and fountain displays in addition to its indoor plant displays, combining to make December its most-visited month.

Even though there's always something to do if you're a gardener, this month marks the beginning of the gardening "off-season." That's just as well because December usually turns out to be one of our most hectic months anyway.

## PLAN

### ALL

Assess your yard's warmer microclimates, those little pockets where you can get away with borderline-hardy plants. Examples, a walled-in courtyard, south- or west-facing masonry walls that absorb heat in winter, and east-facing sides dense evergreens that block cold, northwesterly winds. Spots where the snow melts first are usually sunniest. Spots where the snow piles up are wind tunnels.

Plants that look good in winter can be grouped to make an attractive winter garden out a favorite window. Options include colorful evergreens, shrubs with winter fruits, trees with great bark, and evergreen perennials and groundcovers. Hardscaping features (walls, benches, arbors, boulders) add to the winter effect.

Make your holiday gift list (for yourself and others). Gardeners are always running out of something and make easy gift recipients. How about new pruners to replace the ones you lost under the bushes somewhere? Maybe give a friend a new book (this one?), or how about those elegant

■ *Take inventory of your remaining seeds to determine which new ones you'll need to buy for next season.*

plant markers you never seem to buy? Maybe add the gift that only a gardener can appreciate—a big sack of composted manure. Of course, there's always a garden-center gift card.

Adding plants to your landscape that aren't readily available at the garden center? Ask your favorite locations if they can order them. Most garden centers take special-orders at no extra charge. They work on spring orders over winter, so now's good timing.

Re-make lost or fading plant labels, and add ones for new plants that you planted this season. Save money by making your own homemade labels out of cut-up vinyl blinds or bleach bottles. Use a China marker or wax pencil for the words.

Note the expiration date on pesticide containers and safely dispose of any that are beyond their useful life.

### ANNUALS & TROPICALS

Inventory leftover seeds, and make a list of what you'll need. Next year's seed catalogs start showing up online and in the mail this month.

Jot down this year's first and last frost dates to help you plan future planting times.

The top-selling winter potted plant, the poinsettia, has an undeserved reputation for being poisonous. Eating the leaves might make you nauseous, and some people get a skin rash from the milky sap, but you won't die from eating a bud, as some think.

### BULBS

Garden centers and mass retailers have an increasing array of already-flowering amaryllis, paperwhites, hyacinths, freesias, and other bulbs for those who didn't start their own last month.

### LAWNS

If you didn't do it last month, get your mower ready for next season. Replace the spark plug. Clean gunk and grass clippings from the engine, fan, and undercarriage. Clean and sharpen the blade. Replace the fuel filter, and clean or replace the air filter. Change the oil. Drain old gas, and add fresh gas right before cutting for the first time next spring.

■ *Clean out your lawn mower so it will be ready for next spring.*

## SHRUBS

Those low-heat, low-voltage LED strings of lights pose no harm to woody plants that you're decorating. Just be careful you don't snap branches wrapping them, or fall off the ladder and break one of your own limbs. Secure the lights loosely, not tightly, and remove the lights after the holidays so they don't grow into the bark. Arbors, trellises, and similar garden structures also look nice when lit.

## TREES

If you're planning to buy a live balled-and-burlapped evergreen as a Christmas tree and plant it outside afterward, prepare the hole early this month. The ground may be frozen later. Fill the hole with mulch and cover with a tarp or board. Store the saved soil where it won't freeze when you need it.

## PLANT

### ALL

It's not the ideal time to plant outside, but if you somehow find yourself with a plant in a pot, go ahead and get it in the ground. Water well, and cover the soil with mulch. If the ground is frozen, look for a warm spot along a wall where you can bury it, pot and all, until spring. Or set the potted plant in a larger container insulated with leaves, foam packing peanuts, or mulch. Place it in a protected spot over winter, such as along a heated wall, in a walled-in courtyard, in a cold frame, or in an unheated garage. Check regularly to make sure the soil stays damp.

### ANNUALS & TROPICALS

You'll find way more than just poinsettias for indoor December color these days. The palette includes a raft of choices, from traditional Christmas cactus and cyclamen to tropical kalanchoe and red anthurium to budget-priced orchids. Growers are even producing white-flowering euphorbias (an outdoor annual) and forcing hellebores (a perennial) into bloom for holiday sales.

Don't overlook the houseplant section. These plants add indoor interest now, then can go outside in summer. Some, such as palms, croton, snake plant, and dracaena, make good pot centerpieces.

### HERE'S HOW

#### TO PLANT A LIVE CHRISTMAS TREE

1.  Dig the hole in advance before the ground freezes. Store the excavated soil where it won't freeze, and fill the hole with mulch. Cover with a board or tarp.

2.  Acclimate the balled-and-burlapped tree for three or four days in an unheated garage or porch before setting it up inside.

3.  Set the rootball in a large container where it won't tip or leak water. Keep the ball and its burlap wrapping consistently damp. Pour water over it regularly.

4.  After Christmas, set the tree back into unheated garage or porch for a few days to gradually acclimate it to the cold.

5.  Plant as you would in the growing season. Water well, and cover the soil with 3 to 4 inches of the mulch that filled the hole earlier. Stake if you're planting in a windy area.

When selecting indoor plants, look for stocky leaves and no signs of wilting, bugs, disease, or browning around the leaf edges. A good sign is plants that are pushing new leaf buds. Match the plant's light and other care needs to the conditions you have at home.

Be careful taking your new plants home. Most of these are tropicals that really don't like anything under 50 degrees Fahrenheit. On cold days, the seller should place live plants in a plastic or paper sleeve before you leave the store. Keep the plant in the car with you with the heater on and *not* in the cold trunk.

Check cuttings to see if rooting has happened. Transfer these as needed to larger, individual pots, give them a light dose of a slow-acting fertilizer, and set them under lights.

## BULBS

Start some amaryllis, paperwhite, and hyacinth bulbs every few weeks for continuing bloom through the winter. Watch for sale prices right after Christmas.

Get those just-found spring bulbs in the ground right away. Don't wait until spring or next fall. They'll dry out and die by then. December-planted spring bulbs still have a decent chance of growing, although probably shorter in size and later to bloom.

Stores still may be selling deeply discounted spring bulbs. If the bulbs are firm and not

## HERE'S HOW

### TO GROW AMARYLLIS INDOORS

1. Set the bulb, pointed end up, in a pot nearly filled with potting mix. Plant so that half of the bulb is above the soil line.

2. Firm potting mix around the bulb and water. Move pot to a cool, bright location (60 to 65 degrees Fahrenheit is ideal) and keep the soil damp but never soggy.

3. Turn the pot regularly as the leaves and then the flower stalks emerge. This produces more even, balanced growth. Blooms should occur in six to ten weeks.

4. After flowers fade, cut off the flower stakes at the base. Fertilize every two to four weeks with a diluted bulb or flower fertilizer, continue watering when the soil dries, and continue displaying in a bright location.

5. After danger of frost, gradually acclimate the plant to the outside over seven to ten days, then either continue to grow it as a potted plant outside or plant it in the ground over summer. Fertilize monthly.

6. Stop watering and fertilizing in late August. In early September, move pot back inside and let foliage die back. Or dig up the bulb and store it bare and dry. Cut off foliage when it browns.

7. After about eight weeks, repot in fresh potting mix and begin watering again for a new cycle.

rotting or drying out, the odds are good. One drawback is you may run into frozen soil. Hack through the frozen crust if you must, or wait for an afternoon thaw. Or plant your bargains in winter-resistant pots.

## LAWNS

See November, "Plant, Lawns," page 195 for what to do if you're stuck with bare soil at the end of new construction. Otherwise, deal with patching, reseeding, or overseeding lawns in early spring.

## SHRUBS

Small evergreens will grow in pots for the patio, deck, pool, and this time of year, decorated with lights flanking the front door. Choices available in December include arborvitae, upright boxwood, narrow juniper, dwarf Hinoki cypress, dwarf blue spruce, sheared upright yew, and the mite-prone dwarf Alberta spruce. Use foam, heavy plastic, or otherwise winter-tough pots, and keep these damp all winter when the soil isn't frozen. When they get too big for the pot, either repot into a larger size or plant them in the ground.

## CARE

### ALL

If weather permits, bed-edging is a job that can be done in December. The ground is typically soft and cuts easily. Yank winter weeds while you're out there.

Get out the chipper-shredder and chop up that pile of yard prunings, cut-down ornamental grass, and other yard waste that can be composted or used as mulch.

If you use ice-melting products, switch to more plant-friendly types this winter instead of the more inexpensive rock salt. Salt runoff can lead to excess sodium in lawns and planted beds, which can translate into browning of leaf tips and edges, especially in hot, dry weather. Alternatives are calcium magnesium acetate, calcium chloride, or potassium chloride. Or just scrape off ice or put down sand or wood ashes to improve traction.

Thin mulch can still be topped off this month. Bare soil really should have *some* mulch over winter to prevent erosion.

Just because poison ivy has dropped its leaves doesn't mean you can pull it off trees bare-handed. The oil in the stems is still very much active all year long, and you can get a skin rash by handling leafless poison ivy plants even in December.

## ANNUALS & TROPICALS

Yank ornamental kale and cabbage and any other remaining annuals that finally bit the dust.

Inside, maximize light to your potted annuals and tropicals by keeping the windows clean. Dust and grime cut down a surprising amount of light. Or move leggy plants to sunnier windows or closer to the windows, if you can. Don't let them touch cold glass, though, or you might freeze the tender leaf tissue.

Avoid life-shine products. They might make houseplants look clean and shiny, but they clog plant pores. A better (and less expensive) idea is to use lukewarm water and a sponge to clean dust off leaves.

The obligatory poinsettia does best in bright but indirect light, at temperatures between 55 to 70 degrees Fahrenheit. Make sure water can drain out the bottom. Either poke holes in the foil and set a saucer underneath, or transfer the pot

■ *Every couple of months, use a damp cloth to gently remove dust and dirt from houseplant leaves.*

into a slightly larger decorative pot. Water when the pot is noticeably lighter and the top inch or so of the soil is dry. There's no need to fertilize unless you plan to keep the poinsettia for another year, and even then, fertilizing isn't needed until early spring.

## BULBS

Regularly turn indoor bulb pots (amaryllis, paperwhites, hyacinth) so light is distributed evenly. That prevents the growth and the blooms from leaning to the window side.

Check tender bulbs (cannas, gladioli, dahlia, and so forth) that you're overwintering inside. If you're seeing any early signs of rot, replace the storage medium with dry sawdust, sphagnum moss, or

shredded newspaper in ventilated bags, and look for a cooler, drier storage location. On the other hand, if the medium and storage location is so dry that bulbs are shrinking and shriveling, lightly dampen the medium.

## LAWNS

Turfgrass is dormant now so no care needed. Just stay off of frozen grass as much as you can to avoid crushing the crowns. Walking on wet but unfrozen lawns also compacts the soil.

## PERENNIALS & GROUNDCOVERS

If weather permits, continue cleaning frost-killed foliage out of the perennial beds. If the birds have finished off the seedpods you left behind, go ahead and cut those plants.

## HERE'S HOW

### TO USE LANDSCAPE PLANTS FOR HOLIDAY DECORATING

1. Evergreen prunings make ideal boughs, garlands, roping, and winter arrangements. Take branches you'd remove anyway, such as crossing or overly long branches. Cut back to joints, where smaller branches attach to longer ones or to the trunk.

2. Use landscape gatherings to make a winter pot or window box display. Look for berried twigs of winterberry, holly, crabapple, and beautyberry; branch prunings from evergreen trees and shrubs; bright red stems of redtwig dogwood; rose hips; lime green fruits of osage orange; dried flower heads of red celosia and red amaranthus; and seedheads from ornamental grasses.

3. Use dried flowers such as hydrangea, baby's breath, strawflower, allium, or celosia to add a natural look and a spot of color to Christmas trees and evergreen arrangements.

■ *You can create beautiful holiday decorations using just a few different evergreens of differing colors and leaf textures.*

4. Spray-paint pine cones, seedheads, sweetgum balls, and assorted nuts and display them in baskets or use as accents on larger decorations.

5. Use grapevines, clematis vines, or willow branches to make wreathes.

6. Make a "kissing ball" (an alternative to mistletoe) out of boxwood cuttings stuck into a potato and decorated with ribbon and berries.

## ROSES

If you didn't do it last month, winterize hybrid tea, floribunda, and grandiflora roses by insulating the base of the plants (about 6 to 10 inches up) with soil, bark mulch, chopped leaves, pine needles, wood chips, or shredded bark. Do the same with climbing roses in the state's coldest regions.

As for pruning, some say to let your roses alone now, and prune them at winter's end. Others say roses should be cut back enough after they lose their leaves in fall to prevent wind from whipping around long canes and bending them. If you opt for Door No. 2 and decide to fall-prune, this month is fine if you didn't do it in November.

## SHRUBS

If you haven't already set up protection for shrubs against wind, snow, critters, and other winter threats, do so now.

"Harvest" a few shrub branches from shrubs for use as holiday decorations. See page 208.

## TREES

Snow and ice storms can rip off limbs or even topple whole trees. After a storm, remove broken branches you can safely reach, cutting back to the little ring just outside where the branch attaches (the "branch collar"). Also cleanly carve off torn bark with a sharp knife. No tar or tree paint is needed on wounds.

For large, hanging limbs and other bigger or off-the-ground work, *call a tree company*. As legendary USDA tree expert Alex Shigo often said, one of the most dangerous combinations is a homeowner, a chainsaw, and a ladder.

With badly broken trees or ones starting to lean, removal might be necessary. The overriding concern should always be whether the tree is creating a hazard. Particularly err on the side of caution when there's a target in the path of a big limb or leaning tree, such as a house, power line, or street.

As with shrubs, it's fine to take prunings from evergreen trees to use in holiday decorating.

Recycle the Christmas tree after the holidays. Cut off the branches and intertwine them as insulation around the base of rose bushes. Or grind the branches into mulch with your chipper-shredder. Or rub off the dried needles for mulch and compost, and sink the bare tree in the ground as a vine support. Or if you live in a rural area, toss the tree along a stream bank or brushy area where birds and small mammals can use it for shelter.

## WATER

### ALL

Once the ground freezes, that's it for most of the outside watering, except for exceptions noted below.

Inside, remember that nothing kills more plants—and kills them faster—than too much water. Soggy soil rots roots. Some pointers:

- Be sure your pots have drainage holes.

- Use lightweight, porous, well-drained potting mix for indoor plants.

- Don't be fooled into thinking it's time to water just because the surface dries. Most houseplant roots are in the bottom two-thirds of the pot, so that's what counts. Stick your finger into the soil 1 to 2 inches, and see what the moisture is there.

Another good test is to tip or lift the pot to check its weight. Dry soil is noticeably lighter.

When you water, add enough so that it drains out the bottom. This ensures that water has reached the entire depth of the rootball. Don't let excess water sit. Dump it to avoid hindering continued drainage.

### BULBS

Here's one exception to the December no-water generality: Bulbs being chilled in pots for indoor winter forcing. Bulb pots buried in the ground or in spots that get winter rain are usually fine. But if you're storing pots in an unheated garage, covered window well, refrigerator, or similar no-rain spot, check regularly and add moisture as needed to keep the soil damp. Don't overdo it into sogginess.

## LAWNS

If it's been an unusually warm and dry late fall, and the ground isn't frozen, newly planted grass still benefits from an occasional sprinkling. Established lawns can fend for themselves from here on out.

## PERENNIALS & GROUNDCOVERS

Newly planted perennials benefit from an occasional December soaking if it's been a warm, rainless fall and the soil is unfrozen and dry.

## SHRUBS & TREES

Here's another exception to the December no-water generality: evergreens growing in pots (and to a lesser extent, flowering shrubs). The soil in these should be kept damp whenever it's not frozen. Evergreens in particular keep losing moisture through their foliage all winter, so if the soil goes too dry for too long (more likely to happen in pots than in the ground), they'll brown and possibly die.

In-ground evergreens are usually okay over winter. The exception is newly planted or borderline-hardy broadleaf evergreens (sweetbox, skimmia, camellia, osmanthus), which benefit from an occasional December soaking if the soil is dry and unfrozen. New broadleaf evergreens are at highest risk during an exceptionally cold, windy winter in which the soil stays frozen most of the time, locking up the roots' ability to replenish moisture being lost through the foliage.

## FERTILIZE

## ALL

Wait until the end of winter to begin feeding perennials, groundcovers, roses, shrubs, trees, vines, and the lawn. Don't fertilize over the top of frozen ground. Winter rains and runoff from snowmelt may carry it offsite.

## ANNUALS & TROPICALS

A light application of slow-acting granular fertilizer once a month is usually plenty to meet the slow-growth demands of overwintering potted annuals, tropicals, houseplants, and rooted cuttings.

## BULBS

Indoor-flowering bulbs don't need fertilizer this month, especially ones you're going to toss after bloom, such as paperwhite narcissus. Start fertilizing amaryllis with a balanced, granular fertilizer every two to four weeks after it finishes blooming.

## PROBLEM-SOLVE

## ALL

One thing you can do about deer browsing is lean toward plants that deer don't favor. That at least can help when your neighbor has a tastier selection than you do. The problem is that deer don't read the deer-resistant plant lists, and will eat almost anything rather than starve to death, including thorny roses and jaggy hollies. One good deer-resistant list, if you want to take a crack at it, is published online by Rutgers University at http://njaes.rutgers.edu/deerresistance.

## ANNUALS & TROPICALS

Dry air is an underrated detriment to indoor plants. Static is a sign that your air is dry, a common side effect of home heating. Water-filled pebble trays underneath plants don't help much. A better idea is a room humidifier that puts moisture into the air at optimal levels. Both your sinuses and peace lilies will thank you.

Avoid placing overwintering potted plants near outside doors or heating vents. Even short blasts of cold outdoor air can harm tender tropicals, while regular doses of dry, warm air can brown leaf margins.

Examine your plants regularly. The sooner you catch a problem, the easier it is to deal with. Things to look for are shiny, sticky coating on the leaves; new foliage that is twisted or discolored; fine webbing on the stems; pale or speckled leaves; leaves that are turning yellow; stems that are discolored near the soil line; and a gray or white coating on the foliage.

## BULBS

Voles are mouse-like rodents that are some of the most underrated plant pests. They're active all winter, and they love bulbs. It's not too late to cover bulb beds with chicken wire to discourage voles from tunneling down.

Another vole-fighting option is employing a cat with claws, preferably one with a surly attitude. Cats hate voles, and find it great sport to hunt them all day long. And another option is setting out cage traps or snap traps baited with peanut butter.

## LAWNS

During the growing season, voles stay underground or hide under groundcovers to avoid being eaten by hawks and other predatory birds. However, under snow cover in winter, they venture out into the open lawn in search of food. Their movement makes surface tunnels in the lawn that look like curvy roads built by drunken road crews. Use these vole-fighting strategies for now, and scatter grass seed in the curvy roads in spring to speed recovery.

## PERENNIALS & GROUNDCOVERS

Voles even pick on many perennials and groundcovers, feasting on the tender roots underneath. If your foamflowers suddenly look wilted or disheveled, see if the roots aren't gone. If so, suspect voles.

## ROSES

Lack of light stresses miniature roses growing indoors. These benefit from growing under plant lights or 2 to 3 inches underneath fluorescent lights, set to run fourteen to sixteen hours a day.

If it looks like somebody pruned your roses, it's probably deer. If damage is just low on the plant, it's more likely rabbits. If any roses are falling over, check to see if the roots aren't gone. If that's the case, it's those darned voles again.

## SHRUBS

Animal damage is the main threat this month. Deer especially target azalea, rhododendron, yew, and arborvitae. Rabbits gnaw the bark of young, tender shrubs, and bite off branch tips, making sharp, clean, angled cuts that look like the work of scissors. Underground, voles, chipmunks, and mice could be eating roots. Install or reinforce your

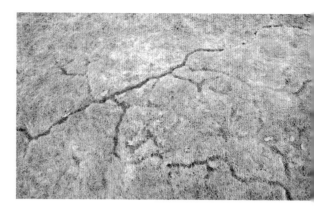

Vole tunneling damage to a lawn.

barriers, and set out traps and repellents if you're seeing any of this.

Watch for browning damage on the street side of evergreens caused by road salt from passing snowplows. Erect a burlap barrier to head off further injury. Soak the plants and ground well in spring if rains don't wash salt off and away for you.

## TREES

That greenish gray crust growing on tree trunks isn't some kind of ominous disease. It's lichen, a fungus and algae growth that's harmless to the plant. Just ignore it. Or admire it.

Trees run into the same animal risks in winter as shrubs. See above for threats and options.

Strong winter winds threaten young and newly planted trees in exposed sites. Either stake them for the winter or erect wind barriers of burlap (not plastic) to block the worst of its force.

## VINES

Some people like the look of English ivy growing up trees, but ivy can threaten trees, not by strangling them or somehow sucking the life out of their branches, but by growing out and over tree leaves. That deprives a tree of its ability to take in sunlight. Stop ivy before that happens. Ivy growing on dead trees, however, doesn't mean ivy killed the tree. Ivy often colonizes trees that are already dead. An ivy-covered dead tree in your yard is worse than an ivy-covered live one because a dead tree is at risk of falling down.

Figuring out what to do when in the garden is tricky enough just considering gardening's own numerous variables. Toss in the weather, and it's like adding a moving target to the equation. Weather can change drastically from one season to the next, not to mention daily—or by the minute. That makes gardening by a calendar a guide more than it's carved in stone.

Go by the averages, and you'll *usually* be fine. But if you can pay close attention to weather vagaries, and are ready to shift gears when conditions on the ground—and in the air—change, you'll fare best no matter what curveballs come along (deer visits notwithstanding). The month-by-month tips in this book give you an excellent starting point, a baseline of what jobs are best done when. By all means, tweak them to suit what you observe in your own yard each season.

If things get off to early start after a warm winter, for example, you might need to move up your pruning or crabgrass-prevention treatments by a week or two. If a cold, snowy winter just won't quit, you might end up doing jobs a week or two later than usual. One way to gauge these shifts is by watching what nature is doing around you. Observations such as when a certain bug appears or when a particular tree leafs out can give an important clue as to how the season is progressing. These happenings are interconnected.

What controls the timing is not the calendar date but changeable factors such as daylight length, air temperature, soil temperature, accumulated "chill time" over winter, and more. Overwintering living organisms such as trees, bulbs, bugs, and even disease-causing fungi have biological or hormonal clocks that monitor and react to these changing conditions. It's a remarkably accurate system, too—much better than how gardeners are so often faked out by a calendar that's having a hard time staying in sync with erratic weather.

People have long been watching nature's clues, especially gardeners and farmers. There's even a science called "plant phenology" devoted to connecting events. America's earliest farmers didn't have biophenometers and other sophisticated weather-measuring equipment to tell them when to plant. They knew it was time to plant corn when new oak leaves had grown to the size of a squirrel's ear. As science developed, growers and most people wrote off those kinds of advice as "old wive's tales." It turns out there's actually some good scientific data to back up the corn-planting-and-oak-leaf connection and other such "superstitions."

Plant scientists and phenologists have been monitoring plant/bug connections and weather data for more than 50 years. They've found that plant bloom times and bug emergence can vary by weeks from year to year, but no matter how screwy the weather is, the *sequence* of living events is amazingly consistent. In other words, gypsy moths might hatch in mid April one year and early May the next, but they always do it when redbud trees are just starting to bloom.

This kind of revelation can be helpful to a gardener. By watching when certain plants do certain things, you can accurately predict when certain pests might be primed to cause trouble.

That's a big edge because by the time most people notice an infestation, the damage already has been done, and it's too late to do anything.

Example: Eastern tent caterpillars on crabapple or cherry trees. These web-forming leaf-munchers overwinter as eggs on tree branches and normally hatch anywhere from late March to late April. They get big very quickly, and if you wait until they're mature, they not only have eaten more leaves, but they're more difficult to kill then. But if you know tent caterpillar eggs always hatch shortly after star magnolias bloom or when forsythias are in full bloom, you can time treatments much better—or at least know when to start looking for tent caterpillars.

A big reason phenology is making a comeback is because farmers and gardeners alike are trying to cut down on pesticide use. A well-timed spray may do the job in one or two treatments instead of three or four that are applied according to the calendar. Also, less toxic products such as soap sprays and horticultural oils generally work well only when they hit bugs at vulnerable life stages, which makes timing more critical.

Besides being a bug- and disease-fighting tool, phenology is useful for knowing when to plant or do other jobs around the garden. For instance, crabgrass begins to germinate once soil temperatures 4 inches deep stabilize at 55 degrees Fahrenheit. You could try to remember that, but it's a lot easier to realize that forsythia blooms under those same conditions, and remember to put down your crabgrass preventer when forsythias are in bloom.

Similarly, when daffodils begin to bloom, that's a signal that enough warmth has occurred to plant the sweet pea seeds outside. And it's warm enough to plant most annual flowers when lilacs are in full bloom.

Plant scientists were able to connect the dots by linking events according to "growing degree days."

A growing degree-day measures the number of degrees a day's average temperature exceeds 50 degrees Fahrenheit. The numbers start accumulating as of March 1. Example: If today is March 1 and the average temperature is 55 degrees, that counts as 5-degree days. If tomorrow's average is 60 degrees, that's 10-degree days. Together, that would add 15-degree days to the running total that began March 1. By putting it all together, it's possible to develop charts that really make the data useful to gardeners. A good online gateway to all sorts of phenological information is the USA National Phenology Network at www.usanpn.org.

One detailed chart that lists bug appearance and bloom times according to growing degree days was developed by Ohio State University entomologist Dr. Daniel Herms and is posted online at www. entomology.umn.edu/cues/Web/049DegreeDays.pdf.

Whether you go by the charts or observe what's happening in your own yard, you'll end up with a customized, changing calendar for your to-do list.

And the bugs will have less of a chance of getting the upper tentacle on you.

## KNOWN LINKS BETWEEN PLANT EVENTS AND BUG EMERGENCE

- **Eastern tent caterpillar:** early bloom of star magnolia or full bloom of forsythia
- **Pine sawfly:** early bloom of ornamental pear or weeping cherry
- **Spruce spider mite:** full bloom of serviceberry or 'PJM' rhododendron
- **Azalea lace bug:** full bloom of Korean spice viburnum
- **Gypsy moth:** early bloom of redbud or crabapple
- **Birch leafminer:** early bloom of silverbell or full bloom of flowering quince
- **Spruce gall adelgid:** early bloom of weigela or full bloom of lilac
- **Lilac borer:** early bloom of deutzia or doublefile viburnum
- **Holly leafminer:** early bloom of black cherry or sweetshrub
- **Euonymus scale:** full bloom of honeysuckle or early bloom of 'Miss Kim' lilac or beautybush
- **Dogwood borer:** full bloom of Washington hawthorn or mock orange
- **Bagworm:** full bloom of Japanese tree lilac
- **Pine needle scale:** full bloom of rose-of-Sharon
- **Rhododendron borer:** early bloom of winterberry holly or full bloom of catalpa
- **Fall webworm:** early bloom of oakleaf hydrangea
- **Japanese beetle:** early bloom of goldenrain tree or full bloom of Japanese spirea

Water gardening offers soothing sounds, wildlife attraction, and a "cool feel" to the summer landscape without the in-ground work of tilling, mulching, and weeding. Besides traditional ponds, water-garden choices include pondless water features and container water gardens.

Pondless features eliminate open, standing water by dropping water down a waterfall and into a buried, screen-and-stone covered vault with a pump in the bottom. The pump circulates water through hidden tubing to the top of the falls.

A container water garden can be any watertight container, ranging from a pot without holes to an old bathtub with the drain sealed. Here's a month-by-month care regime:

## JANUARY & FEBRUARY

- Plan for good plant diversity. Aquatic plants include submerged plants that generate oxygen in the water (anacharis, cabomba); floating plants that shade and filter the water (water hyacinth, water clover); immersed plants that flower and attract beneficial insects (lotus, water lilies); marginal plants for the shallow shelf (canna, papyrus, taro), and bog plants for wet soil around the pond edges (iris, marsh marigold, sedges).

- Check on non-winter-hardy water plants you're storing inside to make sure potted ones remain wet and wrappings of tubers and rhizomes are damp.

- Don't let your pond freeze over, which leads to a toxic buildup of gas that threatens fish. Install a de-icer device, or keep a bubbler or waterfall running. Never chop a hole in the ice. The concussion can harm fish. Gradually pour hot water to thaw openings.

- Get your supplies ready for the new season, and in the case of a new water garden, decide if you're going to add fish and a filter as well as aquatic plants.

## MARCH

- Transplant new shoots or divisions of overwintering plants into separate pots. Take cuttings of ones that you'd like to expand or give away.

- Keep your winter netting over the pond. It catches debris and protects fish from predator birds.

- As winter ends, tidy the pond's edges by clipping off dead stems of perennials and ornamental grasses.

■ *Fish need at least a small opening of unfrozen water so deadly gas doesn't build up in winter.*

■ *A water garden can be tucked into a corner of your yard.*

• Once the ground thaws, it's a good time to dig a new pond. Check local ordinances to determine rules on fencing.

## APRIL

• Pull out and compost green stringy algae.

• Start feeding fish when water temperatures reach 50 degrees Fahrenheit. Never feed more than fish can eat in three to five minutes.

• Remove your winter netting, and install a criss-crossing matrix of fishing line across the water to discourage fish-eating birds.

• Divide and repot hardy water-garden plants that have overwintered at the bottom of the pond.

## MAY

• Pot, plant, and set tender aquatic plants in the water garden after all danger of frost.

• If you use public water to fill your pond or top it off, wait a day to let chlorine dissipate. Or use products that neutralize chlorine or chloramine.

• Wait out cloudy water; that's common as the water warms.

• Be patient if the water is green from algae bloom. As plants cover the water surface, and your filter and oxygenating plants do their

work, this "pea soup" should gradually clear on its own. Don't worry about brown, furry algae on pot and liner surfaces; it's beneficial.

## JUNE

• Begin fertilizing water lilies and flowering aquatic plants with tablets monthly once the water temperature rises above 70 degrees Fahrenheit.

• Remove and rinse filter pads from submerged filters every few days.

• Consider installing night lights or in-pond lights to enhance the water garden in the evening.

• If green water isn't clearing, try these: limit food for fish, reduce the number of fish in the pond, stop fertilizing plants, add more submerged plants, and add more floating or immersed plants so 60 percent of the water surface is shielded from the sun.

## JULY

• Prune off injured or spent foliage and flower shoots from both the water-garden plants and those surrounding the pond (except for lotus, whose pods are one of their best features).

• About 60 percent of the water surface should be covered now with plants to limit unwanted algae and provide hiding places for the fish. Add more plants, if needed. On the other hand, if plants are so overcrowded that they're growing over one another, remove some of them, and compost or give to other water gardeners.

- If plants are growing too fast or stems are weak and floppy, cut back on fertilization. Or move them to a sunnier spot.

- Don't let the water level in the pond or container drop more than an inch or two. The liner should not be exposed to sunshine.

## AUGUST
- If you don't have fish or a pump to move water, use a product with B.t. (*Bacillus thuringiensis*) to keep mosquitoes from breeding in still, open water.

- Fill your pond to the top before going away on vacation.

- Continue to snip off spent foliage to keep water-garden plants looking good in the heat of summer.

- Watch for pots tipping over from plant roots squeezing through the pot's drainage holes or from fish or animals bumping into them. Prune off excessive roots. Use bricks or rocks to secure submerged pots.

## SEPTEMBER
- Tropical water lilies and other tender aquatic plants should go inside (if you're keeping them) when overnight temperatures dip into the low 40s.

- As plants stop growing and die back for the season, divide and repot them.

- Stop fertilizing water-garden plants until next spring.

- Continue feeding the fish until the water temperature dips back below 50 degrees.

- If you're losing water, check for reasons other than a leak in the liner, including a fountain that's spraying water outside the pond, a liner

edge that's pulled down, or a separation in the tubing at a waterfall or filter.

## OCTOBER
- This is an ideal month to drain and clean gunk out of the pond. Every two years is fine. Check for and repair liner leaks while the pond is drained.

- Before the leaves start dropping, cut back taller water-garden plants and stretch netting across the pond to catch leaves and prevent them from rotting in the water.

- Cut back and submerge hardy plants. Get tender ones inside before frost, such as in a basement, non-freezing garage, or old refrigerator.

- Store statuary and breakable containers indoors.

- Stop feeding fish, even if the weather warms after a cold spell.

## NOVEMBER
- Keep the pond from freezing over by installing a water heater or de-icer device. Or keep your pump running to keep the water moving.

- After removing plants, drain, clean, and cover shallow preformed ponds so they will not collect debris over winter.

- Remove and toss or store plants from water-garden containers. Then drain, rinse, and overturn wooden half-barrels and other winter-hardy containers. Take breakable ones inside.

## DECEMBER
- No plant stems or foliage of overwintering hardy water plants should protrude above the water surface. If some have started to send up shoots because of a mild fall, cut them back to the soil level in their pots.

- Jot down what changes you'd like to make next year while everything's still fresh in your mind.

Mulch is any material that goes on top of your soil. It's useful for retaining soil moisture, stopping weeds, moderating changes in soil temperatures, preventing disease-causing pathogens from splashing onto leaves, and, in the case of organic mulches, adding nutrients to the soil as they break down.

You have lots of mulch choices. Some types are more suited for some situations than others. Some are more expensive than others. Sometimes the choice boils down to personal preference. All mulches have their pros and cons.

Organic mulches come from living materials, such as shredded hardwood, bark mini-nuggets, wood chips, or chopped leaves. Inorganic mulches include weed fabric, black plastic, and stone.

The amount used is just as important as the type of mulch. Not enough allows weeds to poke through or doesn't moderate soil moisture and temperate as well as an optimal layer. Apply too much, and you risk shutting off your roots' oxygen supply or denying rain to the soil under a ridiculously thick mulch layer.

The worst mulching offense is "volcano mulching," which is packing mulch up against a tree trunk, sometimes a foot or more, so that it looks like the tree is growing out of a volcano. This encourages the bark to rot, which can kill a tree if enough rotting occurs the whole way around.

Between 3 to 4 inches is an ideal amount around trees and shrubs. About 2 inches is good for perennial flowers and over bulb beds, while about 1 inch is enough around smaller annual flowers.

The idea is to maintain those amounts. Some people dump on more and more each year, even faster than last year's mulch is breaking down. The result is accumulating mulch that can reach counterproductive amounts.

If you already have enough mulch, just cultivate what's there (if necessary), and call it a day. If your 3-inch layer of mulch has deteriorated to 1 inch, just top it off with a fresh 2 inches.

While applying mulch, use your hand to make a ring around each plant so that the mulch doesn't touch the trunks and stems. That avoids rotting and keeps a slight channel open for rain penetration.

Here's a look at thirteen mulches you may run across and what to consider before making your pick:

## SHREDDED HARDWOOD

This is tree wood—mostly branches and inner wood instead of bark—that's run through shredding machines. Sometimes called "tanbark," it's Pennsylvania's most popular mulch and is often sold double- or triple-shredded.

**Pros:** Widely available in bulk; moderate price; very good weed control at optimal amounts; some people like the dark color and natural appearance, especially when freshly applied; knits together well, helping to keep it in place on a bank.

**Cons:** Commonly grows nuisance fungi, especially slime mold and the artillery fungus that shoots sticky black dots on light surfaces; tends to crust and impede rain unless cultivated; lightens as it dries to the consternation of those who like the original black color; breakdown requires redoing it every year or two; can use nitrogen at the soil surface as it breaks down.

## BARK

This is the outer and often corky wood stripped from tree trunks, usually pines or other conifers. It's available in large chunks (nuggets), fingernail-sized flakes (mini-nuggets), or ground into almost soil-like texture (bark mulch).

**Pros:** Less likely to grow nuisance fungi than shredded hardwood; doesn't mat or crust like shredded hardwood; some like the look of nuggets or mini-nuggets, which are slow to break down and quick to dry (slightly lessening plant disease); others like the natural, soil-like look of the ground version.

**Cons:** Mini-nuggets somewhat prone to blowing around in windy spots; nuggets look unnatural to some; mulch version breaks down faster than nuggets; usually sold in bags instead of bulk, making it more labor-intensive to install and more expensive; can use nitrogen at the soil surface as it breaks down.

## WOOD CHIPS

Wood from cut-down or pruned trees that's run through a grinder to produce chip-sized pieces. Usually includes the bark, the wood, and leaves.

**Pros:** Moderately priced and maybe free from companies doing nearby tree-removal or tree-pruning work; good source of nitrogen after they break down; no crusting or matting like shredded hardwood, allowing improved oxygen and moisture exchange in the soil; fairly slow to break down.

**Cons:** Loose pieces can slide down a bank; not everyone likes the "rough" look; may grow nuisance fungi; slight chance of transmitting disease from diseased trees to the same species in a landscape; can use nitrogen at the soil surface as it breaks down.

## COLORED WOOD MULCH

Recycled wood (often pallets, packing crates or boards) is shredded or ground into pieces that are colored with dye and sold in bags.

**Pros:** Holds color for years; recycled use for products otherwise headed to a landfill (assuming nothing is toxic).

**Cons:** Expensive and labor-intensive since it's generally sold in bags; wood source is usually unknown, opening possibilities such as treated lumber, lead paint, or pallets that carried leaking chemicals; coloring sources also questionable, such as coal tar as a source for black; may grow nuisance fungi; breaks down faster than bark; some reports of dye washing off; can use nitrogen in the soil surface as it breaks down; some say potentially harmful to plants, mainly young annuals.

## LEAVES

These are the falling bounty from deciduous trees that can be shredded or chopped into mulch.

**Pros:** They're free; excellent at adding organic matter and nutrients to the soil; good at weed control if you apply enough; no nuisance fungi; good choice around annual flowers and veggies; some like the natural look or the idea of recycling.

**Cons:** Among the quickest of the materials to break down; large whole leaves will mat and impede rain; leaves from diseased trees may allow overwintering spores to reinfect trees in the same species; you may not have or be able to get enough leaves to complete the job or keep enough on.

## GRASS CLIPPINGS

These are best left on the lawn, but if you haven't mowed for awhile or otherwise end up with excess clippings, they can go on garden beds.

**Pros:** They're also free; good source of nitrogen as the clippings break down; makes an ideal soil-enriching blend when used with leaves; no nuisance fungi; good way to recycle materials that many people bag and pay to have taken to a landfill.

**Cons:** Can kill plants if you're using clippings that have been treated with a herbicide; may introduce weed seeds if there were mature weeds in the lawn during mowing; fast to break down; heat from initial breakdown of green clippings can harm stems (let them dry first); large amounts needed for good weed control.

## COMPOST

Decayed organic matter, usually from a mix of materials that might include leaves, grass clippings, spent plants, kitchen waste, ground bark, and/or shredded paper.

**Pros:** Research at Ohio State University found that 2 inches of compost stops weeds as well as 2 inches of wood mulch; adds excellent blend of nutrients to the soil as it breaks down; free if you make it yourself; unlikely to grow nuisance fungi; natural look, almost like soil; discourages plant disease.

**Cons:** Breaks down fast; needs to be added annually; expensive and labor-intensive if you're buying it by the bag.

## PINE NEEDLES

Fallen, browned older needles from white pines or similar long-needled pines. Usually sold in bales and also called "pine straw."

**Pros:** Fairly slow to break down; "breathes" well, allowing good oxygen and moisture exchange in the soil; adds organic matter and nutrients to the soil; no nuisance fungi.

**Cons:** Not widely available in Pennsylvania; expensive when bales can be found; large quantities needed to apply enough for good weed control; some people don't like the look, which isn't as familiar or accepted by Pennsylvanians as Southerners; more flammable than wood or bark mulch.

## COCOA OR OTHER SHELLS

The outer hulls from cocoa beans, buckwheat, nuts or other hard-shelled, pod-producing plants.

**Pros:** Some like the chocolately scent of freshly applied cocoa-shell mulch; good way to recycle a waste product; harder shells are slow to break down; unlikely to grow nuisance fungi.

**Cons:** Light shells are prone to blowing in windy areas; shells are usually sold bagged, making them expensive and labor-intensive to apply; some develop mold in wet weather; cocoa products are potentially harmful to dogs that might try to eat the shells.

## WEED FABRIC

Polyester or similar thin but durable fabric sheets that roll out and can be cut to fit. Openings are cut to insert plants. Sometimes called "geotextiles."

**Pros:** Good at stopping weeds; fairly inexpensive; easier to install than lugging around bags or wheelbarrows; eliminates threat of nuisance fungi, unless topped with wood mulch; doesn't have to be done repeatedly; good choice for non-planted pathways or along 1- to 2-foot house-foundation stripes covered with stone; can be sprayed with herbicides when weeds pop up in pathway or foundation settings.

**Cons:** Can impede oxygen flow into the soil; can trap excess moisture in wet clay as well as impede rain; if you top it with organic mulch, weeds can sprout on top of the fabric as the mulch decays; grassy weeds can grow up through the fabric; not a good choice where you want plants to spread, such as with perennials or a groundcover; wood-mulch topping can grow nuisance fungi.

## BLACK PLASTIC

Rolls of thin, black plastic are cut into sheets and pegged down over the soil. Some is sold with small holes to make it somewhat porous, similar to weed fabric made out of plastic.

**Pros:** Very slow to break down, and so doesn't have to be redone repeatedly; good at stopping weeds; fairly

inexpensive; easy to install; eliminates nuisance fungi unless topped with wood mulch; can be covered with stone in pathways or along house foundations where weeds can be sprayed without harming plants.

**Cons:** Impedes oxygen flow into the soil and traps excess moisture in wet clay; even with holes, slows both of these important processes; weeds can germinate on top of the plastic if you top it with organic mulch for looks; mulch (especially chips and nuggets) readily slide down the slippery surface when used on a bank; not a good choice where you want plants to spread, such as with perennials or a groundcover; wood-mulch topping can grow nuisance fungi.

## STONE

Can range from small, tightly packed material such as crushed gravel (sometimes called "stone dust") to pea-sized pebbles to larger chunks of decorative stone.

**Pros:** You don't have to keep replacing it; some people like the "clean," formal look; doesn't grow nuisance fungi; no fire hazard.

**Cons:** Among most expensive options; heavy work for that one-time installation; doesn't add organic matter to the soil; will sink into soil if plastic or fabric not used underneath; limestone may increase soil alkalinity (a potential problem around acid-preferring plants); larger sizes don't control weeds well, especially as leaves blow in and decay among the stones; can absorb heat in sunny locations (good in cold weather, not so good in summer).

## RUBBER

Ground chunks of tires or other recycled rubber products. It's usually dyed either black or brown.

**Pros:** Very slow to break down; "breathes" well and doesn't mat; holds color well; doesn't grow nuisance fungi; makes a productive use out of material otherwise heading to the landfill.

**Cons:** Comparatively expensive; doesn't add organic matter to the soil; some concern about potential for leaching zinc, aromatic hydrocarbons, and other manufacturing chemicals; can burn hot and fast if catches on fire; can get hot when used in sunny locations; only moderate weed control unless laid thickly; some people object to the odor, at least soon after applying.

To figure how much soil or mulch you'll need for a garden project, calculate the total square feet of the area to be covered. Measure the length and width, then multiply those two to get total square feet. For irregular areas, divide the space into a series of smaller, approximate rectangles, and calculate the square footage of each. Then add the totals. For circular beds, measure the distance from the center to the perimeter (the radius). Then multiply that number by itself. Then multiply that by 3.14 to get total square footage.

The next step is to decide how many inches of soil or mulch you plan to put down. Multiply the number of inches by the total square footage. If you're buying by bulk, vendors generally sell by the cubic yard. To determine how many cubic yards you'll need, divide the total square footage times the mulch depth by 324. Example: You want to add 2 inches of mulch to a bed that's 8 feet wide by 20 feet long. Multiply 8 × 20 to get 160 square feet, then multiply by 2 inches. The total is 320. Divide that by 324 and you get almost 1 cubic yard.

In stores, mulch usually comes in either 2- or 3-cubic-foot bags. One way to determine bags needed is by knowing how far each bag goes. A 2-cubic-foot bag covers about 12 square feet of bed at 2 inches or about 8 square feet at 3 inches. A 3-cubic-foot bag covers about 18 square feet of bed at 2 inches and about 12 square feet at 3 inches.

So in this example where you're trying to cover 160 square feet at 2 inches, you'd need a little more than thirteen of the 2-cubic-foot bags. (160 divided by 12 equals 13.3.) If you're buying 3-cubic-foot bags, you'll need nine of those (160 divided by 18 equals 8.9).

Another way is to divide the total number of square feet of soil or mulch needed by 12 inches to give you a total of cubic feet needed. Then divide that total by the number of cubic feet in each bag to give you the number of bags to buy.

In the scenario where you're covering 160 square feet at 2 inches, your total square footage is 320. Divide that by 12 to come up with 26.67 cubic feet needed. If you're buying 2-cubic-foot bags, you'll again come up with a little more than thirteen bags, (26.67 divided by 2 equals 13.3.)

If you're buying 3-cubic-foot bags, you'll again need almost nine, (26.67 divided by 3 equals 8.9.)

Math overload? Numerous online calculators let you plug in square footage and number of inches needed, then give you totals in cubic yards and/or bags needed.

One is available at the National Gardening Association website at www.garden.org/calculators. Another is available on the Landscape Calculator website at www.landscapecalculator.com/calculators/mulch.

Here's a chart to help you get started with cubic yards:

| SQUARE FOOTAGE TO COVER | CUBIC YARDS OF MATERIAL NEEDED | | |
|---|---|---|---|
| | 2" | 3" | 4" |
| 100 | ½ | 1 | 1+ |
| 200 | 1+ | 2 | 2½ |
| 300 | 2 | 2¾ | 3½ |
| 400 | 2½ | 3½ | 5 |
| 500 | 3+ | 4½ | 6 |
| 600 | 3½ | 5½ | 7½ |
| 700 | 4+ | 6½ | 8½ |
| 800 | 5 | 7½ | 10 |
| 900 | 5½ | 8+ | 11 |
| 1000 | 6 | 9+ | 12 |

One of the top landscaping foul-ups is not giving plants the space they need to grow. Too big or too many plants in too little space soon leads to overcrowded gardens, unnecessary pruning, and ultimately, removals. Plan for the size a plant is *going* to get, not the size at planting. Even that's an estimate that will vary by factors such as the weather, your particular site, and the care you deliver. The "mature" size listed on the plant label is a good starting point. But even these may vary from grower to grower. At least those listings give you an idea of growth habit (about twice as tall as wide) and approximate size.

## SPACING GUIDELINES

- When planting next to a wall or property line, take the mature width and divide in half. Plant no closer than that distance. (Example: A holly that will get 8 feet around should be planted a minimum of 4 feet away from a wall.)

- To determine how close to plant plants to one another, space them the mature width apart. (Example: plant 4-foot-wide spireas no closer than 4 feet apart.)

- If two plants of differing sizes are being planted next to one another, add the two mature widths together and divide in half to determine the minimum spacing. (Example: A 6-foot-wide viburnum and a 4-foot-wide spirea should be planted no closer than 5 feet apart. 6+4=10. Then 10 divided in half equals 5.)

- In borders and foundation plantings, arrange your plants so that the tallest plants are in the back and the shortest in front. In an island bed that you'll be able to view from all angles,

go with the tallest plants toward the middle and the shorter ones around the perimeter.

- A good average for spacing perennials is about 2 feet apart. More compact ones can go 15 to 18 inches apart. Bigger ones can go 2½ to 3 feet apart. Large ornamental grasses can go 4 feet apart.

- A good average for spacing annual flowers is 1 foot apart. Compact ones (wax begonias, for example) can go as close as 8 inches apart. More vigorous ones (lantana, for example) can go 18 to 24 inches apart.

- A good average for groundcovers such as vinca or pachysandra is 12 to 15 inches, although if you're patient, 18 to even 24 inches is fine.

- For planting large blocks of small plants, calculate the total square feet to be covered (multiply length by width in feet), decide on spacing, and use the following chart:

## PLANT SPACING

| SPACING (INCHES) | 25 SQ. FT. | 50 SQ. FT. | 100 SQ. FT. |
|---|---|---|---|
| 8 | 57 | 114 | 227 |
| 10 | 36 | 72 | 143 |
| 12 | 12 | 50 | 100 |
| 15 | 16 | 32 | 64 |
| 18 | 11 | 22 | 44 |
| 24 | 6 | 13 | 25 |
| 30 | 4 | 8 | 16 |
| 36 | 3 | 6 | 11 |
| 48 | 2 | 3 | 6 |

# Resources

- **Bug Guide.net.**
  http://bugguide.net/node/view/15740
  Pictures galore to help ID garden pests plus
  folks willing to talk bugs anytime.

- **Climate reports.**
  www.weather.gov/climate/index.php?wfo=ctp
  Daily climate reports from the National
  Weather Service office in State College.

- **Green gardening.**
  www.iconservepa.org
  Pennsylvania Department of Conservation
  and Natural Resources tips on
  environmentally friendly yard care, recycling,
  native plants, and more.

- **Morton Arboretum Plant Clinic.**
  www.mortonarb.org/trees-plants/plant-clinic
  Help with plant troubles, care tips, answers to
  questions, top varieties, and much more.

- **Penn State bug fact sheets.**
  http://ento.psu.edu/extension/factsheets
  All you need to know from Penn State's
  bug experts.

- **Penn State Plant Disease Clinic.**
  http://plantpath.psu.edu/facilities/plant-
  disease-clinic
  How to send suspected diseased samples to
  Penn State for free diagnosis (Pennsylvania
  home gardeners only).

- **Penn State disease fact sheets.**
  http://extension.psu.edu/pests/plant-diseases/
  general-plant-diseases
  Details on assorted plant diseases you might
  run into.

- **Penn State soil testing.**
  http://agsci.psu.edu/aasl/soil-testing/soil-
  fertility-testing
  How to get your soil tested through Penn
  State's testing lab.

- **Penn State Turf Management.**
  http://plantscience.psu.edu/research/centers/
  turf/extension/home-lawns
  Tip sheets on all sorts of lawn-care topics from
  Penn State's lawn experts.

- **Pennsylvania gardening.**
  http://georgeweigel.net
  George Weigel's site featuring weekly columns
  (archived, too), plus 300 plant profiles, public
  gardens worth seeing, best-of/worst-of lists,
  and more.

- **Pennsylvania IPM Pest Problem Solver.**
  http://paipm.cas.psu.edu/1445.htm
  "Soft" and enviro-friendly ways to deal with pests.

- **Plant diagnostics. University of Maryland.**
  http://plantdiagnostics.umd.edu
  Helps nail down plant problems by walking
  you through questions and pictures. Then
  offers action advice.

- **Poisonous plants.**
  http://cal.vet.upenn.edu/projects/poison/
  index.html
  University of Pennsylvania's database on plants
  that are poisonous to both humans and animals.

- **National Turfgrass Evaluation Program.**
  www.ntep.org
  Data from across the country on top-
  performing grass seed varieties.

- **Weather data.**
  www.nws.noaa.gov/climate/xmacis.php?wfo=ctp
  Any kind of weather data you might want
  from the National Weather Service; monthly
  averages, rainfall totals, minimum and
  maximum temps, and so forth.

- **Weed identification.**
  http://njaes.rutgers.edu/weeds/default.asp
  Rutgers University shows you pictures and
  helps you zero in on common lawn and
  landscape weeds.

## OTHER RESOURCES

- *Basic Composting* by Carl Hursh, Patti Olenick, and Alan Wycheck (Stackpole Books, 2003). How to make your own compost.

- *Foolproof Planting* by Anne Moyer Halpin (Rodale Press, 1990). How to start and propagate your own plants.

- *Pennsylvania Getting Started Garden Guide* by George Weigel (Cool Springs Press, 2014). The particulars of gardening in Pennsylvania along with 170 of the best high-performing, low-care plant choices.

- *The Perennial Care Manual* by Nancy J. Ondra (Storey Publishing, 2009). Plant-by-plant care tips on perennial flowers.

- *The Pruning of Trees, Shrubs and Conifers* by George E. Brown and Tony Kirkham (Timber Press, 2009). How to prune woody plants.

- *Tending Your Garden* by Gordon Hayward (WW Norton, 2007). A photo-rich how-to on caring for a landscape.

- *The Well-Tended Perennial Garden: Planting and Pruning Techniques* by Tracy DiSabato-Aust (Timber Press, 2006). Another excellent plant-by-plant care manual for perennials.

- *What's Wrong with My Plant? (And How Do I Fix It?)* by David Deardorff and Kathryn Wadsworth (Timber Press, 2009). Graphics-rich book to help diagnose plant problems and, if necessary, take action.

- *Woody Ornamental Insect, Mite, and Disease Management* by Penn State University (available at County Extension offices or online at http://pubs.cas.psu.edu/FreePubs/PDFs/agrs025.pdf). Bugs and diseases common to Pennsylvania landscapes and what to do about them.

# Glossary

**Acclimate:** To become gradually accustomed to a different environment.

**Acidic soil:** Soil that has a pH reading of 6.0 and lower. Mildly acidic is 6.0 to 7.0. Lime counteracts overly acidic soil to make it more alkaline.

**Aerate (aeration):** To introduce oxygen into the soil. In lawns, it's commonly done with equipment that pulls cores of soil out of the ground, depositing them on the surface.

**Alkaline soil:** Soil that has a pH greater than 7.0. Sulfur counteracts overly alkaline soil to make it more acidic.

**Annual:** A plant that lives its entire life in one season and dies at the end of that year.

**Anti-transpirant/anti-desiccant:** A product that reduces a plant's moisture loss by coating the foliage with a thin film, usually a type of oil, resin, or wax.

**Arborist:** A person trained to care for trees. Certified arborists have met the qualifications of professional organizations.

***Bacillus thuringiensis* (B.t.):** A bacterium that kills caterpillars by attacking the digestive system. Available as a dust or powder that's mixed in water and sprayed on plant foliage when caterpillars are feeding.

**Balanced fertilizer:** A granular or liquid fertilizer with approximately equal proportions of the three key nutrients listed on product labels—nitrogen (the first number), phosphorus (the second number), and potassium (the third number).

**Balled and burlapped:** Describes trees and shrubs grown in the field, then dug with roots wrapped with protective burlap and twine for transport and sale.

**Bare root:** Plants that are shipped dormant, without being planted in soil or having soil around their roots.

**Basal:** Refers to growth emerging from around the base, trunk, or main origin of a plant.

**Beneficial insects:** Insects or their larvae that prey on pest organisms and their eggs. Examples: ladybugs, parasitic wasps, soldier bugs, predatory nematodes, and spiders.

**Biennial:** A plant that grows over two seasons, usually growing foliage only in the first year, and then flowering, setting seed, and dying in the second.

**Bract:** A petal-like modified leaf structure of a plant stem, growing near its flower. Often, it is more colorful and visible than the actual flower, as in dogwood or poinsettia.

**Bud union (graft):** The point on the stem of a plant where a desirable branch or stem (scion) is attached to a plant growing in the ground (rootstock). Roses are commonly grafted.

**Canopy:** The overhead branching area or "reach" of a tree, including foliage.

**Cell packs:** Multi-compartment containers, usually made out of thin plastic and used to sell small plants, most often annual flowers and vegetables.

**Chlorosis:** A nutritional deficiency in plants, usually indicated by yellowed foliage with green veins. Most common in plants that require acidic soil, it's a sign that plants are unable to take up sufficient iron from the soil.

**Climber:** A plant that grows vertically by means of elongating stems. It may twist or cling to surfaces to pull itself up, or it may need ties to help guide it upward.

**Cold hardiness:** The ability of a perennial plant to survive the winter cold in a particular area. The U.S. Department of Agriculture assigns cold-hardiness ratings by zone based on winter's average lows in a given area.

**Compost:** Organic matter that has decomposed into a spongy, fluffy texture. It adds nutrition to soil and aids its ability to hold air and water and to drain well.

**Corm:** A fat, flat, scaly underground stem that's planted underground, similar to a bulb. Leaves and flowers emerge from nodes on the corm. Examples: crocus, gladiolus, freesia.

**Crown:** The part of a plant at or near the soil surface from which the stems emerge. Sometimes referred to as the "growth point" of a plant.

**Cultivar:** A CULTivated VARiety. A plant that has been bred or selected for having one or more distinct traits from the species and then given a name to set it apart. 'Pardon Me,' for example, is a cultivar of daylily.

**Damping off:** A fungal disease that targets young seedlings. Spores in the soil cause their stems to blacken and collapse. Using sterile potting medium helps prevent this problem.

**Deadhead:** To remove dead flowers in order to encourage further bloom, neaten the plant, and prevent the plant from self-sowing.

**Deciduous:** A plant that loses its leaves seasonally, typically in fall or early winter.

**Direct-seed:** To sow seeds directly into the garden rather than starting them in small pots ahead of time.

**Division:** Splitting apart plants to create two or more smaller, rooted sections. Useful for controlling a plant's size and for acquiring more plants.

**Dormancy (dormant):** The period, usually winter, when perennial plants temporarily cease active growth and rest. Some plants, such as spring-blooming bulbs, go dormant in the summer.

**Drip irrigation:** A water-delivery system that uses supply lines (usually plastic) and emitters that slowly deliver water directly to the soil around plants or pots.

**Drip line:** Can refer both to the outer reaches of a tree's branching canopy where rainfall drips from branch tips or to a line that's part of a drip-irrigation system.

**Establishment:** The time needed for a newly planted or transplanted tree, shrub, or flower to produce enough growth (especially roots) that it's adapted to its new environment. An "established" plant no longer requires the additional care needed immediately following planting or transplanting.

**Evergreen:** A plant that keeps its leaves year-round, instead of dropping them seasonally. These can be needled plants as well as broadleaf ones.

**Fertilizer:** Any material that, when added to the soil, contributes one or more nutrients required by plants. These include nitrogen, phosphorus, potassium, sulfur, magnesium, calcium, iron, manganese, boron, chlorine, zinc, copper, molybdenum, and nickel.

**Floating row cover:** A light-weight blanket, often made out of spun-bounded polyester or similar woven fabric, that's draped over plants to protect them from light frost or bug damage. The covers are porous enough to let in light and rain.

**Foliage:** The leafy tissue of a plant, including needles as well as wider leaves.

**Forcing bulbs:** The process of potting dormant bulbs, then giving them the necessary chilling time before taking them into warmth to encourage earlier-than-usual bloom.

**Frost:** Ice crystals that form when the temperature falls below freezing. Tender plants die when frost kills their leaf cells.

**Fungicide:** A product that acts to prevent, control, or eradicate plant diseases caused by fungi.

**Germinate:** To sprout. Usually refers to the initial growth of seeds.

**GMO:** Refers to genetically modified organisms, which involves altering a plant or animal's genetic makeup by inserting or removing genes.

**Girdling roots:** Roots that circle around the base of a tree or shrub rather than growing outward into the soil.

**Grubs:** Fat, off-white, worm-like larval stage of an insect, most often beetles and especially Japanese beetles. They hatch in the soil, and feed on plant (especially grass) roots until transforming into adults.

**Habitat:** The living environment of a plant or animal. A native habitat of a plant or bug refers to the setting in which it's found naturally.

**Hand-pick:** To eliminate pest insects, slugs, or caterpillars by plucking or knocking them from plant foliage into a container or jar of soapy water.

**Hardening off:** The process of acclimating seedlings and young plants grown in an indoor environment to the outdoors.

**Hardscape:** The permanent, structural, non-plant parts of a landscape, such as walls, sheds, pools, patios, arbors, benches, and walkways.

**Hardware cloth:** A stiff, metal fencing with small openings, usually used to protect trees and shrubs from rodent damage.

**Herbaceous:** Describes plants that have fleshy or soft stems that die back with frost.

**Herbicide:** A product designed to kill plants, typically weeds. Some act on foliage and stem tissues, some act on seeds.

**Hybrid:** A plant produced by crossing two genetically different plants, usually to achieve a desired trait, new color or some other perceived improvement.

**Hydrogel crystals:** Also known as polymer crystals or water-absorbing crystals, these are clear or white dry granules about the size of coarse salt grains that can absorb and hold up to 600 times their weight in water. They're typically sold as watering aids, especially for use in potted plants.

**Insecticide:** A product designed to kill insects.

**Larva(e):** An insect in its immature stage, after it hatches from an egg. Typically either a worm or caterpillar form of a butterfly, moth, or beetle.

**Leader:** The term for the center or main trunk of a tree.

**Lime:** Limestone processed as granules, pellets, or powder for use in adding calcium to soils, thereby making it less acidic and more alkaline (increasing the pH reading). Dolomite limestone also contributes magnesium.

**Microclimate:** Small sections of a property that deviate slightly from the prevailing, surrounding climate. A courtyard with stone walls, for example, likely will have warmer, less windy conditions than the rest of a yard.

**Mulch:** A layer of material placed over bare soil to protect it from erosion, to slow evaporation loss, and/or to suppress weeds. It can be inorganic (gravel, plastic, fabric) or organic (wood chips, bark, pine needles, chopped leaves).

**Native:** Indigenous. Native plants are those determined to have been growing in a particular region before the arrival of European settlers.

**Naturalize:** (a) To plant seeds, bulbs, or plants in a random, informal pattern as they would appear in their natural habitat. (b) The tendency of some non-native plants to adapt to and spread throughout their adopted habitats.

**New wood:** The current year's growth. Usually used in reference to a plant "flowering or fruiting on new wood," meaning the flower buds form on the new growth.

**Node:** A swollen joint or ridged scar on a plant stem from which a leaf or smaller stem will (or could) emerge.

**Old wood:** Growth that's more than one year old. Some plants produce fruits or flowers only on older growth, not that season's growth.

**Organic matter:** Gardening-wise, it's material or debris that's derived from plants. Technically, it's carbon-based material that's capable of undergoing decomposition and decay.

**Perennial:** A flowering plant that lives three or more seasons. Some die back with frost and generate new shoots in spring; others hold their stems and leaves throughout winter.

**Pesticide:** A product designed to kill pests, including bugs, disease pathogens, pest animals, or weeds.

**pH:** A figure designating the acidity or the alkalinity of soil as measured on a scale of 0 to 14, with 7.0 being neutral.

**Pinch:** To remove tender stems and/or leaves by pressing them between thumb and forefinger. It's a pruning technique used to encourage branching, compactness, and flowering or to remove bugs or diseased leaves.

**Photosynthesis:** The process by which plants, collecting energy from the sun by means of the chlorophyll in their foliage, transform carbon dioxide in the air and water from the soil into carbohydrates that fuel their growth.

**Pollen:** The yellow, powdery grains in the center of a flower. A plant's male sex cells, they are transferred to the female plant parts by means of wind or animal pollinators, to fertilize them and create seeds.

**Pollination:** The transfer of pollen for fertilization from the male pollen-bearing organ (stamen) to the female organ (pistil), usually by wind, bees, butterflies, moths, or hummingbirds.

**Pre-emergent:** Acting prior to the germination of a seed. Describes a product that inhibits the sprouting of a seed (as in pre-emergent herbicide).

**Rhizome:** An underground horizontal stem that grows side shoots. Examples: canna, ginger, most iris.

**Rootball:** The network of roots and soil clinging to a plant when it is lifted out of the ground or pot.

**Rootbound (or potbound):** The condition of a plant that has been confined to a container too long, its roots having been forced to wrap around themselves and even swell out of the container.

**Root flare:** The point at the base of a tree where the trunk transitions into the roots. This point starts to widen and should be visible just above grade if a tree is planted at the correct depth.

**Rootstock:** The part of a grafted plant that's growing in the ground and providing the root system. A desirable stem or branch is attached to the rootstock.

**Root zone:** The area that the roots of a plant occupy or can be expected to spread to when mature.

**Scion:** The ornamental or desirable part of a grafted plant. Usually refers to a cutting, shoot, stem, branch, or bud that is attached to rootstock, the in-ground plant that's supplying the root system.

**Self-seeding (self-sowing):** Describes the tendency of some plants to drop or distribute their seeds freely, which then sprout on their own. Can be a wanted or unwanted trait.

**Shearing:** A pruning technique in which plant stems and branches are cut uniformly with long-bladed pruning shears (hedge shears) or powered hedge trimmers. Used in creating and maintaining hedges and topiary.

**Slow-acting fertilizer:** Also sometimes called slow-release or gradual-release fertilizer, this is a product that's water-insoluble, releasing its nutrients gradually as it breaks down. Typically granular, it may be either organic or synthetic.

**Sod:** Sections of soil in which turfgrass plants are already growing.

**Soil test:** Chemical analysis of soil to determine its fertility, pH, and nutrients. This is usually done by private laboratories or state university facilities. Less sophisticated tests can be done by gardeners using kits available at garden centers.

**Spores:** Microscopic particles that allow fungi to reproduce themselves, similar to the function of seeds in a flowering plant.

**Sucker:** A new growing shoot. Underground plant roots produce suckers to form new stems and spread by means of these suckering roots to form colonies. Some plants produce root suckers or branch suckers as a result of pruning or wounding.

**Sulfur:** An element that's both a plant nutrient and a key product in making soil more acidic (i.e. lowering the soil pH). Mixed with water, it's also used as a fungicide.

**Stippling:** A description of plant damage to leaves. Stippled leaves are discolored due to loss of chlorophyll removed by tiny insects that insert small feeding holes throughout the leaf.

**Thinning:** The process of removing selected sprouts from a crowded planting, or removing excess branches from a woody plant.

**Transplant:** The process of digging and relocating a plant. Also, a young plant that is mature enough to be planted outdoors in a garden bed or decorative container.

**Transplant shock:** The stress or damage a plant undergoes after it's been moved from one setting or location to another.

**Tropical plant:** A plant that's native to a tropical region of the world and typically not able to survive frost.

**Tuber:** Enlarged roots that send out shoots and roots from nodes along their surface. Examples: dahlia, cyclamen, perennial (tuberous) begonias.

**Turfgrass:** Short grasses that are mowed and used in lawns as opposed to ornamental grasses, which are left to grow as landscape plants.

**Variegated:** The appearance of differently colored areas on plant leaves, usually white, yellow, or a brighter green.

**Water sprout:** A vertical shoot that emerges from tree branches. These should usually be pruned off.

**Weed preventer:** A product distributed in advance of a weed outbreak that either stops weeds from sprouting or kills them before they develop. Also known as a pre-emergent herbicide.

# Index

# Meet Liz Ball

**Liz Ball** is a Philadelphia-area horticultural writer, photographer, researcher, and teacher whose articles and photographs have appeared in numerous catalogs, magazines, and books. A former contributor to *Green Scene*, the magazine of the Pennsylvania Horticultural Society, and other publications, Liz has authored numerous books on plant and landscape care.

She is still writing her weekly "Yardening" newspaper column after twenty-two years, advising non-gardening homeowners on landscape care. She has been a member of the Garden Writers Association since 1986.

A former teacher of writing, literature, and history at the secondary level, she has taught courses on gardening and on garden writing at local community adult and arboretum programs. She has spoken often to garden clubs, horticultural societies, civic groups, and at the Philadelphia Flower Show.

In her spare time, Liz presides over a 2-acre suburban yard that serves as an informal laboratory and for ongoing plant and equipment testing, research, and workshop presentations. A certified wildlife habitat, it features a backyard wetland, bog garden, vegetable and ornamental beds, small turfgrass areas, a composting operation, and deer fencing.

# Meet George Weigel

**George Weigel** is a garden writer, garden designer, and frequent speaker best known for the garden columns he's written weekly for more than twenty years for The Patriot-News and Pennlive.com in Harrisburg, Pennsylvania.

Originally from Lancaster County, Pennsylvania, George earned a journalism degree from Penn State University and later became a Pennsylvania Certified Horticulturist through the Pennsylvania Landscape and Nursery Association. Besides his newspaper column, George has written for numerous magazines, including *Horticulture, Green Scene, Pennsylvania Gardener, Central Pennsylvania* magazine and *People, Places and Plants.*

He also posts a weekly "e-column" on his website, www.georgeweigel.net, which includes month-by-month garden tips, public-garden profiles, plant profiles, and a library of articles on a wide variety of gardening topics.

George is author of the *Pennsylvania Getting Started Garden Guide* (Cool Springs Press, 2014), and co-author of the medical book, *Striking Back! The Trigeminal Neuralgia and Face Pain Handbook* (Trigeminal Neuralgia Association, 2004), written along with Dr. Kenneth Casey.

Besides writing, George offers garden design and consultations to do-it-yourselfers through his Garden House-Calls business, leads numerous garden trips, and gives dozens of talks each year at various garden shows, garden clubs, and Master Gardener programs.

George is a member of the Pennsylvania Horticultural Society's Gold Medal Plant Committee, a Garden Writers Association member since 1993, and a former board member of Hershey Gardens, where he helped design the 1-acre Children's Garden.

George and his wife, Susan, live and garden in suburban Cumberland County.

# Photo Credits

American Horticultural Society: p. 136 (top)

Steve Asbell: p. 26

Cool Springs Press: pp. 10, 11 (both), 13, 18, 22, 23, 28, 38 (right), 41, 50, 52, 55 (all), 59 (top), 60, 62 (right), 64 (left), 69, 74 (top), 75 (right), 76, 77 (both), 81, 83, 91 (right, top and bottom), 92 (both), 93, 95, 97, 104 (right), 113 (right), 126, 128, 132, 133, 139, 142 (bottom), 144, 148, 157, 158, 163 (all), 164 (all), 167 (all), 179 (bottom), 184 (all), 192, 199, 205

Susan Ellis, Bugwood.org: p.121 (left)

Tom Eltzroth: pp. 156, 166

Katie Elzer-Peters: pp. 16, 17, 25, 32, 36, 43 (all), 44, 46, 56 (both), 57, 59 (bottom), 62 (left), 63, 72 (left), 74 (bottom), 80, 84 (right), 89, 96 (both), 101, 104 (left), 111, 112, 113 (left), 114, 129 (right), 134, 143 (both), 146, 149, 161 (both), 162 (all), 165 (top), 173, 176, 177 (all), 180 (all), 181, 185, 193, 196, 200, 207

JC Raulston Arboretum at NC State University: pp. 178 (top)

Bill Kersey: pp. 19, 39, 54, 75 (left), 186

Crystal Liepa: p. 204

Tim Murphy, University of Georgia, Bugwood.org: p. 201

National Garden Bureau: p. 137 (bottom)

Jerry Pavia: p. 154

Shutterstock: pp. 7, 8, 15, 20, 24, 27, 29, 34, 37, 38 (left), 48, 65, 66, 68, 79, 84 (left), 85 (both), 86, 91 (left), 102 (both), 105, 106, 108, 109, 115 (both), 118, 122, 123, 124, 127, 129 (left), 136 (bottom), 137 (top), 140, 142 (top), 147, 150, 151 (bottom), 153, 160, 171, 172, 174, 178 (bottom), 179 (top), 188 (all), 190, 195, 202, 206, 207, 208, 211, 214, 215

Neil Soderstrom: pp. 72 (right), 165 (bottom), 183, 197

George Weigel: pp. 42, 151 (top)

Wikimedia Commons: p. 121 (right)